P9-DBP-301

PRAEGER LIBRARY OF U.S. GOVERNMENT DEPARTMENTS
AND AGENCIES

The Department of Labor

PRAEGER LIBRARY OF U.S. GOVERNMENT DEPARTMENTS
AND AGENCIES

Consulting Editors

ERNEST S. GRIFFITH

Former University Professor and Dean Emeritus, School of International Service, American University; former Director, Legislative Reference Service, Library of Congress; and author of *The American System of Government* and *The Modern Government in Action*

HUGH LANGDON ELSBREE

Former Chairman, Department of Political Science, Dartmouth College; former Managing Editor, *American Political Science Review;* former Director, Legislative Reference Service, Library of Congress

THE U. S. GOVERNMENT today is a maze of departments and agencies engaged in a world-wide range of programs and activities. Some departments are as old as the government itself; others are newly created or have been expanded or redirected by recent legislation. The books in this series describe the origin, development, function, methods, and structure of specific departments or agencies and explain how far their activities extend and how they relate to other branches of the government and to the public. All are written by authors with firsthand knowledge of their subjects.

The *Praeger Library of U. S. Government Departments and Agencies* is the only comprehensive, detailed source of such information. More than seventy titles are planned for the series; a list of those already published appears at the back of this volume.—THE EDITORS

The
Department
of
Labor

Jonathan Grossman

Blairsville High School Library

PRAEGER PUBLISHERS
New York · Washington

*This book is dedicated to the
employees of the Department of
Labor who, pursuant to the Act
of March 4, 1913, to create a
Department of Labor, strive to
"foster, promote, and develop
the welfare of the wage earners
of the United States."*

Published in the United States of America in 1973
by Praeger Publishers, Inc.
111 Fourth Avenue, New York, N.Y. 10003

© 1973 by Praeger Publishers, Inc.

All rights reserved

Library of Congress Cataloging in Publication Data
Grossman, Jonathan Philip, 1915–
   The Department of Labor.
   (Praeger library of U. S. Government departments and agencies, no. 37)
   Bibliography: p. 295
   1. United States. Dept. of Labor.   I. Title.
HD4835.U4G76   353.83   73-145947

This book is No. 37 in the series
Praeger Library of U.S. Government Departments and Agencies

Printed in the United States of America

Preface

Near the entrance of a museum in Cape Town, South Africa, is a large picture of one carnivorous animal tearing another wild animal apart. Underneath the picture is the legend "For one, life; for the other, death." Perhaps the law of the jungle may govern some societies, but the American dream is of a more humane civilization, with prosperity for all, and of an open society where all people have an equal chance to move upward without tearing each other apart. The Department of Labor, about which this book is written, is one of many powerful forces seeking to make this dream come true.

In a sense, the Department of Labor is more fortunate than most government agencies, for it is one of the departments that seeks to help people directly. Its mission to promote the welfare of workers is central to the national goal of improving the quality of American life. Many of the Department's programs have within them the seeds of greatness. But there is a difference between potential and performance.

Ernest Hemingway, in a Nobel Prize–winning book, described the struggle between an old Cuban fisherman and the biggest fish he had ever seen. After a heroic battle, the fisherman harpoons his mighty antagonist and tows him back to land, but sharks gnaw away the fish's flesh, leaving only his skeleton. It would be too cynical to apply this allegory to the social goals of the Department of Labor, conceived in high hopes and sometimes gnawed to a skeleton by sharks in the sea of politics, administration, and the realities of economic life. A more realistic appraisal must recognize that, though some programs fail, others have varying degrees of success, and a few will make important long-range contributions toward creating a better America.

Department of Labor programs grow out of one of the great traditions of Western civilization—faith in the perfectibility of man. Many Americans believe that mankind can improve itself. Things that are wrong in our society, they feel, can be made right through human intelligence and initiative. Thus, Department of Labor programs are built on such aims as achieving industrial peace, finding jobs for all who are able to work, and training people so that through their own efforts they can rise out of poverty and contribute to society.

This book is a history and portrait of the Department and its work, covering all major segments of the subject except the history and work of the Bureau of Labor Statistics. That bureau is the subject of another volume in the Praeger Library of U.S. Government Departments and Agencies, written by former Commissioner Ewan Clague.

The viewpoints expressed in this book are mine alone, and not the official position of the Department. In extolling its achievements, I have also exposed its failures and frustrations. My hope is that a frank discussion of the Department of Labor and its work will, in some small measure, contribute to furthering its social goals.

To young people with an interest in public service, I would add that they should investigate employment opportunities in the Department of Labor. It is a good place to work. Appendix A summarizes some types of career opportunities available in the Department.

It would take a small telephone book to list the names of my fellow employees, my friends, and members of my family who cooperated with me in writing this book. For reasons of space I mention only William Gerber, Pauline Grossman, Rita Grossman, Judson MacLaury, Max Rutzick, and Jeannette

EFACE   vii

Sobajian, whose help and encouragement were particularly
valuable. However, to all who helped me I say, "Thank you."

JONATHAN GROSSMAN

Washington, D.C.
August, 1973

Contents

CHART

A section of photographs follows page 86 .

The Department of Labor

I

The Early Decades

"The purpose of the Department of Labor shall be to foster, promote, and develop the welfare of the wage earners of the United States, to improve their working conditions, and to advance their opportunities for profitable employment." These words, the second sentence of the Act creating the Department of Labor on March 4, 1913, are the cornerstone upon which the Department has been built. They represent the goal toward which workers began to struggle shortly after the Civil War.

Labor unions developed under severe handicaps in the early years of the American republic. They had grown in strength during the Civil War, but peace brought unemployment and economic hardship. Part of their troubles, labor leaders claimed, grew out of the fact that government departments were dominated by businessmen and represented business interests. What labor wanted, said William Sylvis, president of the National Labor Union in 1868, was "a new department at Washington to be called the Department of Labor, the head of said department . . . to be chosen directly from the ranks of workingmen."

The cry for recognition was echoed and re-echoed. Between 1864 and 1900 more than a hundred bills and resolutions relating to a department of labor were introduced in Congress.

Planting the Seed

In 1867, the House of Representatives created a standing committee on labor, a landmark event marking the first federal recognition of the importance of labor. But the campaign for a department of labor died with the death of Sylvis in 1869. Hopes for revival of the campaign were dampened by the depression of 1873.

Meanwhile labor shifted its strategy, concentrating on efforts to create state bureaus of labor statistics. In 1869, Massachusetts pioneered by creating the first bureau of labor statistics in the world. This new bureau immediately became embroiled in an issue that continues to plague government labor agencies to this day: Was the bureau a "voice of labor," or was it to be impartial?

The first Massachusetts bureau started as the voice of labor reformers. Henry K. Oliver and George McNeill, its first leaders, announced, "It is *not* our belief that the diseases of society could be determined and the right medicine administered by any tabular array of statistics." Their first questionnaires to employers, if fully answered, might have caused the employers to testify against themselves and accept responsibility for poor living and working conditions. The bureau's first report, issued in 1870, gave a history of British working conditions since the thirteenth century, with the themes that the lot of the English worker was one of filth, poverty, and nastiness and that there was a "resemblance between the mother country and our own."

Here, as well as there, will be found, in the labyrinthal slums of cities, in narrow courts, dark lanes, and nasty alleys, wretched tenements, with small rooms, dismal, dark, unventilated, into which the sun, God's free gift, never sends a shimmering ray; packed full of men, women, and children, as thick as smoked herrings in a grocer's box. Here they breed, here they live (!), and here they die, with their half-starved, ill-clad children—death's daily dish. . . . In such dens, if a horse were kept, the society for the suppression of cruelty to animals, should look after his owner.

Employers protested against the reports of the bureau, which they felt merely tried to prove preconceived notions. Protests notwithstanding, the governor of Massachusetts refused to abolish the bureau of labor statistics. The answer to false and partial reports, he said, "must be sought, not in discontinuing the investigation . . . but in lifting it to a higher and broader level." In 1873, he appointed Carroll Davidson Wright to head the bureau and told him to "make it or bust it."

Carroll Wright changed the direction of the bureau's activities. He refused to be "seduced" by partisanship and determined not to volunteer opinions but to present facts impartially. A friend attributed to him the quotation "Figures won't lie, but liars will figure." He conducted wide-ranging investigations that laid the foundations for the bureau's reputation for objectivity. By 1883, twelve states had followed Massachusetts and created labor statistics bureaus of their own, generally patterned after the Massachusetts bureau.

These thirteen state bureaus of labor statistics established a precedent for the national government. In 1884, the House Committee on Labor reported a bill of Representative James H. Hopkins of Pennsylvania to establish a department of labor statistics. Hopkins pointed to the Botanical Gardens, the Naval Observatory, and other institutions supported by the government to enlighten people. How much more important than knowledge of plants or topography, he said, was knowledge about workingmen! The bill passed by large majorities in both houses—in the House by 182 to 19 and in the Senate by 55 to 2. President Chester A. Arthur signed it on June 27, 1884.

FROM BUREAU TO DEPARTMENT

The new agency was named the Bureau of Labor. It was headed by a Commissioner of Labor appointed by the President for four years at a salary of $3,000 a year, with a total budget for the Bureau of $25,000. The Bureau was to collect information on the subject of working people and the "means of promoting their material, social, intellectual, and moral prosperity." The Bureau was placed in the Department of Interior and instructed to report to the Secretary of the Interior. Labor unions urged that the new Commissioner of Labor be a member of the working class. However, President Arthur turned down Terence Powderly, general master workman of the Knights of Labor, and rejected the idea that a labor leader should head the Bureau of Labor. Nearly half a year after the Bureau was established, and a month before the end of his own term of office in 1885, he selected to head the federal Bureau Carroll D. Wright, who was then in charge of the Massachusetts Bureau of Labor Statistics.

A tradition of historical interpretation has developed contending that Wright's appointment was a victory of objectivity over partisanship. He was chosen by Republican "lame-duck" President Arthur but did not accept until he knew that he would be reappointed by incoming Democratic President Grover Cleveland. Of course, there is the practical matter that Wright would not give up a good job in Massachusetts for another job from which he might be fired in a few months. Yet he did establish a precedent by holding office under both Republican and Democratic Presidents for twenty years. Wright also served the cause of objective statistics when he wrote to his boss, the Secretary of the Interior, that the Bureau of Labor could not be shaped to special ends and that its work was "that of pure fact," free from the exigencies of politics.

Carroll Wright's devotion to "pure fact" grew out of deep moral convictions. He believed in the cooperation of "sober, industrious, and thrifty workingmen" with "humane, large-hearted employers." The solution to industrial problems, he felt, could be found in the Ten Commandments and the Golden Rule. Carroll Wright treated facts respectfully, because he believed that, if the Bureau of Labor showed the government the truth, the government would act in a humane and logical way for the benefit of all the people.

The infant Bureau of Labor was an instant success. Organized labor supported it and called for larger appropriations. Wright's objective idealism was in tune with the times and won wide support. Most early reports of the Bureau, ranging in topics from "Industrial Depressions" and "Convict Labor" to statistics on marriage and divorce, were well received. President Cleveland on two occasions recommended that the Bureau be enlarged so that it could investigate the causes of labor disputes and eventually act as an arbitrator.

Supporters of the Bureau called on Congress to transform it into an independent department. The Knights of Labor, at their convention in 1887, recommended a "Department of Labor, the head of which shall be a member of the Cabinet." Terence Powderly, at the request of President Cleveland, prepared twenty-five suggestions on the scope of the proposed department. Congress passed a bill establishing a Department of Labor but dropped the idea of Cabinet representation. One rationalization for scuttling Cabinet representation for the new department was that Cabinet appointments are partisan, whereas the Department's main function was development of objective facts. President Cleveland signed the more limited bill on March 21, 1888.

The new Department of Labor, even without Cabinet status, gained personnel and prestige. Most important, the Commissioner of Labor no longer reported to the Secretary of the Interior but addressed his reports to the President. The Department grew in usefulness and importance. Its reports covered railroad labor, industrial education, working women, economics of the liquor traffic, effects of machinery on labor, labor legislation, compulsory insurance, housing for working people, and other subjects. In addition, in 1895, the Department inaugurated the *Bulletin of Labor,* which under different titles has been published to this day and is now the *Monthly Labor Review.* The Department's devotion to objective facts made it the most important statistical agency of its period. President Cleveland recognized this pre-eminence by designating Carroll Wright to supervise the completion of the 1890 census.

In a sense, Wright became a Presidential adviser on labor matters. In 1894, he acted as chairman of a commission on the Pullman strike. President Cleveland called in the army to deal with the situation because the strike blocked the mails. Violence erupted, and people were killed. The strike was broken when strike leader Eugene V. Debs was jailed for defying a court injunction. Wright's excellent factual reports unfortunately had little influence.

Wright's objective approach was somewhat more useful when President Theodore Roosevelt called upon him in the coal strike of 1902. In that era, the nation depended on coal for heating. With winter approaching, Wright reported to President Roosevelt on the causes of conflict in the coal fields. The head of a coal-carrying railroad denounced government interference in the situation and proclaimed that "the rights and interests of the laboring man will be protected and cared for . . . by the Christian men to whom God in his infinite wisdom has given control of property interests of the country."

President Roosevelt did not accept the thesis that the coal operators expressed the will of God. He called on Wright to participate in a White House conference of coal miners and mine owners. Though the conference failed, the mine owners eventually agreed to accept an arbitration commission in which Wright participated. The workers got less than they demanded but won higher wages and a partial recognition of their union. The Department of Labor had played a constructive role in the settlement.

Although the Department was occasionally successful in its pursuit of social justice through application of impartial facts, when tensions run high and passions are inflamed, neither side listens to moderation and truth. Both sides consider an impartial statement to be giving aid and comfort to the enemy. The violence of the Pullman and Homestead strikes, labor's fierce drive to organize, the "open shop" campaign of great corporations to break unions, the increased use of troops, court injunctions—all these were among the factors that made it difficult to resolve disputes consistently on the basis of data supplied by a neutral and objective Department of Labor.

Increasingly, unions called for a department with a voice in the Cabinet that would champion labor causes. At the same time, commercial interests waged a battle for a Department of Commerce in which the existing independent Labor Department would be reduced to a bureau. The bill for a Department of Commerce incorporating the Labor Department won the support of the Republican majority in Congress. President Theodore Roosevelt agreed because he believed that the interests of workers and employers could thus be harmonized.

The Department of Commerce and Labor was established in 1903 and lasted until 1913. The heads of the new department were prominent businessmen and financiers. Carroll Wright resigned. Labor was subordinated.

Although the Secretaries of the new department considered labor and capital as twin arms of industry that could be served together, conflicts soon appeared. One of the hot issues was immigration policy. Labor opposed the admission to the United States of immigrants who might depress wages and provide a supply of strike breakers. Secretary of Commerce and Labor Oscar Straus believed that America was a land of opportunity with room for immigrants and, therefore, was lenient in applying laws that might keep them out. Labor leaders renewed demands for an independent voice of labor in the Cabinet.

ESTABLISHMENT OF THE DEPARTMENT, 1913

As cleavages between organized labor and capital intensified, labor stepped up its campaign for a department to be operated by and for workers. The American Federation of

Labor successfully backed six union members for Congress in 1906. In 1908, the Democratic Party platform called for the "enactment of a law creating a Department of Labor, represented separately in the President's Cabinet." In 1910, the Democrats won control of the House, and fifteen union members were elected to Congress. Congressman William B. Wilson, formerly an officer of the United Mine Workers, became chairman of the House Committee on Labor.

Congressman William Sulzer of New York introduced a department of labor bill, which the House passed with little opposition on July 17, 1912. For a time, it seemed that the Senate might let the bill die in committee, but on February 7, 1913, Senator William E. Borah reported the bill to the Senate, and it passed without a recorded vote.

President William Howard Taft did not want a department of labor. While he was not opposed to the purposes of such a department, he did not see the need for it. He thought nine departments were enough for the administration of the executive branch.

However, Taft was not a stubborn man. He took graciously his defeat in 1912, when he ran a very poor third behind Woodrow Wilson and Theodore Roosevelt in the "Bull Moose" Presidential campaign. When a supporter boasted that he had voted for him, Taft said to him good naturedly, "Sh-sh. Somebody might hear you."

Taft's realism made him aware that his veto of a department of labor might be misunderstood. And, at best, it would probably have been a futile gesture. Incoming Democratic President Woodrow Wilson had already chosen a proposed Secretary of Labor, and, had the bill been vetoed, the new administration would probably have enacted a similar law. President Taft, on his last day in office, March 4, 1913, reluctantly signed the bill creating the Department of Labor.

President Wilson, in selecting the first Secretary of Labor, made good his campaign promise to be friendly to labor. He chose a workingman, a union leader, and a congressman who had been instrumental in creating the Department of Labor —William Bauchop Wilson.

Recent Secretaries of Labor have included distinguished lawyers, personnel directors, and a college professor. By contrast, William Wilson dropped out of school at the age of nine and then went to work for ten hours a day in a coal mine. At the age of eleven, he became a "half-member" of a union; at fourteen, he was elected secretary of a union local, and soon after was black-listed for union activity. When he could not find a mine job, he worked as a railroad fireman, lumberjack, typesetter, and farmer. Although he had a difficult time supporting his wife and nine children, he continued to organize miners at great personal sacrifice. He was one of the founders of the United Mine Workers and, in 1900, became the union's international secretary-treasurer.

In 1906, William Wilson began his political career by running for Congress in his Pennsylvania district against a millionaire lumberman. He eked out a surprising victory by a narrow margin. He was re-elected in 1908 and again in 1910. Then suddenly he was unexpectedly defeated for re-election by 568 votes when the Socialists split the labor vote. At a time when William Wilson's career prospects looked grim, President Woodrow Wilson appointed him (then fifty years old) as the first Secretary of Labor.

Secretary Wilson quickly explained that the new department was devoted to the welfare of all wage earners, whether organized or not. But unorganized labor had few ways of expressing its needs. Where possible, it was generally agreed, the Department of Labor should seek relations with nonunion workers, but, in practice, the Department has had to deal with unions as the best spokesmen on behalf of all workers.

This concept of devotion to the welfare of labor contained the seeds of conflicts that have persisted through the entire history of the Department. Can a government agency be a class agency? Can it properly act as a representative of a particular group of citizens who are its clients? It was claimed that the Department of Commerce acted for business interests, that the Treasury from the days of Alexander Hamilton represented financial powers, and that the Department of Agriculture worked for farmers. Why, then, should not the Department of Labor represent the workers and the unions? What is more, most Americans are wage earners and, therefore, what is good for workers is good for the country. As William Wilson put it, labor never had "desired to impose an injustice on anybody else. If securing justice to those who earn their bread by the sweat of their face constitutes partisanship, then count me as a partisan of labor."

Strong as these arguments are, there are many who have not agreed. Some have been opposed to labor outright. They have wanted a cheap supply of efficient labor that would allow owners large profits. There have been others who believed that all government agencies represented all the people and that subdivisions into agencies should not make them partisans of class interests. Agencies, they have contended, may administer different functions such as agriculture, commerce, or labor, but they should treat all sides impartially.

The initial Department of Labor was a puny infant. Four bureaus were transferred to it. The largest was the Bureau of Immigration, with 1,700 employees. The 130-employee Bureau of Naturalization was a natural adjunct of the immigration function. A Children's Bureau established in 1912 to report on matters of child welfare was transferred with 15 employees. The Bureau of Labor Statistics, with 100 workers, rounded out the quartet of bureaus.

Congress gave the Department of Labor one new activity that was not transferred from any other agency—the conciliation of labor disputes. This function might have been stillborn because Congress failed to appropriate the needed funds, but Secretary Wilson drew upon other bureaus for money and personnel and created a Conciliation Division to help him achieve his major goal of winning industrial peace.

William Wilson worked on the theory that no strike settlement would last unless it were accepted by both sides. He opposed compulsory arbitration and insisted on voluntary mediation. Conciliators were instructed to act not in a judicial but in a diplomatic capacity. As a matter of policy, he appointed conciliators only when asked to do so by one or both of the parties to a dispute. But the Department's progress as a mediator was insignificant. In the first two years, out of thousands of strikes, the Department of Labor received only seventy-five requests for conciliation.

One reason given for the lack of progress in settling strikes was fear that the Department was biased. Although Secretary Wilson tried to be impartial during negotiations, he strongly believed that workers should bargain collectively. During his first year in office, he told the American Federation of Labor convention in Seattle that the only way employers could deal fairly with workers was to bargain with the unions representing them. In the 1916 annual report of the Department, he described the problem of a solitary wage earner facing a foreman whom he asks for work. Behind the job seeker, he wrote, is a shadowy mass of other workers eager for the job, and confronting him is the foreman upon whose word his livelihood depends. Over the foreman is a superintendent, and "rising above both, rank upon rank, [there are] managers, directors, stockholders." The interests of all but the solitary worker interlock to dictate the lowest wages the market will allow. "At the outer edge of it all," Wilson continued, "a lone wage-worker bargains for work; bargains in a glutted market; bargains individually."

There were reasons other than lack of funds and charges of partisanship for the slow progress of conciliation. On the whole, conciliators tried to be fair, but they faced difficult conditions. Unemployment rose from 4.4 per cent of the labor force in 1913 to 9.7 per cent in 1915. Depression stiffened employer resistance to any discussion of labor demands. Perhaps more important, the American economy had not reached the stage where collective bargaining was an accepted method of settling labor disputes. The public still thought in terms of personal negotiations between an employer and his worker. Many owners, in fact, were outraged at the idea that intermediaries should be needed between themselves and their men. While some businessmen were willing to talk to committees made up of their own workers, others were willing to listen only to individual workmen, not to a committee. As an officer of Bethlehem Steel explained, "We don't employ a committee, we employ a particular individual."

Many employers grew especially vehement about unions bargaining for their members. Such employers considered union leaders to be outside agitators who did not belong in their plants. At a time when only 7 per cent of the labor force was unionized, many owners thought that even discussing conciliation with the Department of Labor was a humiliating capitulation that implied that employees could bargain with them as equals. In such a climate of industrial relations, William Wilson's efforts to mediate, based on collective bargaining, were like "spitting against the wind."

WORLD WAR I LABOR BOARDS

During World War I, the labor movement gained in strength. Instead of unemployed workers begging for jobs, unfilled jobs went begging for workers. War production generated a demand for labor, while at the same time the draft for the army and the virtual end of immigration cut the supply. The number of unemployed dropped from almost 4 million in 1915 to only 560,000 in 1918, which as a practical matter meant a labor shortage. Before the war, many labor leaders were pacifists, but the war to "make the world safe for democracy" won the support of many union leaders. Patriotism and labor shortages enhanced the status of labor and of the Department of Labor.

Congress recognized the new role when it included Secretary of Labor William B. Wilson in the Council of National

Defense set up in 1916. Samuel Gompers, president of the American Federation of Labor, became a member of a distinguished Advisory Commission of the Council and chairman of its Committee on Labor. Gompers and Wilson rallied workers behind a war program that dwarfed into insignificance any previous government activity. Manpower was needed for the armed forces, for a huge shipbuilding program, to build military camps, to produce war supplies, and to maintain peacetime industries.

Labor and government faced a dilemma. Obviously war was no time for social experimentation. Yet, in the prewar period, the average work week had been about fifty-five hours, and factory workers' earnings provided only minimal living standards. War brought additional problems of crowded housing in war centers and rising prices, which doubled between 1915 and 1920. On one hand, workers were caught up in the patriotic fervor that called for sacrifices; on the other hand, the time to make demands was when labor was scarce and desperately needed for the war effort.

In piecemeal fashion, several government agencies began to work with the explosive labor situation. The War Department, in June, 1917, signed an agreement with the American Federation of Labor creating the Cantonment Adjustment Commission. This commission, a landmark in labor history, was the first of the series of wartime labor boards. Its establishment probably represented the first time the federal government had recognized unions. The commission adopted a procedure that at the time was considered "peculiar," when it accepted the wages in a given locality set by an agreement between unions and employers as *the prevailing wage*. This may have been the origin of the prevailing-wage concept, which today is a vital part of government contracts.

War and defense labor agencies proliferated. When labor conditions in the shipyards became chaotic, the government and the American Federation of Labor created the Shipbuilding Labor Adjustment Board, which prevented major shipyard strikes during the war. A National Adjustment Commission dealt with longshore labor problems. A Fuel Administration negotiated with coal miners; a Railroad Wage Commission worked with rail labor; and the War and Navy departments developed a variety of commissions and industrial service sections. Other government agencies struggled with manpower activities in particular industries and geographical areas.

Most of these agencies were associated with the Department of Labor, but the general lack of experience in administering such agencies, combined with the need for speedy action, brought confusion. Secretary of Labor Wilson had made only a little progress in creating some order out of the chaos when, in September, 1917, President Wilson appointed him to head the President's Mediation Commission. This differed from other agencies because it was created by the President and not limited to one area or one trade.

In January, 1918, in a giant step toward a consistent labor policy, President Woodrow Wilson gave to Secretary William Wilson the authority to organize a War Labor Administration. The keystone of the War Labor Administration was the National War Labor Board. This board, appointed in April, 1918, grew out of a previously organized nongovernmental Conference Board. Management and labor, to show their impartiality, each selected one public representative to act as co-chairman. Labor picked Frank P. Walsh, a famous liberal lawyer; employers chose ex-President of the United States William Howard Taft.

The Conference Board had created a labor code for the duration of the war. This "Magna Charta of Labor" outlawed strikes and lockouts in wartime but in return gave workers the right to organize and prohibited employers from firing workers for joining unions. The code called for women to receive equal pay for equal work, recognized the basic eight-hour working day, and established the principle that all workers are entitled to a living wage. The code assured labor that, in return for its support of the war, wartime needs would not be used as an excuse to oppress workers. Labor was assured that, while working to save the world for democracy, the government would preserve social justice at home.

On April 18, 1918, Secretary of Labor Wilson appointed the members of the Conference Board to the new National War Labor Board. This board was to apply the principles of the code to actual disputes. The National War Labor Board became a kind of supreme court for labor relations.

Most contestants in labor disputes accepted the board's decisions, though there were some notable instances of defiance. President Wilson in June, 1918, warned the Western Union Telegraph and Postal Telegraph companies, the first two recalcitrants, "it is imperatively necessary in the national interest that the decisions of the National War Labor Board be accepted by both parties to labor disputes." Postal Telegraph yielded, but Western Union Telegraph defied the board and refused to rehire men who had been fired for joining a union. The President then placed Western Union under the control of the U.S. Post Office. When Smith and Wesson, a munitions company in Springfield, Massachusetts, offered to turn its plant over to the government rather than comply with board orders, the War Department took over the company.

Labor as well as employers felt the sting of the board's actions. When workers in Bridgeport, Connecticut, struck in defiance of the board and the decision of a Department of Labor umpire, the President ordered them back to work. He threatened to bar them for a year from certain war industries if they refused, and he added, "the draft boards will be instructed to reject any claim of exemption based on your alleged usefulness on war production." The strikers went back to work.

Technically the War Labor Board's position as part of the War Labor Administration brought it under the supervision of Secretary of Labor Wilson. He recommended to the President the appointment of the board's members and received the board's reports. But the members' stature and the board's judicial authority made it, in fact, independent. It is doubtful whether exercise of the same authority directly under the Department of Labor, which had been accused of holding a pro-labor bias, would have been nearly as effective. In the seven months between its creation and the armistice on November 11, 1918, the board markedly reduced the effect of strikes and brought about, as briefly noted above, historic changes in the relationship of workers to their employers.

Other agencies of the War Labor Administration did not develop as rapidly as the National War Labor Board. Hindsight being clearer than foresight, in the light of difficulties that were to develop during the war, it is easy to criticize the timidity of Congress and the Secretary of Labor for not acting sooner on behalf of labor peace and of equity in labor relations. Yet there was danger of overreacting. Prominent patriots argued that, if you could conscript men to fight overseas, you could, and should, conscript them to work on farms and factories. The "work or fight" order of April, 1918, expressed the feeling that men exempt from military service should still serve their country when needed. Secretary Wilson, however, explained the difference between drafting men to defend their country and drafting them for other people's profit. The War Labor Administration, nevertheless, acted to encourage workers to select jobs that would serve the national interest.

Secretary Wilson assigned to the Information Division of the Bureau of Immigration the task of channeling workers into war industries. During the war, the division became the core of the current United States Employment Service. It placed 3 million workers in war-related jobs.

The War Labor Administration coordinated many other manpower services. A Farm Service Division directed thousands of workers to farm jobs and was entrusted by the Immigration Service with importing temporary farm labor from Mexico, thus foreshadowing a controversy that intermittently erupted for the next half-century.

A Boys' Working Reserve helped with local harvesting and

was a forerunner of youth labor programs in later decades. A Division of Negro Economics, operating under a Negro university professor, tried to reduce racial discord as blacks left Southern farms for Northern factories. A Woman in Industry Service recruited women for new jobs. A Training and Dilution Service encouraged employers to break down skilled jobs into easy components that could be performed by less skilled labor. Several divisions of the War Labor Administration tried to increase production by providing better working and living conditions. The United States Housing Corporation built five thousand houses, apartments, and dormitories in war-production centers and ran a hotel for working girls in Washington, D.C. A Child Labor Division fought the exploitation of children in war-related work. A Working Conditions Service recommended improvements in low wages, long hours, and unsanitary working conditions.

In an effort to unify the wide-ranging functions of the War Labor Administration, Secretary Wilson appointed Felix Frankfurter as his assistant, made him chairman of a newly created War Labor Policies Board, and directed him to provide coordination and policy guidance. In contrast with the autonomous National War Labor Board, which acted in a judicial capacity and dealt decisively and conclusively with strikes, the newer Policies Board dealt in a more general way with such problem areas as recruiting manpower and setting wage standards and working conditions. The work of the Policies Board represented a dovetailing process, linking a variety of government agencies involved with labor. The board established policies but depended on the operating agencies to put them into effect.

Frankfurter understood labor problems, knew his way around politically, was energetic, and was a strong administrator. His board, establishing a momentous precedent, successfully incorporated social goals into the provisions in government contracts. For example, war production contracts called for a procedure to settle labor disputes, barred child and convict labor, and established the eight-hour day with time and a half for overtime.

Frankfurter's War Labor Policies Board was only partially successful in its efforts to rationalize the use of manpower and made virtually no progress in creating orderly wage standards in the various industries and geographical areas. One problem it faced was that the National War Labor Board, though theoretically strictly a judicial agency, had great prestige and established precedents that the War Labor Policies Board was virtually forced to follow. Consequently, the new board did not achieve one of its major objectives, that of serving as the unifying force of the War Labor Administration.

Despite its shortcomings, the parent War Labor Administration chalked up a substantial record of achievement. It established recognition of the fact that labor was not just another commodity that might be needed for the war. While the War Labor Administration cooperated with the production agencies that used labor and that actually controlled labor relations, it succeeded in establishing policies that protected workers. In a sense, the handling of labor during World War I was a bargaining process between labor and government in which workingmen supported the war, and in return the government supported collective bargaining and improved working conditions.

IMMIGRATION WORK

After World War I, immigration became the most important concern of the Department of Labor. In 1921, Congress passed the first major law setting up bars against immigration. There had been, since 1882, limited restrictions, such as the exclusion of Chinese and of people who could not pass literacy tests. But the 1921 law broke the tradition of the "open door."

Immigration was at the heart of the American heritage. Almost all Americans are descendants of immigrants. In the early days, settlers were welcomed. An average of a million immigrants a year came to the United States in the decade before World War I. The situation was almost unique in the history of the world, for the immigrants were not conquerors or slaves but had the potential of becoming fully equal with the old settlers. America was the land of freedom and opportunity. While the adjustment to the new country frequently was painful, immigrants could and did make their way up in a relatively open society.

William B. Wilson and James J. Davis, the first two Secretaries of Labor, are examples of the American immigrant dream. When William Wilson was eight years old, his father left Scotland for a job in a coal mine in Arnot, Pennsylvania. As soon as he had saved enough money, he sent for his wife and children. Because he was not in the best of health and could not support his large family, nine-year-old "Billy" went to work in the mines loading coal carts. From these beginnings, he worked his way up to the successive statuses of coal miner, union official, congressman, and Secretary of Labor.

The second Secretary of Labor was also an immigrant. The father of James J. Davis left Tredegar, Wales, to work in Pennsylvania, where he earned passage money for his wife and six children. In America, eight-year-old "Jimmy" worked as a water boy in a steel mill. When he was thirteen, as Davis tells it, "there were about 120 of us kids in the rolling mill, and we got fifty cents a day. When we decided to organize, they made me President—and we struck . . . for fifty-five cents a day—and we got it!" He became a steel "puddler" in Elwood, Indiana, went into Republican politics there, and was chosen town clerk. Then he became an organizer for a fraternal society, the Loyal Order of the Moose. He was paid on a per capita basis, increased membership to eighty thousand, and became rich. His detractors commented that he was the only man who ever successfully milked a moose. When President Warren G. Harding appointed him Secretary of Labor, Davis commented, "Is there another country in the world where a poor immigrant boy . . . could become a member of the President's Cabinet?"

One of the most vital responsibilities of the "immigrant boys" who had become Secretaries of Labor was the control of immigration. Immigration was largely a labor problem. Frequently without resources, immigrants needed immediate income and took almost any job at almost any wage. As a group, immigrants worked at poorer jobs and accepted lower wages than native workers. Because of this, there had been some opposition to foreign workers for a long time. The passing of the frontier, with its opportunities for earning a living from the land, and the increased number of immigrants competing for jobs led organized labor to join with other groups in a fight against unlimited immigration.

World War I cut the torrent of new immigrants to a trickle, but wartime passions set aflame another issue: what to do about the "un-American" immigrant. In 1917 and 1918, Congress clarified the powers of the Secretary of Labor to deport aliens who advocated anarchy, assassination of public officials, or overthrow of the government by force.

One of the basic issues Secretary William B. Wilson faced was whether to deport people only for subversive acts or merely for membership in a subversive organization. As the ideology of the Bolshevik Revolution spread outside of Russia and U.S. officials received live bombs in the mail, fears arose of a radical plot to overthrow the U.S. Government. There was growing xenophobia. Every Italian became a potential anarchist; every Slav, a Bolshevik. The Department of Justice, in 1919 and 1920, raided homes and meeting places of radicals, seized thousands of aliens, and demanded that the Department of Labor deport them.

Secretary of Labor Wilson refused. People would be arrested, he said, only on the basis of sworn affidavits with specific information, and would be confronted with evidence and given an opportunity for rebuttal. After "these safeguards of American liberty" had been provided, and if the alien were still found to be "deportable," Secretary Wilson reported to the President, "we will deport him."

After Secretary Wilson became ill, Assistant Secretary Louis Post continued this policy. In spite of public protest, Post canceled about three thousand warrants for arrest and released four hundred of about one thousand aliens in custody.

A congressman brought in a resolution to impeach Post. Post explained that he did not favor freeing aliens who were guilty and that, when he canceled a deportation warrant, this was because of his honest "finding [of] a verdict for the defendant." The dramatic highlight of the spectacular congressional hearings on the impeachment resolution came when a congressman who had opposed Post told him, "I believe you have followed your sense of duty absolutely."

Although Wilson and Post had provided trials that protected the rights of thousands of threatened immigrants, they did not fight against all deportations. As a matter of fact, nearly 250 aliens, including the well-known anarchist Emma Goldman, were sent to Russia on the army ship *Buford,* sometimes called the "Red Ark."*

Although the hysteria over immigrant radicals abated, when Secretary of Labor James J. Davis took office on March 5, 1921, immigration was his most important problem. About 75 per cent of the Labor Department's employees dealt with immigration and naturalization.

---

* Nearly twenty years after the failure to impeach Post, a conservative congressman asked for the impeachment of Secretary of Labor Frances Perkins because she did not deport labor leader Harry Bridges. Secretary Perkins thought the evidence against Bridges was insufficient to warrant his deportation. Because Bridges had become so prominent, however, she spoke to President Franklin D. Roosevelt about the case. She told the President that Bridges was an Australian who had come to the United States in 1920, had worked as a longshoreman, lived in a boarding house, behaved in an orderly fashion, and played the mandolin. He had become a leader of striking longshoremen and was accused of being a Communist. Roosevelt laughed about the dangerous mandolin-player and told Secretary Perkins "not to let our imagination run away with us" and only to deport Bridges if the evidence supported such action. Secretary Perkins found in favor of Bridges, and the House Judiciary Committee dismissed the impeachment proceeding against her as having no merit.

At this time, the issue of limiting immigration had reached the boiling point. Unemployment had increased to about 5 million, and the United States was trying to absorb soldiers returning to civilian life. At the same time, immigration accelerated, with more than 800,000 arriving in the year ending June 30, 1921. The press carried sensational stories about more than 10 million would-be immigrants from war-stricken Europe ready to swarm into the United States.

In May, 1921, departing completely from tradition, Congress passed a new restrictive immigration law that limited numbers of immigrants to 3 per cent of the number of foreign-born people of each nationality in the United States in 1910. It provided for a maximum of 357,000 immigrants, plus non-quota immigrants from Mexico and British North American areas.

A 1924 revision of the law reduced the quotas from 3 per cent to 2 per cent, reduced the total to 164,000, and changed the base from the percentage of foreign-born people in 1910 to the percentage according to the census of 1890. Provisions were added to prevent immigrants from becoming public charges and to weed out undesirables. A further change in 1929 again reduced the total and emphasized preference for admission of immigrants of Western and Northern European nationalities.

Secretary Davis would have made the laws even more restrictive if he had had his way. He pointed out that, though the immigration laws had partially closed the front door, the side door from Western Hemisphere countries remained open. Otherwise ineligible immigrants would go to these countries, establish residence, and then come to the United States. For example, in 1924, immigration from other American countries reached nearly 300,000.

The immigration laws created a big business in "bootlegging" aliens. Under a law permitting alien seamen to stay in the country sixty days, some ships came in with double crews, with aliens paying as much as $1,000 for the privilege of being seamen. These "seamen" deserted in American ports and disappeared. Thousands of aliens also came in on forged passports or crossed the Mexican or Canadian border illegally. Some who entered on student visas did not return home after completing their studies.

Once in the country, many illegal immigrants fraudulently gained citizenship. To cope with this problem, beginning in 1924, the Secretary of Labor required immigrants to register so that their legal status could be proved. Registration laws were strengthened in later years. Labor Department officials rooted out corrupt immigration and naturalization practices, and, in the early 1930's, in New York, thirty-seven racketeers were indicted and thirty government employees were punished for falsifying naturalization papers.

In 1924, Secretary Davis established a border patrol of men trained in law, investigation techniques, fingerprinting, jiujitsu, the use of firearms, and tracking and trailing. In a single year, 1930, the border patrol caught 269 smugglers of aliens and 20,815 aliens who had been smuggled.

Many illegal aliens were deported. In 1922, about 4,000 of them were expelled. Ten years later, 19,000 were deported and 11,000 left voluntarily after they had been caught. Deportees included criminals, prostitutes, and anarchists, but most often harmless people whose only crime was that they wanted to live in the United States. It is impossible to determine how many "illegal" immigrants escaped the dragnet, but, in 1936, the Immigration Service estimated that there were fewer than 100,000 aliens who, if detected, could be deported.

The quota acts reduced immigration; the Depression virtually halted it. Officials applied the law to prevent immigrants from becoming public charges so strictly that, in 1933, there were only 23,000 immigrants. At the same time, many aliens emigrated. After flowing in one direction for three hundred years, the stream of migration reversed itself, and, in the early 1930's, more people left the country than entered.

At the end of the 1930's, immigration revived a little. The

rise of Adolf Hitler in Germany sent refugees searching for new homes. President Franklin Roosevelt, when discussing the plight of terrorized Jews, told Secretary of Labor Perkins that a few extra people would not threaten the nation's prosperity. In 1939 and 1940, about 80,000 Jews comprised more than half the immigrants admitted. Additional thousands over-stayed temporary visas. Because deportation could mean death, most "illegal" visitors were not deported to Nazi-con-trolled countries.

Yet even refugee immigration was reduced. Rumors spread that Nazi spies had infiltrated the country in the guise of refu-gees. Under "special care" directives, U.S. consuls abroad cut the flow of refugees so that, in 1941, only 47 per cent of the already limited German-Austrian quota was used. It is prob-able that, as a result, tens of thousands who might have been saved by coming to the United States died instead in concen-tration camps.

The minor revival of immigration in the late 1930's was a trickle compared to the torrent in the "open door" period. The newcomers in the Depression decade constituted about one-twentieth of the 10 million immigrants who had arrived in the decade before World War I. When the Department of Labor had been organized in 1913, immigration had been a labor problem. By the 1930's, immigration was a relatively unimportant activity. In 1940, much of the government re-sponsibility was shifted to the Justice Department.

The Department of Labor today retains a few vestiges of its former immigration functions, particularly as they relate to the labor market. The Department selects immigrants in the category of those who come to the United States for jobs. Within the quotas, the United States gives preference to those who will benefit the nation. The Secretary of Labor also can bar immigrants who might take away work from Americans or might depress wages by working for extremely low pay.

Since enactment of the Immigration Act of 1965, the De-partment of Labor issues a certificate, which every immigrant looking for a job must get before he can obtain a visa. However, because the number of immigrants is determined by quotas, there is no set relationship between the number of such certifications in any year and the total number of immigrants admitted to the United States in that year.

Because more immigrants want to come to the United States than the law allows, efforts are made to evade the law. Sailors still "jump" ships in U.S. ports, and thousands cross the Mexican and Canadian borders and melt into the population.

Professional and technical workers are automatically certified for American entry. It is ironic that among the major exporters of highly skilled manpower are several of the developing nations, such as the Philippines and India, which need the skills of these specialists at home but cannot afford to pay the salaries they can command. This flow of *émigrés* to the United States constitutes the "brain drain," which benefits the United States.

In its early years, the United States was a country whose "streets were paved with gold" and through whose open door unskilled and skilled alike entered to seek wealth and freedom. Today, the United States still draws people from the ends of the earth. But the door is only slightly ajar.

President John F. Kennedy, grandson of Irish immigrants, parodied the famous poem inscribed at the Statue of Liberty in New York Harbor: "Give me your tired, your poor, your huddled masses yearning to breathe free." Kennedy added, "as long as they come from Northern Europe, are not too tired or too poor or slightly ill . . . never joined any questionable organization, and can document their activities." He could also have added, "and as long as there are only a few of them."

DAVIS, DOAK, AND DEPRESSION

Although immigration control was the most important activity of the Department of Labor in the decade after World War I, other activities also loomed large. Secretary Davis was especially involved in efforts to conciliate labor disputes. President Harding had picked him as a man with a big heart who had sympathy for both the capitalist and the workingman. Because most strikes were ultimately settled by negotiation and ended in compromise, Davis felt it was a tragedy when the settlement had to be preceded by a long-drawn-out struggle. Gaining half a loaf by compromise was better, he felt, than trusting to the vicissitudes of industrial warfare. One of his notable achievements came when, collaborating with Secretary of Commerce Herbert Hoover, he persuaded the United States Steel Corporation to give up the twelve-hour workday. Davis was proud of the record of the Department's Conciliation Division and pointed out that, in addition to strikes settled, the service deserved credit for helping to avoid strikes, even though its activities of this kind were generally not known to any but the directly interested parties.

Davis continued to support the work of the Department in improving work conditions for women and children. He tried through publicity and by working with states to promote child welfare. He fought for larger appropriations for the Children's Bureau and for keeping it in the Department of Labor.

Although the Employment Service set up during World War I had been largely dismantled after the war, Davis continued to operate a skeleton of the organization. The Bureau of Labor Statistics fared better. Its cost-of-living statistics served as the basis of several strike settlements, and the bureau furnished a continuous picture of the American worker, his wages, his hours of work, and his standard of living. "Without such information," Davis noted, "all labor policies of the department would be adopted in darkness and would almost be futile." Labor statistics provided a factual basis for labor measures and labor policy.

In 1930, while still serving as Secretary of Labor, Davis campaigned for and won a seat in the U.S. Senate. He resigned as Secretary of Labor upon taking his seat as a senator. One of the few Republicans who survived the Democratic election landslides during the Roosevelt Administrations, he was twice re-elected and served until 1945.

William N. Doak, who succeeded Davis, was the first American-born Secretary of Labor. Like his predecessors, he was mostly self-educated, his formal education having ended with a business-school course in Bristol, Virginia. Doak went to work at seventeen as a $1.30-a-day railroad yardman, joined a union, and in time became legislative representative of the Brotherhood of Railroad Trainmen and editor of the union magazine. He worked for Republican candidates in various elections, campaigning for Presidents Warren Harding, Calvin Coolidge, and Herbert Hoover—among others. President Hoover appointed Doak Secretary of Labor over the protests of the American Federation of Labor.

Doak tried to follow policies similar to those of his predecessor. He believed in unions and labor negotiations but felt that strikes were weapons of last resort and should be avoided except in extreme cases. He believed that workers deserved high wages, but he opposed government intervention and subsidies aimed at raising wage levels. "It was never intended," he said, "that the central government should be used as a charitable institution." He advocated individualism, character training, and confidence in American ideals.

But circumstances forced Doak, at least partially, to change his views. At the end of the booming 1920's, Secretary of Labor Davis had predicted that there would be no more depressions. When the Depression did strike, the Hoover Administration, including Secretary Davis, predicted that it would soon be over. When Doak took office, about 5 million workers were looking for jobs. During his incumbency, unemployment reached a peak of at least 12 million people. One out of every four workers could not find a job.

The Department of Labor was closer to the unemployed than any other branch of the government. As the tragedy of joblessness became acute, Secretary Doak urged employers to maintain current wage levels and argued that giving labor its fair share helped to sustain buying power. He suggested a six-hour day and five-day week to spread out the work, and he introduced the five-day work week for Department of Labor employees. He also supported a program of public works and unemployment insurance to level the effects of recurring cycles of poverty and joblessness.

By the time the Hoover Administration came around to advocating government counteraction, the Depression had reached catastrophic proportions. Fear and resentment gripped the nation. In the election of 1932, the voters repudiated the Republican Administration.

As a result of the Administration's failure to foresee and adequately counteract the Depression, later critics looked upon Doak as one of the worst Secretaries of Labor and considered his predecessor, Davis, not much better. However, both men held the prevailing views of their times. They both believed in progress through American ideals and had faith that these concepts would continue to bring a rising standard of living to American workers. The magnitude of the Depression caught them by surprise.

Secretary Doak was in a particularly difficult position. He loyally supported President Hoover, insisted that the President was misunderstood, and campaigned on his behalf. As the Depression deepened, the President became the victim of bitter jokes and popular hatred. The very name "Hoover" became a dirty word to some, and shantytowns were dubbed "Hoovervilles." President Hoover was hurt by the popular contempt and sadly remarked, "My men are dropping around me."

Had Doak been an angel with halo and wings, he would still have been branded as incompetent. His successors of the opposite party probably judged him too harshly, but the truth is that he demonstrated no great qualities of leadership, and he seems to have been a rather ordinary man.

II

The New Deal and World War II, 1933–45

In November, 1932, when Franklin D. Roosevelt was elected President, it seemed impossible that economic conditions could get worse. But the impossible happened. By March, 1933, when Roosevelt took office, conditions were worse.

Estimates of unemployment ranged between 13 million and 18 million, or from 25 per cent to 35 per cent of the labor force. But many of those who did work had miserable jobs, which constituted a type of hidden unemployment. Based on a 1926 Department of Labor index of 100, payrolls had nose-dived by the time of Roosevelt's inauguration in March, 1933, to 33.4, or one-third of what they had been seven years earlier. Coal was the sickest industry in the United States. In some mining towns, nobody had a job, grocery stores could not operate, teachers were not paid, and nearly everybody was bankrupt. Reports showed that in Pennsylvania only two out of every five workers had full-time work. Yet, no matter how startling the statistics, they do not reveal the despair of a job-less father trying to feed his family, the hopelessness of hungry people waiting in line for bowls of soup, or the pervasive, haunting terror that corroded American economic life.

President Roosevelt, in his historic first inaugural address, said, "This great nation . . . will revive and will prosper. So, first of all, let me assert my firm belief that the only thing we have to fear is fear itself." He assured the nation that he would put people to work, "treating the task as we would treat the emergency of a war."

THE DEPARTMENT DURING THE NEW DEAL

On the firing line in the war against unemployment was the new Secretary of Labor, Frances Perkins—competent, dedicated, and committed to social betterment. Yet, except for her ability, she was a most unlikely Secretary of Labor. All three Secretaries who had preceded her had had working-class backgrounds. Frances Perkins was a descendant of the Revolutionary War patriot James Otis and came from a blue-blooded New England family. None of the previous Secretaries had been college graduates; she had been the president of her class at Mount Holyoke College. In addition, she had received training in social work at Hull House in Chicago. Reserved, disliking noise to such a degree that she did not own a radio, with an ethical and intellectual approach to labor problems, she could not sidle up to the bar for a beer with union leaders or join them in their leisure activities.

When President-elect Roosevelt summoned Frances Perkins in February, 1933, and said to her, "I want you to be the Secretary of Labor," she argued with him that she was not a bona fide labor person. But she had served Roosevelt as industrial commissioner in New York State, and Roosevelt trusted her. Most important, Roosevelt wanted to break precedent by appointing the first woman Cabinet member in American history.

Help for the Unemployed

The immediate problem was assistance to the unemployed. Basically, Secretary Perkins was an old-fashioned individualist who felt that people should take care of themselves. Her radicalism consisted of her belief that every worker has a right to a job. When people are without jobs because of conditions beyond their control, she felt, the government should step in. But it should do only what an individual cannot reasonably do for himself.

In 1933, many people desperately needed money to live. The New Deal created numerous programs to meet the need. A bewildering, overlapping, and sometimes conflicting alphabet of agencies sprang up—CCC, FERA, CWA, WPA, NYA, PWA, USES, and NRA—all aimed at putting people to work. The Department of Labor recommended and justified many public works projects. In addition, the "conception of finding special work for those who could not be absorbed on straight public works," Secretary Perkins summarized in a 1939 report, "also sprang from a meeting of labor leaders, government officers, and others in the Department of Labor."

One of the first Department programs was the Civilian Conservation Corps (CCC). President Roosevelt told Secretary Perkins that young men would love to leave the city and work in the woods. He looked upon the CCC as a means of both conserving natural resources and providing work for young men. Between 1933 and 1939, the Department of Labor recruited for the CCC about 2 million unemployed, unmarried men between eighteen and twenty-five years of age. These young men, along with a few war veterans and some experienced woodsmen, worked in forest and park camps. Most of the men received board plus $30 a month, of which they sent $25 home to their families.

Another unemployment weapon was FERA (Federal Emergency Relief Administration). When Secretary Perkins came to Washington, she had on her desk more than two thousand plans to fight unemployment. One of those who had developed these plans was Harry Hopkins, whose ideas were based on New York experience. Secretary Perkins arranged a meeting for Hopkins with President Roosevelt, who made him federal relief administrator. FERA spent $4 billion on food, clothing, shelter, medicine, and other human needs. In Hopkins's words, FERA "bought more of courage than it ever bought of goods."

One of the articles of Secretary Perkins's faith was that work was better than handouts. Work could preserve a man's skill and save his self-respect. The Civil Works Administration (CWA), which was established pursuant to that faith, created 4 million temporary jobs during the bitter winter of 1933–34.

The Works Progress Administration (WPA), which grew out of the CWA, was also a make-work program. Critics complained that putting people on jobs that were not worthwhile was wrong. With so large an improvised program, some projects were indeed ridiculous, such as digging a ditch and filling it up. On the other hand, many projects, ranging from construction and operation of playgrounds to programs of adult education, had value. Over a period of six years, the WPA provided jobs for 8 million people.

One of the WPA projects was a survey that showed in 1935 that 3 million young people between the ages of sixteen and twenty-five were on relief. In that connection, President Roosevelt tried to help youth by establishing the National Youth Administration (NYA). The NYA gave jobs to school dropouts, paid for part-time work to help students stay in school, and provided a job guidance and placement program. By 1936, the NYA was helping half a million or more young people yearly.

A point of confusion on the already confused roll of alphabetical agencies is the distinction between the WPA and the Public Works Administration (PWA). Basically the PWA built large-scale, permanent works such as schools, hospitals, public housing, and river-control projects, spending 70 per cent of its funds on materials and 30 per cent on wages, in contrast to the temporary projects of the WPA, for which 25 per cent of funds went to nonlabor costs and 75 per cent to labor. Secretary Perkins supported both programs and helped to turn back the arguments of those who opposed public works because they cost more than relief or make-work projects. Owing to the need for planning and a long lead-time, the PWA got under way slowly, but it provided many jobs along with useful public facilities.

Another New Deal achievement was the revival of the United States Employment Service (USES). This World War I unit had deteriorated to a virtually useless organization. Miss Perkins, from her New York job, had criticized the service in 1930, when President Herbert Hoover on the basis of inaccurate information given him by the Employment Service told the press that employment was picking up. She issued a press release stating flatly that President Hoover was wrong and that unemployment was increasing.

As Secretary of Labor, Frances Perkins became the boss of USES. Under the Wagner-Peyser Act of 1933, she turned it into a vehicle for energetically seeking jobs for the unemployed. The law provided federal matching funds to the states to encourage them to establish their own employment services. Where such state agencies did not function, a National Re-employment Service operated as a special division of USES to fill the gap. In no instance was the Re-employment Service permitted in areas covered by the state employment services. In the meantime, more and more states joined the USES federal-state system, so that, by 1936, forty-two states were affiliated as part of the nationwide system. During the Depression years, the Employment Service in the Department of Labor selected workers for relief projects and placed 26 million people in jobs.

These and other government programs helped directly to meet the needs of the jobless for money and jobs, but in accordance with the concept of free enterprise the major emphasis in government policies was on stimulation of private employment. Secretary of Labor Perkins wanted those who worked on relief to earn more than those who did not work at all, but she also wanted higher pay scales for jobs in the economy than for jobs on relief. At times, she implied that those who remained on relief were less capable and needed kindly government supervision.

The National Recovery Administration

Because of her faith in private enterprise, Secretary Perkins was among the early advocates of the National Recovery Administration (NRA), which suspended the antitrust laws to stimulate business. The competitors in an industry proposed codes of fair competition. The Department of Labor and its advisers contributed to the labor sections of these codes, which set standards of wages, hours, and working conditions. Essentially, the NRA aimed at putting people back to work by raising wages, increasing purchasing power, and thus stimulating the economy. This amounted to "priming the pump." No employer under this system could gain advantage by cutting prices on the basis of "sweating" labor. Prices would go up, but business could act decently because it could do under the NRA what had been previously unlawful.

The American people responded enthusiastically to the NRA. Its symbol of a blue eagle bearing the legend "We Do Our Part" soon appeared in almost every shop window and factory. The idea behind it was explained by the President: "Soldiers wear a bright badge on their shoulders to be sure that comrades do not fire on comrades." The economy began to recover. The NRA signaled a possible end of the Depression and the revival of the American spirit. Frances Perkins said it seemed as if the dead had come to life. But opposition developed. The NRA contained the seeds of economic dictatorship, permitting individual industries to legislate for their members.

Some employers held out against the NRA on principle. Henry Ford refused to sign the code that obligated him to bargain with his workers. Other employers challenged the NRA in the courts. One case involving a code that fixed minimum wages and maximum hours in the live chicken–slaughtering trade in Brooklyn, New York, came before the Supreme Court. On May 27, 1935, the court declared the NRA unconstitutional because, in allowing industries to establish codes to prevent "unfair competition," it delegated legislative authority and because, in enacting certain provisions of the National Industrial Recovery Act, the federal government had exceeded its power to regulate interstate commerce.

By this time, the worst was largely over. Many people were back at work at higher wages and with better working conditions. Some useful elements of the NRA survived. The New Deal tackled the problem of putting into more palatable form many features of the NRA, including the guarantee of workers' rights to join a union, the abolition of child labor, and the enforcement of fairer labor standards and better working conditions.

Labor Unions and the NRA

The NRA gave unions a new status. Section 7a of the National Industrial Recovery Act affirmed the right of workers to organize and bargain collectively through representatives of their own choosing. But Section 7a was only a declaration of principle. It left unresolved such concrete issues as how much support the government would provide for collective bargaining and what should be done about the closed shop, company unions, and related aspects of labor representation. The application of Section 7a had to be hammered out in combat within the unions, within the government, and between employers and unions.

Secretary Perkins tried to act with reason, but, in the battle over Section 7a, the voice of reason faded to a whisper. She supported the right of workers to bargain collectively. But she was as much concerned with the right of workers not to join unions as with the right of unions to organize workers. Neither unions nor employers were satisfied with her position.

One of the first conflicts in this regard broke out in the steel industry. Labor organizations as well as employers were supposed to be represented in the drawing up of an industry code. But the steelworkers' union had never recovered from the strike of 1919. When Secretary Perkins told the President that Department of Labor representation for steelworkers violated the rule that the Department was nonpartisan, Roosevelt compared the fight against the Depression to a war that called for emergency measures. He said, "The Secretary of Labor ought to be the Secretary *for* Labor . . . if anybody says that's unorthodox lay it on to me."

To enable her to do the best job of representation, Secretary Perkins visited steel plants and steel towns. She spoke to workers at their jobs, at meetings, and in their homes. The steel companies and public officials cooperated everywhere except in Homestead, Pennsylvania, a steel company–dominated city, where authorities prevented her from talking to workers. In this instance, as tension mounted, she took the workers to the post office, which was beyond the local authorities' jurisdiction. She spoke to the workers and listened to their complaints. The incident convinced many workers that the government wanted to be fair.

At the signing of the NRA steel code, Secretary Perkins wanted government, management, and labor all to approve. Because there was no national steel union, she invited William Green, president of the American Federation of Labor (AFL), to attend, and he agreed. When she tried to introduce Green to the heads of the steel companies, Secretary Perkins recalls in her memoirs, they "backed away into a corner, like frightened boys." They were afraid that others in the steel industry might find out that they had talked to a labor leader.

If labor organizations were weak, Section 7a was almost meaningless. Therefore, the section was used as a rallying point for the cause of stronger labor unions. In the coal industry, where John L. Lewis was a strong labor leader, he waved Section 7a like a flag and told miners that it was their patriotic duty to join the union. Sidney Hillman and David Dubinsky, representing the men's and ladies' garment industries, respectively, also used Section 7a to build their unions.

In 1933, before the NRA, unions had declined in strength to fewer than 3 million members. This was the first time since World War I that there were so few union members. A few months after the establishment of the NRA, AFL unions alone added nearly a million members. Yet the effect of Section 7a should not be exaggerated. It took new legislation and several great organization drives over another decade for unions to reach their zenith. Nevertheless, by the time the Supreme Court killed the NRA, unions had gained strength and fighting spirit.

Employers countered the growth of dynamic unions by developing company unions. Between 1933 and 1935, they created almost four hundred such unions. Secretary Perkins accepted these unions when they were the free choice of workers, but she considered most of them "war brides" married hastily under pressure of industrial conflict. As arbitrator in a dispute in which U.S. Steel tried to use a company union to beat a drive by an independent union, she decided that the company union could not sign wage agreements. This action virtually sounded the death knell for company unions in that period.

The National Labor Relations Board

Aside from Secretary Perkins's role vis-à-vis company unions, the Department of Labor was out of the mainstream of new developments in labor relations during the 1930's. Senator Robert Wagner of New York was the driving force behind the landmark labor law in 1935 that bore his name.

Secretary Perkins helped Wagner in the planning that led to the establishment in 1933 of the National Labor Board. This board, created by executive order, handled disputes under the NRA. It was set up outside the Department of Labor, thus raising the question of which cases would be handled by the Conciliation Service in the Department. But an agreement determined which labor cases were NRA violations, which ones went to the National Labor Board, and which ones went to the Conciliation Service in the Department of Labor. Secretary Perkins said, "I find no sense of jealousy, no sense of conflict." But some officials felt her claim had a hollow ring.

Secretary Perkins liked the premise of the National Labor Board that it would seek voluntary agreements. But the Board lacked the authority to make its decisions effective and could not cope with the increasing number of strikes triggered by conflicting interpretations of the National Industrial Recovery Act. Some labor leaders began to refer to the NRA as the "National Runaround."

Senator Wagner submitted a bill to create a stronger board, whose powers would be based on legislative authority. Secretary Perkins opposed this bill and gained instead the President's approval for a National Labor Relations Board, established by executive order, which reported to the President through the Secretary of Labor. Miss Perkins helped to select the chairman of the Board. This development would have been a victory for the Department of Labor if the board idea had worked.

The Board did not succeed. It had a hard job to do but lacked the power to do it. The Board's most serious weakness was that it could not require unwilling employers to bargain with unions.

Congress finally turned to Senator Wagner's program. The Wagner Act, as passed by Congress and signed by the President on July 5, 1935, reasserted the principles of Section 7a of the National Industrial Recovery Act and spelled out in statutory law the rights of workers to organize and bargain collectively. It prohibited employers from interfering with these rights, enumerated various "unfair" practices such as firing employees for union activities and refusing to bargain with unions, and established a strong National Labor Relations Board.

Secretary Perkins and President Roosevelt both felt the Wagner Act was one-sided, protecting the rights of labor only. Wagner answered that such seemingly just criticism was meaningless in the practical world of labor relations. No one assailed traffic laws on the ground that they regulated the speed of automobiles without also regulating the speed at which pedestrians could walk. Employers, he argued, had nothing to fear; it was labor that needed protection.

Roosevelt accepted the Wagner Act to avoid a break with unions and with Senator Wagner. Secretary Perkins hoped that the new National Labor Relations Board would be placed in the Department of Labor. Wagner, however, called for an independent board arguing that the country might think a board within the Department of Labor was too biased. Wagner won.

The Great Strike Wave

A strike wave marked the period of the NRA and the Wagner Act. During the early stages of the Depression, workers were afraid to strike, but, after the New Deal brought a little prosperity, the accumulated frustrations began to erupt. Between 1930 and 1934, the number of man-days lost in strikes rose sixfold to 19.6 million and then to a pre–World War II peak of 28.4 million in 1937.

Department of Labor conciliators scurried about the country, trying to dampen the fires of industrial warfare. Secretary Perkins hardly had taken office when her Department helped to mediate a bloody trucking strike in Minneapolis in which teamsters won the right to be represented by their own union. In San Francisco, striking longshoremen turned down a Department of Labor compromise, and after two strikers were killed in July, 1934, other unions joined with the longshoremen for the first general strike since 1919. Some Cabinet members, fearing revolution, called for drastic measures. Secretary Perkins, however, thought it unwise to shoot it out with strikers, and Roosevelt backed her up. The general strike collapsed after four days, and the longshoremen ultimately accepted arbitration. In textile strikes, deputies killed six strikers in South Carolina; in Rhode Island, textile workers fought with troops. The bitterness of the antagonism is illustrated by the comment of a trade journal: "A few hundred funerals would have a quieting influence." In September, 1934, the various groups of textile workers accepted defeat.

The 1936 sit-down strike at General Motors is among the most important events in American labor history. On December 28, 1936, 1,700 workers stayed after work at two plants in Flint, Michigan. Besides desiring higher wages for its members, the United Auto Workers wanted to become the "sole bargaining agency" for employees at General Motors. The corporation said that it would bargain with the union on wages but that employment with General Motors would "depend on the ability and efficiency of the workers—not on membership or nonmembership in any labor organization. . . . You do not have to pay tribute to anyone for the right to work." The union continued to insist on recognition as the sole bargaining agency in pursuance of provisions of the Wagner Act.

Staging a sit-down strike simply meant that the workers continued to stay in the plant after their day's work was finished. The workers knew that, if they remained in the plant, strike breakers could not fill their jobs. Moreover, in a mechanized industry where all work is interrelated, the sit-down enabled a few workers to tie up an entire industry. A handful of sit-downers paralyzed giant General Motors so effectively that in February, 1937, the company produced only 151 cars.

General Motors officials looked upon the sit-down as an invasion of property rights and refused to negotiate until the strikers evacuated the plants. Secretary Perkins and President Roosevelt agreed that sit-down strikes were illegal, but, as Roosevelt said, "You don't shoot a man because he trespasses on your property." Another reason that General Motors did not want a bloody eviction of the workers was that public reaction to such violent action might make it difficult to sell cars for a generation.

Secretary Perkins tried to convince General Motors that its self-serving avowed concern for workers was not as effective a way to end the strike as flexibility and common sense. She wanted company and union officials to talk things out, but General Motors president Alfred Sloan refused.

The country was emerging from the Depression and General Motors had a better chance to sell cars than it had had for many years. The strike hurt the workers, hurt the economy, and hurt General Motors. The company finally, in a face-saving effort, agreed to negotiate if the President personally requested it to do so.

President Roosevelt had never met William Knudsen, the production head at General Motors. But he phoned him and said pleasantly, "Is that you, Bill? I know you have been through a lot, Bill . . . but Miss Perkins has told me about the situation. . . . I hope very much indeed that . . . your people will meet a committee." The President and Knudsen exchanged expressions of admiration. A few days later the strike came to an end, though it took time to work out the details.

Face-saving aside, the outcome was a great victory for the United Auto Workers' Union. Regardless of legal or moral issues, the sit-down technique was, at that time, effective.

The government role had been decisive. The Department of Labor insisted that the government was impartial. But there are degrees of "impartiality." If the government had impartially refused to intervene, that would probably have meant the defeat of the union. The government's impartiality in insisting that the two parties bargain in good faith, combined with the tenacity of union supporters, made it possible for the union to organize. In the months following the strike, union membership increased to 400,000 and the United Automobile Workers became a great union and a force to be reckoned with in the country.

The side effects of the union victory over General Motors not only included the unionization of the other major auto manufacturers but also created the climate for collective bargaining in other mass production industries. In the steel industry, for example, Secretary Perkins influenced President Roosevelt to get the major companies to bargain with the Steel Workers Organizing Committee (SWOC), and the resulting contract signed in March, 1937, was another union victory.

But the "little" steel companies, important as a group, held out. Secretary Perkins appointed a distinguished mediation board to deal with this problem, but the effort failed. In a violent strike marked by the wanton killing of 18 men and the wounding of 168, the union was beaten. In the past, such a defeat would have ended unionization in these companies for a generation. But government influence, not on the terms of settlement but on the principle that both sides should bargain in good faith, enabled the union to ride out the defeat.

The vigorous drives to organize the workers in mass production industries created both anticipation and terror in the hearts of the old-line labor leaders of the American Federation of Labor. The unions that had survived best after World War I were those of skilled workers organized by craft. Their leaders did not know how to handle industry-wide organization of unskilled and semiskilled workers. In the words of a labor reporter, they felt about mass production workers the way an old man "feels about a young and desirable woman. He wants her, and he is afraid."

When the American Federation of Labor rejected unrestricted organization of mass production industries in 1935, a Committee of Industrial Organizations (CIO) split away. Secretary Perkins appealed to the warring factions to settle their dispute, but she kept "hands off" in deciding on the merits of the controversy. President Roosevelt, beginning in 1938, sent annual appeals for peace to both the CIO and the AFL. He told the leaders, at first in general terms, that the fight had gone too far. Then, in February, 1939, he sent identical letters to leaders on both sides, inviting them to meet under his auspices. Committees met at the White House, but President Roosevelt told Secretary Perkins prophetically, "I don't think they have the slightest intention of making peace."

The split in labor's ranks caused serious problems for the Department of Labor and the Roosevelt Administration. John L. Lewis, leading the CIO, was a source of special difficulty. He freely expressed his view that the government did not give labor enough support. When Roosevelt, exasperated by the obstinacy of both management and labor during the "little steel" strike, unguardedly invoked "a plague on both your houses," Lewis retorted, "It ill behooves one who has supped at labor's table . . . to curse with equal fervor and fine impartiality both labor and its adversaries when they become locked in deadly combat." In the 1940 election, Lewis attacked Secretary Perkins savagely and appealed to workers to vote against Roosevelt, saying that, if Roosevelt were reelected, he would resign as head of the CIO. Most workers voted for Roosevelt. When Roosevelt won the election, Lewis kept his promise.

The instinct of the workers was correct. Although Roosevelt was neutral on specific issues, he was friendly to workers and their goals. When he first took office, there were fewer than 3 million labor union members in the United States. By 1940, membership had tripled to nearly 9 million. It reached almost 15 million by the end of World War II, which was the period of the greatest growth of labor unions in American history.

The Fight for Decent Pay and Working Conditions

In contrast to her secondary role in labor relations, Secretary Perkins was the star of the dramatic events leading to enactment of the Fair Labor Standards Act of 1938. When Roosevelt asked her to become Secretary of Labor, she warned him that if she accepted she would want to put a floor under wages, set up a ceiling over hours of work, and abolish child labor. She made the achievement of these ends a major goal of the Department of Labor.

During the Depression, labor standards had collapsed. While millions had been looking for work, other men, women, and children had been working long hours for pitifully low wages. Sweatshops had been the order of the day in many industries. In 1933, President Roosevelt promulgated under the National Recovery Administration a document called the President's Re-employment Agreement, by which employers who signed committed themselves to paying not less than $15 weekly for a forty-hour week. This was followed by specific codes establishing wage and hour standards on an industry-by-industry basis.

At the time, there was serious doubt whether a federal law regulating wages, hours, and working conditions was constitutional. Secretary Perkins turned to the tedious task of gaining the same ends by persuasion. A Division of Labor Standards in the Department of Labor cooperated with state governments on a variety of laws and standards covering such matters as workmen's compensation, safety and health, shorter hours, child labor, and minimum wages.

Secretary Perkins also told the President that the Department of Labor had studied legislation for a national program that could salvage labor standards set by the NRA and that she had a plan "locked up in the lower left-hand drawer of my desk." During the 1936 campaign, Roosevelt promised he would try to find some way of establishing fair labor standards. After his re-election, Roosevelt asked Secretary Perkins, "What happened to that nice unconstitutional bill you had tucked away?" She sent her proposal to the White House for study.

The opposition to labor standards at that time was fierce. When a bill on the subject was introduced in Congress in 1937, even labor unions opposed it, fearing that minimum wages would tend to become the maximum. It was one of the few programs that both organized labor and organized manu-

facturers sought to defeat. The bill passed in the Senate but
died in the House Committee on Rules.

President Roosevelt called a special session of Congress in
November, 1937, at which he stated that the exploitation of
child labor, the undercutting of wages, and the stretching of
hours of work of the poorest paid workers prolonged depressions and placed burdens on those least able to bear them. In
the legislative struggle that followed, Roosevelt suffered his
first major defeat on the floor of the House. Many observers
believed that wage-hour legislation was doomed.

Roosevelt, however, did not surrender. When Congress re-
convened in January, 1938, he said that he wanted to end
starvation wages and intolerable hours of work. Secretary
Perkins pushed for adoption of a revised and watered-down bill.
The President's hand was strengthened when two supporters of
the wage-hour regulations won spectacular victories in key
special elections in Florida and Alabama. As soon as the election results were announced, previously reluctant congressmen stampeded to support the measure. On June 25, 1938,
President Roosevelt signed the new law. The Fair Labor
Standards Act, which had been a rejected orphan, now found
many would-be fathers.

The Act set minimum nationwide standards. The work
week was first set at forty-four hours, with reductions to forty
hours over a three-year period and time-and-a-half payment
for overtime work. The higher overtime pay was an inducement to employers to spread the work among wage earners.
The minimum wage was set at 25 cents an hour, rising to 30
cents a year later, and 40 cents over an additional period of
time, varying from industry to industry. Children under sixteen were prohibited from working in many industries, and
employment of those under fourteen was banned in all covered
nonagricultural fields.

The Fair Labor Standards Act was a precedent-making
achievement in its time. It covered an estimated 12.5 million
workers who were either engaged in interstate commerce or

producing goods for interstate commerce. It immediately raised the pay of 300,000 workers and shortened work hours for a million more. The law was a giant step toward a "fair day's work."

The Birth of Social Security

Perhaps the most enduring landmark of her career was Frances Perkins's contribution to the creation of Social Security. From a halting start, Social Security has become a basic element in this country's economic structure.

Social Security during the Depression was only one aspect of the great war against destitution. Public works and work relief were emergency measures. But President Roosevelt wanted to lay the cornerstone of a system that would outlast the Depression. He spoke of every child at birth having an insurance policy to protect him against economic hazards of unemployment, sickness, and old age. He wanted a simple and all-inclusive system "from the cradle to the grave"—a phrase he used long before it was popularized in England during World War II.

On practical grounds, the initial plan had to be restricted. Secretary Perkins chose insurance against unemployment as the first priority. Just as a manufacturer protected machinery when it was idle, so society, she said, should care for its workers when they were unemployed through no fault of their own. Employers should contribute to a fund that would assure workers of a floor under their earnings should they become unemployed. If the unemployment dragged on beyond the time the insurance would cover, then the worker, according to Secretary Perkins's thinking, would be entitled to a relief job.

Popular sentiment for old-age insurance was even stronger than that for unemployment benefits. With the possible exception of blacks, no part of the population suffered more than the old. Depression had dragged substantial people, who had worked and saved, downward into the ranks of paupers—with no savings, no jobs, no job prospects. Life became steadily bleaker as men and women declined physically and financially over the years. Dr. Francis Townsend, an unemployed sixty-two-year-old physician, expressed the spirit of the times as he told of looking out of his window and seeing "three haggard, very old women . . . stooped with great age" clawing at the contents of garbage cans in the alley below him. With missionary zeal, he organized a movement for a federal pension for everyone over sixty, amounting to $200 a month, at that time a large sum of money, provided they did not work and spent the money immediately. This would take people off a labor market where there were too many workers and not enough jobs, and it would pump money into the economic system. Secretary Perkins opposed the Townsend Plan and similar campaigns as being irresponsible and perhaps leading to national bankruptcy. But she understood the economic disease from which such a movement grew, and she worked for responsible remedies.

President Roosevelt appointed a Committee on Economic Security made up mainly of Cabinet members. Secretary of Labor Perkins was chairman. She attended every meeting, worked out compromises of differences, and presented to the President a program for the Administration to submit to Congress. She then helped guide the program through Congress and made hundreds of speeches on its behalf.

Secretary Perkins had hoped that the administration of Social Security would end up in the Department of Labor, but, as with other measures, she lacked the required political support to achieve this goal. Many opponents argued that Department of Labor administration would favor workers. The bill, when it finally emerged from Congress and was approved by the President, placed Social Security outside the Department of Labor under the administration of an independent board.

The Social Security Act of 1935 provided two kinds of insurance for workers. The first type was for unemployment, to help the worker over the difficult period after he had lost his job. The employer paid the premium. The second type of insurance covered old age. Here the employer contributed one dollar for every dollar of premium collected from the worker, with the government holding the money for the benefit of the worker in his old age. Although Secretary Perkins lost jurisdiction over Social Security, she achieved acceptance of her principle that working people would be provided for during unemployment and in their old age, not as a matter of charity but as a matter of right.

If these first arrangements for unemployment and old-age insurance had been administered purely as insurance, they would have covered very few people, the benefits would have been delayed a long time, and the amounts would have been pitifully small. Even in the bill that was passed, Social Security copied many features from private insurance, where benefits had to be paid out of funds supplied by premium payments. Therefore, many workers who were already unemployed or old were not covered. But the government is not a profit-making insurance company, and, even at the beginning, it made many exceptions to provide some benefits not warranted under strict insurance principles.

With the passage of time, Social Security laws have been repeatedly broadened, and many people have been covered and benefits increased, beyond the limits that would be justified strictly on the basis of premiums paid. Social Security still has an insurance aspect, as benefits are often related at least partially to premiums. But today these laws have some features that, instead of being insurance-based, actually form part of a body of social legislation protecting most Americans. Secretary of Labor Perkins helped to plant in fertile soil a seed that yielded a fruitful crop to future generations of Americans.

THE DEPARTMENT DURING WORLD WAR II

The great spurt of social reforms sponsored by the Department of Labor came to a halt with U.S. involvement in World

War II. Government took on a new role in which the Department of Labor did not participate pivotally. Secretary Perkins, to be sure, argued that "the Department of Labor was not weakened by the war. It was strengthened. It got larger appropriations" for its programs. But she was engaging in an exercise in apologetics. Unlike what had happened in World War I, when the Secretary of Labor was the War Labor Administrator, war agencies during World War II regularly bypassed the Department of Labor.

The low status of the Department of Labor resulted from many factors. Secretary Perkins did not get so excited about wartime needs that she abandoned peacetime standards. She did not fear labor shortages, because she remembered the large number of men and women unemployed during the Depression. Although she did not condone strikes, she understood that for the first time in many years workers were not afraid to risk their jobs to enforce their demands. Factually, she was right; politically, she was wrong. Her reasoned attitude reflected neither the very real employer fear of labor shortages nor the strong public anger against strikers in wartime.

President Roosevelt's attitude toward administrative management was another reason why the Department of Labor was pushed into the background. Roosevelt thought a little rivalry between government officials was stimulating. He favored extensive use of temporary agencies. If these agencies developed bad practices born of wartime needs, he felt, these practices would be eliminated with the agencies' demise after the war.

The Department of Labor was left with only its peacetime functions plus a few special wartime duties. Secretary Perkins referred to the Department as the "wheelhorse" that helped other war agencies. When conflicts developed between various agencies over manpower, the President asked her to "take the lead in getting them together." At Roosevelt's direction, she sat in on so many committee meetings that attendance at such meetings became her principal wartime job.

Energetic political and labor leaders brushed the Secretary of Labor aside in developing wartime manpower policies. Roosevelt relied heavily in this area on Sidney Hillman, a union leader, who became a powerful member of the Advisory Commission of the National Defense Council. Hillman built up a large staff of labor advisers, and the army, the navy, and other war agencies did likewise. Frequently, when there was a problem, "troubleshooters" from different agencies would offer conflicting advice, and the first problem was for the "adjusters" to settle their own differences.

When labor unrest threatened war production, Secretary Perkins suggested that a National Defense Mediation Board, with representatives of management, labor, and the public, be created. The Board, established in March, 1941, did not last long. In a dispute over the closed shop in "captive mines" (mines owned by steel companies) producing coal for United States Steel, the Board held that workers did not have to join the union in order to work in the mines. The CIO labor representatives resigned and crippled the Board.

The President then revived the World War I idea of a labor-management conference. The Japanese had just attacked Pearl Harbor, and the nation was suddenly plunged into war. The President, at a White House meeting, appealed to leaders to submerge their differences for a common cause.

A Second National War Labor Board

Labor and management representatives pledged that there would be no strikes in wartime and that they would settle disputes by collective bargaining. If they could not agree, it was decided, a new National War Labor Board would have final authority. This board, though similar to its World War I predecessor, recognized that labor problems concerned not only workers and owners but the public as well. In addition to the labor and management members of the World War I board, public members were added to the new War Labor Board, and a chairman was picked from one of the public members.

The War Labor Board met at the Department of Labor but was an independent agency. The Conciliation Service in the Department of Labor dealt first with strike problems, but the tougher disputes went to the War Labor Board. Although the no-strike pledge was often violated, it had some effect. The ratio of man-hours lost because of strikes to man-hours worked during the war ran only from two-tenths to four-tenths of one per cent, which is better than the average ratio of these figures in peacetime.

The War Labor Board worked against one of the worst economic problems in time of war, inflation and its most prominent effect—intolerable increases in the cost of living. In World War II, an Office of Price Administration tried, with limited success, to control prices. To reduce nonmilitary demand for goods, the government increased taxes, rationed scarce commodities, and promoted savings through war bonds. As another anti-inflation measure, the War Labor Board tried to hold down wages. The Board permitted exceptions for "catch-up" increases, for maintaining labor standards, for remedying inequities among workers, and for promoting the prosecution of the war. However, the bulk of improvement in wages came through fringe benefits and the time-and-a-half provision for hours worked in excess of forty hours a week.

Some unions were not satisfied with the increases allowed by the War Labor Board. The coal miners, under John L. Lewis, went out in a series of bitter wartime strikes. No matter what the government or the army could do, the simple fact remained that, in Lewis's words, "You can't mine coal with bayonets." At the end of a series of complicated moves, the miners got much of what they had demanded. In a face-saving settlement on the issue of portal-to-portal pay, miners, though they were not paid for the actual amount of time they spent in travel, received extra pay for forty-five minutes a day.

Other unions or employers occasionally defied the War Labor Board. In some cases, the President resorted to "plant seizure." The government took over and symbolically managed the plants, while the employers and employees continued operations because they were working under the American flag. Most of the plant seizures were in war industries, though occasionally a nonmilitary operation was taken over in order to maintain the authority of the Board. One of the most famous was the seizure of the Montgomery Ward mail-order firm, in the course of which soldiers bodily carried out the elderly, dignified president of the company. Secretary Perkins did not think it was a good idea for the army or any other government agency to run a business, but at times it seemed the best of several bad alternatives to enable the country to get on with the war.

Senators and congressmen introduced many antistrike bills to satisfy the popular resentment against men who went on strike while others were endangering their lives. One bill enacted in 1941, the Smith-Connally Act, called for a "cooling-off" period before a strike could be called. Actually, modern strikes are not based on anger, and "cooling-off" often results in a heating-up period, during which both sides use the time to fortify their positions. Yet it was one way of trying to harness workers and employers to pull together in the national interest.

The War Manpower Commission

Passions were also stirred in a debate over "national service." President Roosevelt was impressed by the national service system in Great Britain, where every man or woman over eighteen could be assigned where he or she was most needed. But Britain was smaller and more homogeneous than the United States and was more seriously threatened with imminent destruction. In the early war years, the United States was still more worried about unemployment than labor shortages. Yet it seemed to many only fair that, if some men were called for military service, others should be subject to call for labor service.

At first, the President considered a centralized manpower program administered by the Department of Labor, with policy established by representatives of management, labor, the military, and the Selective Service. But the Labor Department was considered too "soft" on labor, and the President bowed to public pressure. He created in April, 1942, a War Manpower Commission.

The War Manpower Commission fell short of the idea of "national service." It operated on a voluntary basis without legal support. Unions opposed giving it too much power, because that might end in conscription of labor for private profit. Secretary Perkins thought it a giant government bureaucracy competing with existing agencies and establishing dangerous controls over human beings. Paul McNutt, the War Manpower commissioner, wanted to run for President and probably had too many political ambitions to take strong action on manpower assignment. He followed a cautious, fence-sitting course.

As manpower gradually became a limiting factor in meeting schedules for war production, the War Manpower Commission tried to coordinate the work of other government agencies in channeling workers to places where they were most needed. It tried to use in this way the United States Employment Service, which had become its operating arm. Because USES had been primarily an agency for referring people to relief jobs and, after 1938, for certifying workers for unemployment insurance, it faced difficulty in winning recognition of its new role from the military, civilian procurement agencies, and private employers. Most workers continued to be hired through peacetime procedures. Yet, in 1944, USES placed more than 12 million workers compared to about 4 million in

1940. Toward the end of the war, the War Manpower Commission began to emerge as the central manpower organization for the war effort.

Despite the eclipse of the Department of Labor and the limitations of the War Manpower Commission, manpower mobilization during World War II was a success. Jobless workers provided a huge pool on which the country drew. Between the spring of 1940 and the spring of 1945, unemployment declined by 7 million. In addition, 6 million women and 4 million youths joined the labor force. Retirements slowed up. Older people, the physically handicapped, and other victims of job discrimination got decent jobs. Workers moved from lower-paid jobs to higher-paid war work. Labor was never really short, national service was never needed, and manpower needs were handled by the incentives of higher pay and better working conditions.

Aftermath of War

One of the sad paradoxes of World War II was that it took a war to end the Depression. War created full employment, which provided working people with decent jobs for the first time in a decade. World War II widened the nation's horizons with respect to its economic capability and increased the expectations of American workers for a better life.

Among the beneficiaries of the demand for labor during the war were black workers. The Department of Labor had been concerned with the problem of racial discrimination in employment during the Depression. Secretary Perkins wrote to the President's wife, Eleanor Roosevelt, that her department was setting an example by appointing blacks to professional positions. But it is hard to fight discrimination when everybody is scrambling desperately for work. After several false starts, in June, 1941, President Roosevelt established a Fair Employment Practices Committee to combat discrimination. Although this innovative agency faced many difficulties, it argued with some effect that increasing the output of war goods would reduce war casualties, by increasing production and providing soldiers with the weapons with which to fight. Although it did not accomplish all that it had hoped, and its enemies killed it after the war, the agency established a precedent in dealing with job discrimination.

Perhaps the Labor Department's most effective war activity was the preservation of labor standards. Contractors claimed that labor laws interfered with speed and efficiency. The Department resisted the drive, conducted under the guise of patriotism, to repeal or suspend labor laws limiting child labor, safeguarding women, and protecting workers against job hazards. If any law interfered with a particular program in a particular factory, the Department of Labor agreed to suspend the law for the factory affected, while making sure that the workers' basic needs were met.

The war required many factories to operate seven days a week, twenty-four hours a day. Machines could work all the time. People could not. The Labor Department maintained the principle of the eight-hour day, though it allowed a six-day week. Plants could remain in continuous operation by using three or more shifts of workers. Secretary Perkins agreed that a forty-eight-hour week increased production over the peacetime forty-hour week, while the time-and-a-half pay for the extra eight hours gave workers substantially more income for their extra effort. But she held that additional hours over forty-eight a week caused more accidents, more absenteeism, and a deterioration of quality without much more output. The United States won the war with a forty-eight-hour work week, with its basic labor standards intact, and with most workers in better jobs earning more weekly pay than they had before the war.

FRANCES PERKINS: AN APPRAISAL

Shortly after Roosevelt's death, Frances Perkins resigned as Secretary of Labor. In her twelve years, the longest period for any Secretary of Labor, she had proved to be one of the best, and one of the worst, Secretaries. On one hand, her tenure made the Department of Labor a seedbed for social progress. On the other hand, the Department of Labor was not assigned the new labor functions that emerged in this period of vast social change.

Secretary of Labor Perkins did not have much political backing. With notable exceptions, she had little support from unions, the press, or Congress. It is too sweeping to say that labor leaders did not like her. Only rarely did unions attack her. Though her interest in unorganized workers, child labor, blacks, the disabled, the aged, and other groups of workers had union acquiescence, unions simply were not enthusiastic about the Department of Labor. Secretary Perkins was impartial in the civil war between the American Federation of Labor and the newer Congress of Industrial Organizations and was attacked by both sides. Although it was against her nature to look down on labor leaders, as an educated Puritan lady she could not be "one of the boys." The sentiment toward Frances Perkins was probably caught by Wendell Willkie when he ran for President against Roosevelt in 1940. Willkie told his labor audience, "I will appoint a Secretary of Labor directly from the ranks of organized labor." When the cheers died down, he added, "and it will not be a woman either."

Secretary Perkins had the poorest press image of any Cabinet member. As expressed by one magazine, "Of all the game in the Roosevelt preserve, Secretary of Labor Perkins has been the most frequently chased and most savagely harried." Intellectual, modest, with a sick husband whom she shielded from the public eye, she avoided human-interest interviews of herself as either a career woman or a homemaker. She had no flair for publicity, and her press conferences had the reputation of being the dullest in town.

Her relations with Congress were even worse than with the newspapers. In her formal appearances, she did well, for she knew what she was talking about. Although Senators Harry S.

Truman and Robert F. Wagner liked her, most congressmen did not. Of course, some of them would have opposed any Secretary of Labor. But her tendency to lecture on social philosophy made congressmen feel like dull schoolboys. Secretary Perkins brought many able employees to the Department of Labor, but her defense of appointments based on merit angered many patronage-hungry congressmen.

Congress hit back by cutting appropriations for the Department of Labor and locating functions outside the Department. There were several good reasons for making the National Labor Relations Board independent, but one of the more realistic causes of the Department's failure to get it was Secretary Perkins's lack of influence. And, though she wanted Social Security in the Department of Labor, she could not muster the strength to hold it. For a time, the U.S. Employment Service was transferred out of the Department. The U.S. Housing Corporation, in the Department of Labor since World War I, was moved over to the Treasury. Even though Secretary Perkins willingly let the Immigration Service go to the Department of Justice, she recognized that acceptance of the loss was a retreat from a position where her humane views could have been effective.

In the perspective of history, Frances Perkins achieved much; from the internal view, however, under her administration the Department of Labor was stunted in growth at the time of great expansion of the federal government. In 1932, Herbert Hoover's last year as President, appropriations for the Department of Labor totaled $15 million; the highest appropriation for any of the war years between 1941 and 1944 was $14.1 million. While federal employment shot up from 600,000 in 1932 to more than 3.5 million at the end of World War II, Department of Labor employment dropped from 6,000 to 5,230 in the same period.

If Frances Perkins was among the worst Secretaries of Labor from a bureaucratic viewpoint, in terms of long-range social change she was one of the best. Although concerned with the Department of Labor as an organization, she was more concerned with the nation as a whole. Her effort on behalf of the unemployed, her drive to create humane standards of work and wages, and her activities on behalf of social welfare probably had a greater permanent influence on American social history than the activities of most of her administratively more successful New Deal associates.

III

Recent Decades—1945 to the Present

News from Warm Springs, Georgia, on April 12, 1945, shocked the nation: President Franklin Roosevelt was dead. Harry S. Truman, the "little man" from Missouri, was sworn in as President.

Truman assumed the Presidency during a period marked by serious labor problems. It was the irony of the times. On one hand, Americans had more savings and purchasing power than ever before; on the other hand, there was industrial warfare caused by cutbacks, the closing of war plants, and a fear of unemployment.

Truman saw himself as the heir of the Economic Bill of Rights promulgated by Roosevelt in 1944, under which everyone would have a right to a job, shelter, and education. Truman's concern was to keep nearly the same high level of employment in peace as had been reached in war. The resulting Employment Act of 1946 declared as a national policy the promotion of maximum employment. The Act was aimed at fighting the widely predicted catastrophic postwar unemployment.

Predictions of a wave of unemployment, based on the traumatic memories of the Depression, were logical, convincing, and wrong. Mass unemployment did not materialize. In a quarter of a century following passage of the Employment Act, the unemployment rate averaged 4.6 per cent compared with rates of 15 per cent to 25 per cent during the Depression years. The Employment Act had been called a pioneer law, which might establish a new direction for history. Instead, it turned out to be a symbol. Some of the lesser provisions have had the most far-reaching effects. The Employment Act created the important Joint Economic Committee of Congress and the Council of Economic Advisers to the President. The purpose of these organizations has been to promote higher quality of economic life, the goal that President Truman's Employment Act set for national policy.

THE TRUMAN ERA: SCHWELLENBACH AND TOBIN

President Truman was sympathetic to labor. Yet this sympathy did not allay his conviction that organized labor had to consider the good of the public as a whole. As labor-management relations worsened, the public turned against labor, and Truman faced an uphill battle on most of his prolabor proposals.

In this tumultuous situation, Truman called upon his Senate crony Lewis B. Schwellenbach to become Secretary of Labor. Schwellenbach found the concepts of the New Deal akin to his own philosophy, and Roosevelt in 1940 had appointed him a judge of the U.S. District Court for eastern Washington. It looked as if, in Schwellenbach, the nation had a man who could handle tough labor leaders and industrialists. He was a good mediator in his own right.

Schwellenbach had hardly assumed office when he was engulfed by a strike wave. During the first year following V-J Day, more strikes broke out than in any previous year of American history. Work stoppages involved 5 million workers and resulted in 120 million man-days of idleness.

Disputes about wages and fringe benefits were the most common cause of strikes. Union members totaling 14.5 million were in no mood to slide back from their earning levels of the war years, while management, under controlled prices, was equally determined to hold the line on wages.

The War Labor Board, which had handled labor disputes during the war, was transferred to the Department of Labor after hostilities ended. Schwellenbach had the machinery to make settlements but often could not use it. Instead of persisting along the Labor Board line, he tried to strengthen the Conciliation Service, which he liked because he felt that disputes could be settled if the participants sat down together, talked things over, and compromised. During the peak strike year of 1946, the Conciliation Service helped to adjust more than fifteen thousand disputes. About three out of four were settled peacefully.

In some disputes when conciliation failed, Schwellenbach turned to fact-finding boards. Bringing to bear the informed findings of a panel of public-spirited men, backed by public opinion, sometimes worked. In many cases, however, it did not.

Schwellenbach discussed the problem of industrial peace with the President. As a result, Truman called a Conference of Labor and Management similar to the one held after World War I. Like its post–World War I counterpart, the conference accomplished little. The hope that the two sides could find some way of resolving their differences without stopping production was frustrated. While the conference was floundering, a strike erupted at General Motors, where management had emphatically turned down the union demand for a 30 per cent wage increase as "unreasonable and inflationary." After a 113-day strike involving 200,000 workers, General Motors agreed to about half of the union's 30 per cent demand. This increase, amounting to 18.5 cents an hour, had already become the pattern in other major industries.

The three most serious strikes during the first six months of 1946 broke out in the steel, coal, and railroad industries. The President recruited John R. Steelman, chief of the Conciliation Service, to help directly in this situation and put him on the White House staff. Ostensibly, Steelman's new position was intended to strengthen the hand of the Secretary of Labor. Actually, Steelman became more influential personally and undermined Schwellenbach's position. Even with Steelman's skill, the government had to allow an increase of $5 a ton in the price of steel (to offset a wage hike), seize and operate the coal mines, and take over the railroads.

The strike wave diminished around the summer of 1946. Truman, backed by Schwellenbach, abolished wage and price controls because they were no longer useful. Although big strikes were less frequent, strong antilabor sentiment swept the country. The public blamed the unions for inconveniences caused by strikes.

In the fall of 1946, labor suffered its worst political defeat since the New Deal era. On the first day of the Eightieth Congress, seventeen bills were proposed to amend the Wagner Act or to curb unions. The antiunion campaign culminated in the Taft-Hartley bill. Secretary Schwellenbach testified vehemently, but in vain, against it. Truman, on June 20, 1947, vetoed the bill as contrary to economic freedom and as government interference in collective bargaining. Congress overrode the veto by a large majority.

The new Taft-Hartley law (officially the Labor-Management Relations Act) remains to this day the basic legislation on unions. One of its chief provisions outlawed the "closed shop"; this provision meant that a man could be hired even if he were not a member of the union. However, if a contract provided for it, a worker—once he had been hired—could be forced to join a union to keep his job. The law also provided for "cooling-off" periods in national emergencies and prohibited certain union practices designated as unfair, including secondary boycotts and compulsory political contributions from members. In practice, though the Taft-Hartley Act weakened some unions, it did not cripple labor and did not turn out to be the "slave labor" bill that some of its opponents had called it.

One of the provisions of the Taft-Hartley Act removed the Conciliation Service from the Department of Labor and made it an independent agency. Secretary Schwellenbach fought hard to retain control of the service, but it became the independent Federal Mediation and Conciliation Service. Its transfer took away most of the Secretary's authority in this field.

When Schwellenbach had become Secretary, one of his first goals was to increase the influence of the Department of Labor and bring back into its fold some of the twenty-odd independent federal labor agencies. He wanted to make the Department more than a statistics-collecting agency. President Truman had indicated his support.

At the end of the war, several agencies were brought back to the Department before they were disbanded. These were the National Wage Stabilization Board, the Shipbuilding Stabilization Committee, the Wage Adjustment Board, and the Retraining and Re-employment Administration. The Apprentice-Training Service and the U.S. Employment Service were also brought back into the Department.

However, after the election of 1946, the Department became the number one target of the Eightieth, or "meat-axe," Congress. It did gain the function of safeguarding veterans' re-employment rights, but generally it was reduced to a skeleton consisting of a stripped down Bureau of Labor Statistics, a tiny Women's Bureau, the Bureau of Labor Standards, the Wage and Hour Division, and the Public Contracts Division.

Schwellenbach came to be caught in a chain of events that destroyed him. His grand plans for reorganizing government labor functions into a strong Department of Labor crumbled. He was trapped in the middle of the great postwar strike wave.

Then, during a maritime strike in 1946, he fell and hurt his back severely. Family problems added to his frustrations. An associate reported:

> He'd married late in life and he had a wife who was enough to drive any man into the asylum. . . . Oh, poor fellow, he had no consolation anywhere. . . . He would love to have me come up to his office. . . . He would call me in at 12:30 . . . and I'd find myself there at 3:00. . . . He'd lean back in his chair and he would start reminiscing and talking about things in the old days. . . . I would just sit and say, "Yes" . . . and sometimes I would just have to say, "Well, Mr. Secretary, I'll just have to leave you alone now, you have a lot of things to do, I'm sorry I took so much time."

In the spring of 1948, Schwellenbach was stricken with a respiratory disease. He was reported to be recovering, but he suddenly died on June 10, 1948.

By the time of his death, the Department of Labor appropriations had been cut from $113 million in fiscal 1947 to about $15 million the following year. By fiscal 1949, the number of employees in the Department dropped to 3,340, the smallest staff since the days of President Calvin Coolidge.

After Schwellenbach's death, President Truman appointed Maurice Tobin Secretary of Labor. Tobin, born in 1901 to Irish immigrant parents in Roxbury, Massachusetts, was a promising choice. He had been elected mayor of Boston in 1938 and governor of Massachusetts in 1944. Having been defeated for re-election in 1946, he was planning a comeback in 1948 through a primary that threatened to split the Democratic Party. The President offered Tobin the position of Secretary of Labor, and Tobin accepted. The move was smart politics on Truman's part. It helped the Democratic Party and strengthened the Department of Labor. Tobin brought to the Department labor support, and he became the first Catholic Secretary of Labor.

Tobin dedicated himself to repairing the damage that had been done to the Department. But, before he could implement his plans, Truman had to be re-elected. Tobin spent his first few months as a campaigner. In the less than three months between his appointment as Secretary and election day, he made 150 campaign appearances for the President. His quick wit, good looks (he had been called the best-looking Secretary the Department ever had), and political nature were a bonus to Truman's campaign.

Truman won, and Tobin, who had helped him to achieve his victory, concentrated on rebuilding the Department. In March, 1949, the Hoover Commission (the Commission on Organization of the Executive Branch of the Government) reported to Congress that the Department of Labor had been denuded of responsibilities and should be given more essential work to do. The commission called for restoration to the Department of many functions it had lost, as well as for delegation of new responsibilities related to its purposes. The U.S. Employment Service, the unit administering unemployment insurance, the Bureau of Employees' Compensation, and the Employees' Compensation Appeals Board were transferred to the Labor Department from the Federal Security Administration. The Secretary of Labor was authorized to enforce labor standards and coordinate the administration of laws relating to wages and hours on federally financed or federally assisted construction.

Tobin saw Truman's election victory as a mandate to change the Taft-Hartley Act and was given the task of drafting the labor proposals for the Administration. He assailed the law as a piece of propaganda designed to discredit the labor movement, and he predicted its repeal thirty days after the start of the Eighty-first Congress. However, he proved to be a poor prophet. Two years later, he modified his stand and asked only for greater flexibility in government intervention in labor disputes.

Secretary Tobin was an avid advocate of New Deal legislation. He supported legislation against discrimination in employment because of race, color, religion, or national origin;

advocated equal pay for women; proposed grants to states for promoting safe work places; and asked for changes in the Social Security law to include sickness and disability insurance. He also came out for a national housing program, federal aid to education, and a liberal farm-support program. Most of these proposals died in Congress.

Tobin, however, could be proud of three gains. The Fair Labor Standards Act amendments of 1949 raised minimum wages and strengthened the ban on child labor; the Federal Workmen's Compensation Act amendments liberalized benefits; and the Social Security Act amendments extended coverage to 10 million additional workers.

The outbreak of the Korean conflict on June 24, 1950, led the Department again into a wartime role. An executive order on September 9, 1950, assigned to the Secretary of Labor the job of mobilizing manpower to meet needs for military and essential civilian production. Tobin's role was complicated when the President established the Office of Defense Mobilization (ODM) and appointed Charles E. Wilson, president of General Electric, as defense mobilizer. Tobin battled with Wilson over control of manpower activities.

Tobin, with the support of labor leaders who insisted that manpower policies are best developed in the Department of Labor, carried his case to the President. It can be said that, at best, Tobin gained a compromise that prevented the dismantling of the Department and preserved for it a respectable role in the mobilization program, particularly in recruiting, training, and draft deferments for essential jobs.

Tobin issued general order number 48 assigning new responsibilities to appropriate Labor Department units. The order and its later amendments created the Defense Manpower Administration to supervise and coordinate defense manpower activities in the Department. On the local level, Tobin created a network of labor-manpower committees in industrial centers on the principle that local manpower problems could best be solved by local people. The organization operated within the framework controlled by the director of ODM, Charles Wilson.

When Dwight D. Eisenhower was elected President in November, 1952, Tobin resigned. In his four and a half years in office, he had failed to accomplish much that he hoped to achieve. He did not become the President's top labor adviser; he did not make the Department of Labor the center of man-power mobilization in the Korean War; his intense efforts to repeal the Taft-Hartley law were defeated; and he failed to re-gain the Conciliation Service, which had performed one of the Department's more important functions.

Yet Tobin left the Department of Labor in a far better position than it had been in when he had joined it in 1948. The Hoover Commission reorganization plans made the De-partment of Labor a true Cabinet department. And Tobin was close enough to the President to wield some influence. The appropriations of the Department of Labor had gone up sub-stantially, and in the Tobin years the number of employees increased from 3,340 to 7,443. Tobin reversed the downward trend, laid the foundation for future progress, and started the Department on its comeback trail.

THE EISENHOWER YEARS: DURKIN AND MITCHELL

What does a Secretary of Labor do under a Republican President? Although some union men are Republicans, labor is generally considered to be a part of the Democratic power base. When General Dwight D. Eisenhower won the Presiden-tial election in 1952 by a landslide, the Republicans swept back into power for the first time in twenty years. Rich men dominated the Cabinet. When Martin P. Durkin, a labor leader and Democrat, was appointed Secretary of Labor, the remark was coined that the Cabinet was made up of "nine millionaires and a plumber."

Durkin's appointment was an effort by Republicans to cooperate with the unions. Durkin had several political attri-

butes. He was an Irish Catholic who had probably been recommended by Francis Cardinal Spellman of New York. His
record, according to one of Eisenhower's favorite expressions,
was "as clean as a hound's tooth." He was president of the
United Association of Journeymen and Apprentices of the
Plumbing and Pipe Fitting Industry and the first member of
the American Federation of Labor to become Secretary of
Labor. Republicans hoped that his appointment would give
labor unions a sense of participation in the new Administration.

Durkin was surprised and pleased when Eisenhower ap-
pointed him Secretary of Labor, and he pledged loyalty to the
President. He thought Eisenhower had agreed to revise the
Taft-Hartley Act, for Eisenhower had said during his cam-
paign, "America wants no law licensing union busting. Neither
do I." In his State of the Union message in January, 1953, the
President said he would send recommendations concerning the
Taft-Hartley law to Congress.

Durkin ran into several problems with the Republican
Congress and Administration. He tried to appoint a Congress
of Industrial Organizations (CIO) union leader as an assistant
secretary, but the White House would not clear the nominee.
Durkin had trouble getting other appointments approved.
Congress cut appropriations, and the number of Department
of Labor employees dwindled. Then, too, Southern textile
manufacturers obtained an injunction impairing Durkin's authority to fix minimum wages on government contracts.

But the most bitter conflict erupted over proposed revisions
of the Taft-Hartley Act. Durkin made revision of the law his
chief goal. After repeated meetings with other government
departments and the White House staff, he believed he had
an agreement on nineteen amendments that the President
would recommend to Congress. But some Republicans were
incensed at modifying the ban on the closed shop and secondary boycotts and objected to Durkin's "all or nothing" in-

transigence. They enlisted the aid of Vice-President Richard Nixon, and Eisenhower put aside Taft-Hartley law reform.

The White House staff denied that Eisenhower had ever committed himself to action on this matter. Durkin felt otherwise. Whether Durkin misunderstood or whether the White House reversed itself is not clear. After eight months in office, Durkin resigned because he felt that the President had let him down.

Durkin's stormy exit further impaired the already difficult role of the Department of Labor under the Republicans. When James P. Mitchell took office in October, 1953, the *New York Times* reported that "he was like a man heading into the jaws of an Arctic gale in a sun suit."

Mitchell was the first "industrial relations type" to become Secretary of Labor. He had been a civilian labor adviser to the War Department during World War II, had later served as assistant secretary of Defense for Manpower, and had become a high-priced industrial relations man in private industry. As an Easterner and the third Irish Catholic in succession to be Secretary of Labor, he added balance to the Cabinet.

Some labor leaders who knew him felt he was fair-minded, with a good heart and a thick hide—assets in the difficult role in which he was cast. Nevertheless, they considered that his business background in a business-oriented Administration made his appointment "incredible." President George Meany of the American Federation of Labor, in his blunt manner, noted that "Jim Mitchell will be as good a Secretary of Labor" as the Secretary of Commerce would "let him" be.

Republican Jim Mitchell met the challenge of being a good Secretary of Labor. In a sense, this has always been the worst Cabinet position, for there are virtually insoluble problems inherent in the job. By law, the Secretary is required to promote the well-being of the working people of the United States. When this has involved prolabor partisanship, antilabor interests have attacked the Department for using a public agency for special pleading. Partiality to business would be as dangerous as partiality to labor. A Secretary of Labor at war with the labor movement would be a liability to any Administration.

Mitchell offered a way out of the dilemma. He tried to win the confidence of all sides by declaring that the Department of Labor was dedicated to fairness to every segment of the economy. Other Secretaries of Labor had made similar statements, but Mitchell tried harder to live up to the standard of impartiality. He gained both prolabor and nonlabor support for the idea that workers' needs are intertwined with the needs of the American people as a whole. Workers and their families make up the bulk of the population, and what is good for them is—most of the time—good for everybody. On the few occasions when workers' specific interests conflict with public interest, the Department of Labor, in Mitchell's view, owes its allegiance first to the national welfare, for it does no good to protect labor's interest and hurt the economy of which labor is a part.

In theory, no one can oppose fairness, though in practice it is often difficult to determine what is fair. By intense and careful cultivation of political and union leaders, Mitchell convinced most observers that he acted with integrity. This enabled him to provide easy access between labor and the White House, which was important to both parties and made it possible to increase the effectiveness of the Department.

One of Mitchell's great successes was in becoming the President's man on labor affairs. He did not have above him any special labor adviser to the President who sat in the White House, and he stopped the "end runs" by which other people bypassed the Secretary of Labor and spoke directly to the President. For example, when Kenneth Royall, a former Secretary of Defense who knew Eisenhower, was retained by the strike-bound Louisville and Nashville Railroad, Mitchell warned him that the President wanted to follow a hands-off policy. If Royall went to the White House, it was made clear,

Mitchell would bring over labor leaders to tell their side of the story. Royall did not see the President. Mitchell's success in asserting his authority resulted, in part, from Eisenhower's view that, the less he saw of labor problems, the happier he was, as long as there were no kickbacks.

Mitchell also asserted the independence of the Department of Labor when the Secretary of Commerce suggested that Commerce and Labor jointly prepare recommendations for the Administration on revisions of the Taft-Hartley Act. Mitchell politely refused and prepared his own recommendations. His position did not make any difference in the law, because Congress rejected all changes, but Mitchell had again asserted the role of the Department of Labor in the Administration.

Mitchell also re-established his hegemony over other federal labor agencies. He met with the heads of these agencies, and he influenced appointments to the National Labor Relations Board, the Federal Mediation and Conciliation Service, and other federal labor bodies. Members of those agencies who did not cooperate with the Department of Labor were sometimes replaced. Succeeding Secretaries of Labor often continued the precedent Mitchell established of suggesting to the President nominations for positions in other federal labor agencies.

Mitchell got along relatively well with unions, particularly considering that some of the unions attacked the Eisenhower Administration as a tool of big business. Although labor leaders would never have selected Mitchell had they had a choice, they recognized him as a management man who had in the past bargained in good faith with unions and who believed in collective bargaining. While they could not look to him for favors, they knew that he was not an enemy, and they could count on his support if unions were treated unfairly.

There are difficult problems in summarizing specific accomplishments under any particular Secretary of Labor. Most achievements evolve over a long period, and the base is laid by many civil servants, whose experience and recommendations help shape policy. Many changes have a history of small steps with an occasional giant step, and a great deal of misplaced credit is often given to the head of an agency.

Yet, when progress is made, the vigor and influence of the Secretary are in part responsible for the progress. The Department of Labor under James Mitchell chalked up significant accomplishments in achieving greater safety for workers on the job, improving unemployment insurance, getting a higher minimum wage, increasing protection for farm workers, helping older workers to get jobs, backing blacks in their long climb up the ladder of economic opportunity, and laying the base for a broad manpower program. The Department also gained in internal strength through the centralization of organization and a promotion policy based as much on merit as on politics. Although much has been done in these fields both before and after Mitchell served as Secretary, an objective assessment shows more than average progress in the seven years and three months during which Mitchell served as Secretary of Labor.

THE NEW FRONTIER AND THE WAR ON POVERTY: GOLDBERG AND WIRTZ

When President John F. Kennedy appointed Arthur Goldberg Secretary of Labor, Goldberg told newsmen that his predecessor, Jim Mitchell, had done an outstanding job and had raised the status of the Department of Labor. But, Goldberg added, he expected to do better, because, instead of being handicapped, like Mitchell, by a Republican Administration, he was working with President Kennedy in building a "New Frontier." Would Goldberg make good on his boast?

Arthur Joseph Goldberg was the youngest son of eleven children of an impoverished Jewish immigrant family from the Ukraine. He had worked his way through school and distinguished himself as a labor lawyer. He had helped devise the agreement for the American Federation of Labor–Congress of Industrial Organizations (AFL-CIO) merger and had won a reputation for his battle against both Communists and racketeers in the labor movement. Because Goldberg had been one of the President's earliest and most valuable labor supporters, Kennedy insisted on his appointment, over the protest of labor leaders who said that Goldberg was "of" but not "in" the labor movement. But labor finally gave its grudging assent.

Kennedy's custom of encouraging all Cabinet members to comment on all subjects suited Goldberg's nervous energy and wide-ranging interests. In a short term, he made hundreds of speeches, appeared dozens of times before Congress, went on several trips abroad, and visited many states in the United States, learning about conditions firsthand. His activities extended far beyond labor matters. He dealt with the urgency of the Soviet challenge and made proposals dealing with foreign affairs, the nuclear bomb, and psychological warfare. He participated in efforts to expand trade and worked out import quotas for Japanese cloth. On the home front, his interests varied from the rate of economic and scientific growth to the building of a federal office complex between the Capitol and the White House and government promotion of culture and the arts. Considering that the Department of Labor was the smallest Cabinet department, the scope of Goldberg's activities was so astonishing that he was nicknamed the "Davy Crockett of the New Frontier."

Although active in many fields, Goldberg focused his major concern on labor programs in general and management-labor relations in particular. He made the creation of a better climate between workers and employers his number one goal. Although he advocated high wages and decent working conditions, he observed that business had to be prosperous to afford them. On the industry level, Goldberg suggested human relations committees that would help both sides to get to know each other long before crises at the expiration of a contract.

On the national level, he supported a tripartite Presidential advisory committee on which representatives of employers, unions, and the public would work toward a common goal.

Although Goldberg favored collective bargaining, he made it clear that bargainers had to be responsible enough so that they would not endanger the economy and give comfort to our enemies abroad. The nation, he said, could not afford the luxury of big business and big labor fighting it out while innocent third parties suffered. In Goldberg's view, the government should not dictate specific terms, but it could provide broad guidelines, and it needed an array of weapons to persuade bargainers to make their agreements conform to the public interest.

Hardly had Goldberg taken office when his theories were put to a test. A tugboat strike in New York Harbor in midwinter brought the threat of a fuel famine. Goldberg flew to New York, negotiated for fourteen hours continuously, and won agreement on a substantial pay raise. Meanwhile, he succeeded in having the thorny issue of reducing the number of workers on each tugboat shunted to a special study commission. Over and over again, Goldberg intervened in solving labor disputes, with a remarkably good batting average. Perhaps his best-publicized effort came when the Metropolitan Opera canceled its 1961–62 program because of labor problems. Both the President and Secretary Goldberg felt that this was a national cultural asset that should not be sacrificed. Goldberg, acting as an arbitrator, saved the opera season. A more important achievement economically was the settlement on a noninflationary basis of an impending steel conflict without a strike.

Neither labor nor management was thrilled with Goldberg's intervention. Although both sides conceded his skill as a negotiator, some felt he concentrated so much on getting a settlement that he forgot about the equities. Several management people could not forget about his long association with the labor movement as a lawyer, and a few labor leaders felt that Goldberg knew too much about labor unions and the tricks of the trade. As one union leader noted, Goldberg knew where the "bodies were buried." On one hand, management sometimes expressed the fear that Goldberg's policies might lead to government regimentation. On the other hand, President George Meany of the AFL-CIO on one occasion exploded, claiming that the government was "infringing on the rights of a free people." Yet the fact that both sides criticized Goldberg is added evidence that Goldberg was determined to be impartial.

The Department of Labor, during the Goldberg period, became deeply concerned with the unemployed. Unemployment had risen from under 3 per cent in 1953 to 7 per cent in the spring of 1961. Although not nearly as bad as the catastrophic unemployment of the Depression in the 1930's, these unemployment rates were more than statistical information. They were human tragedies to people who were bewildered, suffering, and angry. Goldberg described three types of unemployment. Transitional unemployment, such as that of workers between jobs and of young people leaving school to join the labor force, was serious. Still more serious was cyclical unemployment, involving workers who would have to wait to be rehired when times got better. Saddest of all was the technological unemployment of those whose jobs had been blown away by the winds of change.

The Administration responded to the ravages of unemployment by extending unemployment insurance benefits for thirteen extra weeks and by trying to handle automation in such a way that the progress would become a blessing and not a curse. Goldberg arranged a program to help workers who had lost jobs because of expanded foreign imports. Perhaps most important of all, the job-training feature of the Area Redevelopment Act of 1961 and the Manpower Development and Training Act of 1962 were seeds of an enlightened manpower program that is still growing and evolving. (See Chapter VI.)

The concern for disadvantaged wage earners likewise manifested itself in programs for dealing with "wetbacks," Mexicans who swam the Rio Grande to get jobs in the United States, and "braceros," the Mexican "stoop labor" who made up much of the migrant labor force that followed the crops during harvest time. In addition, Secretary Goldberg led in the fight for equal employment opportunity. Toward the end of his tenure, 30 per cent of the Department of Labor's employees were blacks. He extended this fight for fair employment to industry and was next in command to Vice-President Lyndon B. Johnson in getting industry to adopt plans for progress in providing jobs for minorities.

Friends and critics alike agreed that Secretary Goldberg was among the most able and active members of President John F. Kennedy's Cabinet. No Secretary of Labor after leaving the Department had as distinguished a subsequent career. On his departure, President Kennedy wrote that his regret at Goldberg's leaving the Cabinet was matched only by the pleasure of naming him to the Supreme Court and that Goldberg had been a wise and invaluable member of the innermost councils of the Administration. And President Kennedy supported Goldberg's boast when he took office that he would do even better than Mitchell's fine performance, for the President noted that Goldberg had brought to the Department a "stature and significance which have never been surpassed."

As Arthur Goldberg donned the robes of Supreme Court justice, the under secretary of Labor, Willard Wirtz, moved up to the secretaryship. It is often difficult for a subordinate to step into the shoes of an eminent predecessor, but the intellectual and idealistic Wirtz had the skill and experience to become a distinguished Secretary. A lawyer and law professor by profession, Wirtz had served as a public member of the War Labor Board during World War II and as chairman of the National Wage Stabilization Board after the war. He had also been a law partner of Democratic Presidential candidate Adlai Stevenson.

Secretary Wirtz's interests were different from those of his predecessor. He felt that the job of industrial peacemaker should belong to the Secretary of Labor only as a last resort. He used the metaphor that instruments too often used become dull. Ironically, he spent the first few weeks in office mediating several major strikes. The Chicago Northwestern Railroad was on strike at the time he became Secretary of Labor. Wirtz, when questioned about mediating the strike, commented, "I rode the Northwestern for 50 years. . . . I hope they are not asking for equal time."

Although forced by circumstances to intervene in many strikes, Wirtz could remark at the end of his term of office:

> The typical Department of Labor scene . . . at the start of the five-year period [1963–68] was of haggard men spending the night glaring at each other across the bargaining table, while the press and radio and television crews kept death watches in the corridors. By the end of the period, the Labor Department was no longer even a regular newsbeat for most of the Washington press.

Although the Department no longer furnished as many screaming headlines about strikes, Wirtz believed that it had shifted its emphasis to even more important work in the field of manpower.

In the early 1960's, the Department of Labor concerned itself intensively with unemployment caused by automation. The Manpower Development and Training Act of 1962 (MDTA), passed while Goldberg was Secretary, was a pioneer law of great historical significance. In its original form, it reflected the hope that education and training might deal with the ravages of automation. The manpower agency would both assist individuals by upgrading their skills and contribute to national economic strength and growth.

Later, however, Secretary Wirtz shifted the emphasis of the Department. Unemployment decreased, and automation proved less damaging than feared. The Department began to tailor its programs to aid those who suffered from poverty rather than from new technology. Priorities were changed to increase help to the young, the old, minorities, the hard-core unemployed, and others. The Department of Labor supplied some of the most important "weapons" in the "War on Poverty." Wirtz was a member of the inner circle of those who, with President Johnson, drafted plans that led to the Economic Opportunity Act of 1964.

One Department of Labor activity passed into history during the Wirtz administration. Braceros, the Mexican farm laborers, had been allowed for many years by treaty to come into the United States for seasonal farm work. At first, the Department tried to ensure some kind of minimum wage to protect these workers and to prevent ruinous competition with American labor. At the peak of the program in 1956, a total of 445,000 Mexicans worked on American farms. American farmers, especially on the West Coast, wanted the treaty extended because they felt American workers would not do stoop labor in the fields. Wirtz argued that Americans would work if given sufficient wages and humane working conditions. In 1965, the program of importing braceros was phased down, and by the end of 1968 the bracero problem ceased to exist, though some wetbacks have continued to enter the country illegally and occasional exceptions have been made for some foreign workers under unusual conditions.

The major change in the Department of Labor in the Wirtz years was its increasing involvement in a variety of social programs rivaling the alphabetical agencies of the New Deal. Among these activities were the Neighborhood Youth Corps, New Careers, Operation Mainstream, WIN (Work Incentive Program), JOBS (Job Opportunities in the Business Sector), and OFCC (Office of Federal Contract Compliance). Parts of these programs went well; others, badly. There were overlapping, duplication, and jurisdictional warfare within the

Department of Labor and with other agencies. Yet, on balance, millions of people were helped, and these programs for the most part carried through to later administrations. (See Chapter VI for a discussion of separate programs and organizational problems.)

Wirtz's successful tenure as Secretary of Labor was marred by a painful blowup on the eve of the 1968 election campaign. The underlying causes of the conflict between the President and his Secretary are difficult to determine and are partly a matter of conjecture. Wirtz seemed to feel that the Department of Labor should have a more important part in determining economic policy than it had. Also, he had an intellectual independence that made it difficult for him to echo every nuance of Administration policy.

In 1968, Secretary Wirtz broke with the President over the Vietnam war. President Johnson, about to immerse himself in negotiations with North Vietnam, may have resented Wirtz's somewhat more "dovish" stand on peace efforts. At this time, Secretary Wirtz ordered a controversial reorganization in the Department. He was surprised when, on October 12, 1968, the President rejected the reorganization. Wirtz ordered it anyhow, saying that it was a departmental matter that did not need Presidential approval.

The President asked Wirtz to rescind the reorganization. Wirtz declined three times to obey the President. At a face-to-face meeting in the Cabinet room in the White House, Johnson told Wirtz, "I want this done or your resignation." Wirtz replied that, as was customary, he had submitted a letter of resignation for the convenience of the President at the time he became a Cabinet member and that the President could remove him. Johnson retorted that he did not want to remove anyone; he wanted his orders carried out.

Wirtz refused to withdraw the reorganization order but sent his resignation to the White House. Johnson worried that a public flare-up would create difficulties for the Democrats in the approaching Presidential election campaign. He sent emissaries to persuade Wirtz to retract the order and withdraw his resignation. Wirtz compromised and postponed "effectuation of the projected action."

Wirtz and Johnson partially repaired their relationship when at their last Cabinet meeting Wirtz said to Johnson that he, more than any other President, had aroused the country to meet human needs.

Although the breakdown of personal relations was dramatic, it did not alter the even more important fact that Wirtz served as Secretary during a period of economic growth and social progress. Although submarginal groups continued to suffer as always, on the average 1963 to 1968 was a period of diminishing unemployment, increased job opportunities, rising real wages, improved living conditions, and soaring expectations. It would require an exaggerated ego on the part of the Department to claim that it was the cause of the general economic well-being. Much of the progress was the result of economic and social forces to which the Department of Labor was only remotely related. Yet the Department contributed to the over-all results. It was during Wirtz's administration that the department brought together the pieces of many programs with the central purpose, as Wirtz wrote in his last annual report, of working "to see to it that every American has a full and equal opportunity to earn a decent living."

THE NIXON ERA: SHULTZ, HODGSON, AND BRENNAN

In the Presidential election of 1968, Republican Richard M. Nixon edged out Democrat Hubert H. Humphrey in the race for the Presidency. Although most labor leaders support the Democrats, a Republican Administration does not necessarily doom the Department of Labor. A Republican President needs good relations with unions and tries to select a Secretary who gets along with labor. Under President Eisenhower, Secretary of Labor James P. Mitchell enhanced the prestige of the Department. When Nixon became President, he sought a man who, like Mitchell, would strengthen his Administration and at the same time be acceptable to labor.

George Pratt Shultz came to the Labor Department highly regarded by both management and labor. He had had experience as a negotiator and had served as a consultant to former Presidents and Secretaries of Labor. As a top union official put it, Shultz was "the best qualified" of those whose names were submitted for approval.

A dean of the Graduate School of Business at the University of Chicago, Shultz has been called an "intellectual conglomerate." Although thought to be unexciting personally by some, Shultz was shrewd and energetic. For ten days before his confirmation hearing, he was seen in the office of practically every member of the Senate Committee on Labor and Public Welfare.

Secretary Shultz enjoyed exceptionally good working relations with President Nixon, who told him not to be reluctant to speak up on both labor and nonlabor matters. Shultz helped draft many of Nixon's speeches and several major programs, including federal revenue-sharing, the reorganization of the federal government, and the full-employment budget. Shultz also explained Administration measures to the press and on television. Although his television coach advised him that he should speak up and that his glasses slipped badly and should be tightened, Shultz, in his scholarly and academic way, was an effective advocate of the President's program.

Of all the Nixon Cabinet members, Shultz was perhaps the most intellectual and most thoroughly grounded in economics. He believed that inflation could be curbed by a strong fiscal policy, but he was not among those in the "sledgehammer school" who believed in cooling the economy through higher unemployment. The hard facts of political life forced him to accept modification of his oft repeated statements that wage-price guidelines were impractical. Even after the President imposed controls, Shultz looked upon them as a temporary evil that would be abolished as soon as a healthy noninflationary economy was restored. Rather than keep controls, Shultz hoped to use the federal budget in a way that would be noninflationary and at the same time foster social goals. He believed manpower programs could be the bridge between social and economic policies.

Shultz thought one way to reduce poverty was through manpower programs. Such programs, he felt, together with welfare, health, and other services, would help move people out of poverty. From a modest beginning in the early 1960's, manpower programs have assumed major proportions in the Department's budget, involving about $4 billion. This amount is greater than the total annual federal expenditures during the early 1930's. As in many rapidly expanding areas, a bewildering array of new projects had been added piecemeal, resulting in a patchwork of programs and conflicting responsibilities both within and between agencies. Shultz vigorously supported a comprehensive manpower system to provide for integrated planning and allocation of resources. Through the Manpower Training bill proposed in 1969, the Department of Labor hoped to create a framework for partnership between the federal, state, and local governments. At the same time, the bill would have consolidated programs administered by the Department of Labor. Although the proposal died in Congress, President Nixon, after his re-election in 1972, introduced revenue-sharing manpower programs through administrative changes within the framework of existing laws.

Under Shultz, the Department of Labor pushed ahead, with varying success, in many fields. Expanded manpower-training programs sought to cope with the problem of raising many people out of poverty through training and support services. The Department continued to sponsor a wide range of programs for young people and tried to modify the much criticized Job Corps. Job "banks" in many cities took advantage of improved computer technology to improve on the traditional function of the Department to match "jobless men" with "manless jobs." The Department used government buying power to create equal job opportunities for blacks and other minorities by steering contracts to firms that followed fair employment practices. Other vitally important programs included efforts to extend unemployment insurance, to bring about safe and healthy conditions in factories and other places of work, and to revolutionize the welfare system by encouraging people on relief to work. (See the following chapters for detailed descriptions of these activities.) By contrast, one of the few fields in which Shultz tried to reduce the role of the Department of Labor was the settlement of strikes. He felt that strikes were not as critical as often described and that, with rare exceptions, management and labor should be left to settle their differences through collective bargaining.

His successes notwithstanding, Shultz had many frustrations. His greatest disappointment was the continued increase in unemployment. When he became Secretary of Labor, unemployment stood at a low 3.4 per cent. In 1970, when he was promoted to the newly created Office of Management and Budget, joblessness had risen to 4.7 percent, and it continued to rise to about 6 per cent at the beginning of 1972. In spite of the difficulties, Shultz conveyed a spirit of progress and concern for the public interest. In his brief, eighteen-month span in office, he proved to be among the more creative Secretaries of Labor.

In 1970, President Nixon promoted Under Secretary James D. Hodgson to be the twelfth Secretary of Labor. Hodgson had held successive personnel positions at Lockheed Aircraft Corporation for almost a quarter of a century and had risen to the position of vice-president in charge of industrial relations. He had never been in the public eye and had no political following. Hodgson's chief qualification was his lifelong interest in what he called "people business." He liked working with problems that directly affect human beings.

In the spring of 1972, some students from Secretary Hodgson's hometown of Dawson, Minnesota, asked their "local boy who made good" some questions. Hodgson was intrigued when one student asked, "Just what does a Secretary of Labor do?" The Secretary gave the following example of a day in the life of a Cabinet officer. It was not a specific day, but it represented the typical daily pace, schedule, and duties.

6:45 A.M.   The day begins. . . . While eating breakfast I read all the political and sports news, plus "Peanuts," in the local morning paper, the *Washington Post*.

7:30 A.M.   My car picks me up at our apartment in northwest Washington, and as the driver wheels me down Rock Creek Parkway toward my office, I read the labor and economic news in the *New York Times* and make notes about things I want my staff to work on that day.

8:00 A.M.   I arrive at the office, walking the last mile for exercise if the weather is good. I scan the *Wall Street Journal,* get my Executive Assistant started on the list of chores I've prepared, and at

8:30 A.M.   I hold a Department staff meeting . . . review the status of the pieces of new legislation I'm attempting to get Congress to pass. I get reports on the latest labor crises . . . I review the latest figures on unemployment, and the cost of living and wage rates . . . Then at

9:30 A.M.   I'm back in my office for a 15-minute cram session—boning up on the new $2 billion Manpower Revenue Sharing Bill . . . Then promptly at

10:00 A.M.   I walk into the Senate committee room and take my seat before 10 senators, a dozen reporters, and a battery of TV cameras. Here I read a 20-minute statement telling how President Nixon and I think our proposed Manpower Bill is the greatest thing since sliced bread. Next I spend two hours parrying queries from Democrat Senators who somehow don't always agree with me. Then . . . at

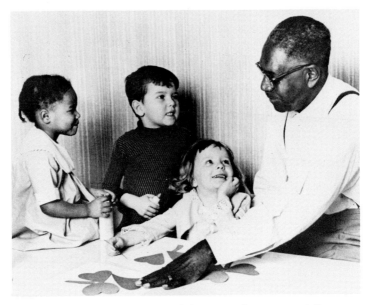

The Department's Operation Mainstream finances part-time employment for older workers. Here a senior aide works at a day-care center. (*Photo courtesy of the National Council of Senior Citizens*)

The Department's Concentrated Employment Program assists the hard-core unemployed. This girl is being trained for what has been traditionally a man's job.

Instruction in English is an important part of Project SER, which works to give Mexican Americans a better chance "to be."

The Department is involved in "promoting the welfare" of every sort of worker. *Top left:* Because alienated people often do not come into an employment office, Outreach workers sometimes recruit participants in their homes. *Top right:* Conditions for "stoop workers," who move from crop to crop, still need drastic improvement. *Below:* This engineer found employment through a manpower program for placing engineers and scientists.

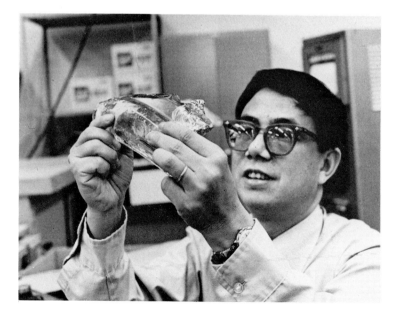

Above: Today, union, management, and Department of Labor officials usually negotiate peacefully and in a rational manner. In 1973, this group met to discuss the controversial issue of Penn Central Railroad crew size.

Left: Legislation now protects the right of workers to health and safety in their work place. Here an industrial hygienist from the Department's Occupational Safety and Health Administration attaches a sampling device to a worker to measure his exposure to silica dust.

Below: In the 1970's, meetings of Department staff are characterized by informality and active staff participation.

On July 6, 1892, strikers and Pinkerton guards clashed during the Great Homestead Strike at the Carnegie Steel Company. Early strikes were often accompanied by violence.

Left: In the early years of this century, strikers carried banners printed in their native tongues.

Right: Sewell Avery, head of Montgomery Ward, was carried out of his office by soldiers when he refused to abide by a decision of the World War II National War Labor Board.

Early labor leaders fought hard for a "voice of labor" within the government. To the left is a photo of Carroll D. Wright, the first federal Commissioner of Labor, who established the precedent that labor statistics be free from the exigencies of politics.

Below: Shown here are the three men responsible for the creation of a Cabinet-level Department of Labor in 1913 *(left to right)*: President Woodrow Wilson, President of the American Federation of Labor Samuel Gompers, and Secretary of Labor William B. Wilson.

Around the turn of the century, laborers often endured miserable work-ing conditions. *Above:* Working girls were forced to work long hours in dark and ill-ventilated workshops. (*Photo from M. B. Schnapper,* American Labor: A Pictorial History, *Public Affairs Press, 1972*) *Below:* In coal-mining areas, children hired as "breaker boys" sorted coal while the thick dust penetrated every portion of their lungs. (*All photos from U.S. Department of Labor unless otherwise noted.*)

Workers at "bell time" have been a familiar sight in American cities for over a century. Above is a Winslow Homer drawing of workers leaving a New England factory in 1868. The photograph below was taken in 1973. Styles in headgear have changed.

Franklin Roosevelt's Secretary of Labor, Frances Perkins, was the first woman to become a member of a President's Cabinet. *Below:* Secretary of Labor Arthur J. Goldberg learns about working conditions firsthand. Here he dons a hard hat to meet structural iron workers.

Right: Trade unionist Peter J. Brennan is sworn in as the thirteenth Secretary of Labor.

12:30 P.M.   I have lunch with a dozen visiting labor leaders from Western Europe. . . . Now it's

1:30 P.M.   And I break off for a short staff briefing on next year's $7 billion Labor Department budget before taking a three-minute drive to the White House . . . at

2:00 P.M.   The President joins us for a short Cabinet meeting. He tells all the Cabinet officers that we're spending too much of the taxpayers' money and then he outlines plans for his upcoming trip to the Soviet Union. . . . At exactly

3:00 P.M.   I leave for Secretary Richardson's office [HEW], work out a new message to send to Congress for increasing Social Security payments, and we devise new programs to provide better medical care for our older people.

Here I am interrupted by a message from the President . . . appoint[ing] an emergency board in the latest railroad dispute, so I rush back to the White House . . . for a 4:00 P.M. briefing of the press and TV. . . .

4:30 P.M.   finds me back at my office with a score of phone calls. . . .

5:30 P.M.   My Under Secretary comes in with a list of candidates for a Presidential appointment to the National Labor Relations Board . . . and at

6:15 P.M.   I call in my secretary to dictate an outline of an upcoming speech and replies to several letters. . . . At

7:00 P.M.   Maria [Mrs. Hodgson] comes into my office with a clean shirt . . . and we're off to a reception at a local hotel for Minnesota Congressman Al Quie from Northfield [of the House Committee on Education and Labor] and duck out because we have an

8:30 P.M.   dinner for 12 at the Australian Embassy. . . . Dinner is over. It's now 11:00 P.M., and we head for home. . . .

Work is six and sometimes seven days a week. Maria and I
    are out five nights in seven, mostly on government so-
    cializing. And . . . nothing like a vacation exists.

Why does anybody do this sort of thing? Hodgson asked
himself and answered his own question by observing that the
"excitement is great, the people are talented, and the work
fascinating." But the real appeal, Hodgson explained, is the
rare opportunity, that few human beings are lucky enough to
have, to work for the advancement and welfare of the nation
and its people.

During the Hodgson period, the Department administered
the first new public employment program since the 1930's;
promoted stabilization of wages and employment in the construction industry; and achieved productivity improvement
break-throughs in collective bargaining. Partly as a result of
a long campaign for equal job opportunities, the black-to-
white proportion of unemployment dropped in 1971 below the
pathological two-to-one ratio, and Secretary Hodgson hoped
in 1972 that equal employment opportunity would wipe out
the differential altogether by the end of the decade.

When a friend asked Secretary Hodgson which of his accomplishments satisfied him most, he felt like a father who was
asked which of his children he loved best. One answer was
that he loved all of them. But, if forced to make a choice,
Hodgson said that he would select as his most satisfying
achievement the passage and administration of the Williams-
Steiger Act of 1970, which set standards of safety and health
on the job for about 60 million wage earners in more than 4
million work places.

Hodgson became Secretary at a difficult time, when relations between President Nixon and organized labor were
worsening because of differing views on the effort to curb inflation. When Hodgson first became Secretary, a *Wall Street
Journal* reporter observed that organized labor would have
preferred someone who was more prounion. But it accepted

the new Secretary cordially as a competent industrial relations expert with experience at the bargaining table. This moderately cooperative relationship evaporated when Hodgson, in supporting the President, suggested that the average worker preferred the President's program to create more jobs and protect the purchasing power of the worker's dollar over the course advocated by many labor unions, which, he believed, led to higher prices.

Careers often are determined by seemingly insignificant incidents. When AFL-CIO President George Meany attacked the Nixon wage freeze, White House aide Charles Colson dictated over the telephone a statement that he asked Hodgson to issue. Hodgson, on his way to the White House for a meeting, asked Joseph Loftus, the distinguished ex-labor reporter who was his special aide, to fix up Colson's statement and issue it. Loftus felt he had no authority to tamper with White House material and released it. The sentence in the statement that infuriated Meany said that he was "sadly out of step with the needs and desires of America's working men and women." Hodgson, who had carefully cultivated relations with many labor leaders, learned the truth of Ralph Waldo Emerson's couplet

> He who has a thousand friends has not a friend to spare
> And he who has one enemy will meet him everywhere.

Although Meany must have known that Hodgson was not the source of the attack, Hodgson was a good target. He was vulnerable because he had no political constituency of his own and he was in an exposed position as an Administration spokesman. Meany, in his speech at the AFL-CIO convention in the fall of 1971, imitated the Secretary's gestures when he answered questions at an AFL-CIO executive committee meeting and commented that Hodgson was like "a little league umpire I see around the neighborhood. He makes every decision with the same gesture. The trouble is, you can't tell whether one is safe or not."

Meany made life difficult for Hodgson when he bypassed him and dealt directly with President Nixon or such powerful Administration advisers as George Shultz, then director of the Office of Management and Budget. And, at a press conference, the AFL-CIO president baited the Secretary of Labor by suggesting that someone ask him about Hodgson because "I have a good answer." When the planted question was asked, Meany relished his reply: "I don't pay too much attention to the Secretary . . . because, in the final analysis, if you have a problem with the landlord, you don't discuss it with the janitor."

Meany did not stop with mockery. He carried on an "off with his head" campaign in a labor drive to get rid of Hodgson. Shortly after the election of 1972, Hodgson resigned.

President Nixon selected, as the thirteenth Secretary of Labor, Peter J. Brennan, president of the New York Building Trades Council. Brennan, a life-long Democrat, had supported many Presidential policies and rallied "hard hat" labor for President Nixon's election. His appointment revived the original tradition of the Department of Labor—Presidential appointment of the Secretary of Labor from the ranks of working people.

IV

Organization of the Department

Has the federal government become too complex and too remote? Has it become a tangle of bureaus, agencies, programs, and special projects that are at once too cumbersome and too fragmented to deal with today's problems?

Many Americans think so, and several Presidents have recommended reorganization of the executive branch of the federal government. President Nixon has called for the abolition of seven existing Cabinet departments—Agriculture, Commerce, Housing and Urban Development, Interior, Transportation, Labor, and Health, Education, and Welfare. In their place, four new Cabinet departments would be organized, each around a major purpose of government. Most of the Department of Labor's functions would be divided between two of the four new departments, the departments of Human Resources and of Economic Affairs.

One observer noted that the proposed Department of Economic Affairs was originally called the Department of Economic Development, with the acronym spelled DED and pronounced "dead." The pronunciation may have been prophetic.

President Lyndon Johnson in 1967 had also recommended a widespread, though not so sweeping, reorganization. At the heart of his proposal was a merger of the Department of

Labor and the Department of Commerce; this arrangement had existed between 1903 and 1913 but had been terminated because organized labor wanted its own department. When both business and labor leaders rejected the 1967 proposed reorganization, the plan, which had been born amid great fanfare, was quietly buried.

The difficulty in reorganizing the Cabinet departments does not mean that such a reorganization is not needed. However, there are obstacles. Almost every American schoolchild learns to enumerate Cabinet officers. Departments have a tradition and a history. Economic and social interests with attachments to existing departments, rightly or wrongly, fear they may lose their voice in the government if "their" department is eliminated. In Congress, seniority arrangements would have to be realigned and committees reshaped in the wake of a Cabinet reorganization.

President Nixon made a strong case for reorganizing the Cabinet departments so that government would be more responsive to national needs. Although as yet he has been unable to streamline the Cabinet structure, he has achieved some of his goals through his new Domestic Council, through the new Office of Management and Budget, and through substantial reorganization within the separate Cabinet departments.

GROWTH AND CHANGE

Although most Cabinet departments continually reorganize to meet changing needs, the Department of Labor has changed more than most. Since the day it was created in 1913, it has been the smallest Cabinet agency. Secretary of Labor James J. ("Puddler Jim") Davis wrote to President Calvin Coolidge in 1924, "Being at the tail end of the Cabinet, after all the others have taken up their questions with you, I somehow feel that I ought not take up more of your time." The Department gained some prestige under President Franklin Roosevelt, but after World War II a hostile Congress reduced it to near impotence.

Starting in the 1950's and accelerating during the 1960's, the Department of Labor reshaped itself from largely a statistical agency into a doer and creator with challenging responsibilities. Its most important challenge is the obligation to give all Americans a chance to earn a decent living. One indication of the change in the status held by the Department of Labor is the increase in personnel from a post–World War II low of 3,300 employers in the late 1940's to about 12,000 in the early 1970's. However, because most of the Department's current goals are achieved through grants and contracts to states, localities, and private enterprise, the rise in financing is even more dramatic. Appropriations multiplied better than three hundredfold from $15 million in 1948 to more than $5 billion in 1972.

This incredible growth sparked a revolution in organization, based on strengthening the management control of the Secretary, establishing a unified Manpower Administration, and assigning the work of the Department to subordinate agencies according to program categories such as manpower development assistance, employment assistance, wage and labor standards, labor-management relations, and data collection. This logical organization is buttressed by a strong departmental management system, progressive financial management, and effective instrumentalities for policy development, evaluation of programs, and research. At the same time that control was centralized to a greater degree than before, operations were decentralized.

THE DEPARTMENT TODAY

A skeleton sketch of the Department's organization (see chart on page 94) does not take into account individual ability, personal relations, and circumstances that make a job important under one administration and unimportant under another. Allowing for such variations, the top management of the Department of Labor consists of a Secretary, an under

U.S. Department of Labor

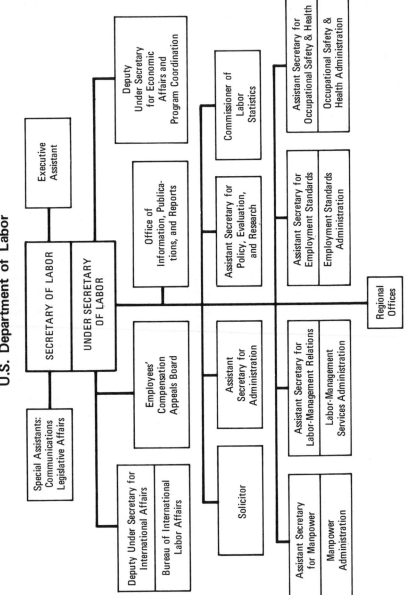

secretary, a solicitor, six assistant secretaries, and a commis-sioner of Labor Statistics—all but one appointed by the Presi-dent and approved by the Senate.

At the apex stands the Secretary, in whom all of the Depart-ment's authority and responsibility are vested. He has a dual responsibility, first as the President's staff adviser on labor-related issues and second as the chief administrator of the Department of Labor. He has an executive assistant, special assistants for communication, legislative affairs, and other re-sponsibilities, and a director for information, publications, and reports.

The under secretary stands next in line. He acts as alternate for the Secretary and serves as head of the Department in the Secretary's absence. He has several deputies, and the indepen-dent Employees' Compensation Appeals Board is in his office for administrative purposes. Although the job was created in 1946, it is basically the same as the position that had been held by the principal assistant secretary since 1913. Among the distinguished men who have held this position are Louis F. Post, the liberal who was vindicated in impeachment proceed-ings in Congress; David A. Morse, who became director-gen-eral of the International Labor Organization (ILO); and James J. Reynolds, the skilled labor mediator. Two under secretaries, Willard Wirtz and James D. Hodgson, later be-came Secretaries of Labor.

The solicitor is the lawyer for the Department. He advises the Secretary, directs legal proceedings arising under laws ad-ministered by the Department, and coordinates proposals for legislation. The many new fields in which the Department is pioneering generate a vast amount of legal activity.

The commissioner of Labor Statistics is the heir of the orig-inal Commissioner of the Bureau of Labor in 1884 out of which the Department grew.* Now, as then, he is an important

---

* For a complete history and description of this bureau, see another volume in this series: Ewan Clague, *The Bureau of Labor Statistics,* New York: Praeger, 1968.

economic factfinder. He directs the Bureau of Labor Statistics, which is world-renowned for its integrity. The slightest inference of partisanship in its output, even when unfounded, brings outraged protests in its defense. Among the most important of its many statistical activities is the preparation of the consumer price index and the reports on employment and unemployment for which management, labor officials, and politicians wait each month with bated breath.

To citizens inexperienced in the ways of the federal government, the title "assistant secretary" does not sound impressive. But the politically appointed assistant secretaries in the Department of Labor are heavyweights who carry out the policies of the Secretary.

The assistant secretary for Policy, Evaluation, and Research is often the Department's practical intellectual. He studies plans to improve the welfare of workers, evaluates the effectiveness of the plans, and directs research on programs to meet the human resources needs of the nation. A similar position was first held by Daniel Patrick Moynihan, who, while in this office, developed provocative ideas on work and welfare, a topic that is one of the crucial domestic issues of the 1970's. During the Nixon Administration, two administrators with an intellectual bent, Jerome Rosow and Michael Moskow, have held this think-tank post.

The assistant secretary for Administration and Management is the business manager of the Department. This job was originally that of chief clerk, held for nearly a quarter of a century by Samuel J. Gompers, son of the president and cofounder of the American Federation of Labor. In recent years, under the guidance of Leo Werts and Frank Zarb, the position of assistant secretary for Administration and Management has grown in scope to support programs in management-systems development, organization, program and budget review, and personnel. Because the incumbent in this position provides a continuity of work during changes of administrations, he is less politically oriented than other assistant secretaries.

Four assistant secretaries have major responsibilities for both policy and operation. The assistant secretary for Manpower directs the Manpower Administration, which spends most of the Department's money and directs most of its activities. The assistant secretary for Labor-Management Relations supervises a Labor-Management Services Administration. The less he has to do with strikes, the happier he is, for he is anxious that they be settled before they get to his office. But, in time of crisis, he may be the most important man in the Department.

The assistant secretary for Employment Standards deals with minimum wages, child labor, job discrimination on account of age, race, or sex, and other work standards. The newest assistant secretary heads the Occupational Safety and Health Administration, which has the mission of ensuring safe and healthy work places for nearly 60 million workers. At one time, there was also an assistant secretary concerned with international labor, but his position has been changed to that of deputy under secretary in charge of the Bureau of International Labor Affairs. (Separate chapters in this book describe each of these activities.)

In Washington nothing is more ephemeral than the power of a political appointee. An official can go home one evening feeling that he is indispensable to a program and may drop into oblivion the next morning. Normally, dramatic changes come when an election sweeps one party out of power. But, after the 1972 Presidential campaign, the Washington *Star* reported on December 14 that, of the nine top jobs, "President Nixon announced today that six Labor Department officials at sub-cabinet level will be leaving their posts." Most surprising was the forced resignation of Geoffrey Moore from the traditionally nonpolitical position of commissioner of Labor Statistics. Financial writer J. A. Livingston noted that Moore was recognized for "statistical competence" and immaculate objectivity. However, as a noncareer official, Moore was vulnerable.

Because career civil servants are more durable and often have more expertise, Secretary James Mitchell tried to provide greater stability by encouraging a system of career deputies to back up key political appointees. James E. Dodson and Millard Cass were career men who served for many years with distinction. When Secretary of Labor Willard Wirtz introduced Leo Werts, a top career official, to President Johnson, the President, playing with the similarity of names, teased them by saying, "I know which Werts really runs the department." Under President Nixon career civil servants lost some of their influence because the President felt that political appointees were more likely to carry out changes in policy. But career men like Ben Burdetsky (labor statistics), Alfred Albert (solicitor's office), Robert Hall (heading a welfare-reform study), and Tom Kouzes (management) are a few of many career officials who provide continuity and stability for departmental programs and policies.

THE BATTLE FOR CENTRAL CONTROL

A unified organization evolved slowly at the Department of Labor. At one time, the position of the Secretary of Labor was not unlike that of a medieval king trying to establish his authority over feudal baronies. Several Secretaries fought for many years to convert the loose confederation of semi-autonomous bureaus into a centralized department.

The politically appointed assistant secretaries led the fight for unification. At first they were looked upon as a "policy staff," while career professionals exercised "line" authority over "operations." Most Secretaries in recent years have felt that policy-making and operations functions are not easily separated. Gradually they placed their "staff" assistant secretaries in "line" positions, with authority over the operation of departmental programs.

The long-established traditional bureaus waged a fierce jurisdictional war, sometimes with strong public and congressional support. They argued that they could carry out programs more effectively than consolidated new organizations. They fought centralization on issues both great and small, and Secretary of Labor Willard Wirtz recalled one acrimonious dispute over whether some bureaus would allow their phone calls to be handled through a departmental switchboard. But most battles were over much more important matters.

Perhaps the fiercest of the skirmishes was the struggle for a unified Manpower Administration. When Manpower Administrator Stanley Ruttenberg appeared before a House Appropriations Committee in 1965, the chairman of the committee told him, "My mind is made up on the question of this reorganization in your department." The Bureau of Employment Security and the Bureau of Apprenticeship and Training, he said, "will stay on regardless of who is secretary tomorrow or next year, or five years from now. . . . Congress has always supported these two agencies."

Although temporarily defeated by Congress, several years later, Secretary Wirtz and Stanley Ruttenberg (then an assistant secretary) again moved to assert control. In the meantime, they had chipped away at the old-line bureaus by strengthening the authority of regional directors and by assigning new programs to new bureaus. Many new activities ended up in the Bureau of Work-Training Programs, which also took on-the-job-training away from the long-established Bureau of Apprenticeship. However, the Bureau of Employment Security, the chief target of the attack, remained the largest bureau in the Department and continued to direct the U.S. Employment Service, unemployment insurance, and various other programs.

Then, on October 21, 1968, Secretary Wirtz announced, "The Bureau of Employment Security and the Bureau of Work-Training Programs are hereby abolished." The Manpower Administration took over the functions of the two bureaus and prepared to carry them out as a "line" operation.

Secretary Wirtz was surprised when the state governors

came to the defense of the Bureau of Employment Security and was shocked when President Johnson ordered him to rescind the reorganization. However, fearing a blowup on the eve of the 1968 Presidential election, he agreed to postpone the implementation of his plan.

Shortly after President Nixon assumed office, Secretary of Labor George Shultz put into effect a similar, though not identical, reorganization. Like the plan that President Johnson had rejected, the Shultz proposal abolished the Bureau of Employment Security and merged its job-placement activities with the programs formerly supervised by the Bureau of Work-Training Programs. The new organization was named the United States Training and Employment Service. Secretary Shultz, also, while centralizing policy and authority, continued the trend of decentralizing operations in order to bring day-to-day services closer to the people.

When Secretary Shultz explained his reorganization to news media and showed them the old organization chart, he said that it looked like a "wiring diagram for a perpetual motion machine." By contrast, he remarked, the chart for his new reorganization was neat and simple.

Some reporters were skeptical. Many career officials still feel they can carry out programs better without extra layers of administration. Perhaps, as already has happened in other Cabinet departments, a future Secretary may think that a super-agency that spends most of the Department's money is like the "tail wagging the dog" and may decide to "cut it down to size."

V

Traditional Aid to the Jobless

The Manpower Administration, a giant organization, in the early 1970's spent about $5 billion per year—nearly 90 per cent of the Department of Labor's funds. It directs a wide array of manpower activities. (Traditional services in this field are described in this chapter; newer manpower, training, and work-experience services are recounted in the next chapter.)

Two important traditional units of the Department of Labor that provide help to the unemployed are the United States Employment Service (USES), whose basic function is to help job seekers find jobs for which they are qualified, and the Unemployment Insurance Service (UI), which pays workers who have been laid off from jobs.

Former Manpower Administrator Stanley H. Ruttenberg has criticized these units as outdated institutions created by one wave of social change, which have turned into a breakwater against subsequent waves. Others feel that USES and the UI have been responsive to changing needs of job seekers and employers in times of depression and prosperity, in times of war and peace. They say that proposals to reform the two services are unrealistic schemes of well-meaning idealists who do not understand the facts of economic life. Where does the truth lie?

The United States Employment Service

The United States Employment Service, along with 2,400 public employment offices in state systems, is the largest and most significant agency dealing with manpower in the United States. Since its creation, it has been attacked by conservatives opposed to the idea of government help to people looking for jobs and, more recently, by liberals claiming that USES has failed to help the "disadvantaged" who need its services most. But detractors and supporters alike agree on its importance.

The roots of the system go back to the Information Office created in 1907 in the Bureau of Immigration and Naturalization. Under the direction of Terence V. Powderly, former general master workman of the Knights of Labor, the Information Office tried, without much success, to encourage immigrants to look for jobs in sparsely settled areas so that they would not congregate in the slums of large cities. When the function was transferred in 1913 to the newly created Department of Labor, the emphasis shifted to finding jobs for unemployed workers. In 1915, the function became the basis of the United States Employment Service, which helped mobilize workers for the homefront war effort. In the 1920's, the myth of permanent prosperity diverted concern for the unemployed, and USES deteriorated. From its remnants, the Wagner-Peyser Act in 1933 created the present United States Employment Service.

The basic structure of USES and many issues that confront it have not changed much over the last forty years. The Employment Service is a federal-state partnership, with a small federal staff and thirty thousand employees completely financed by the federal government. The staffs of the state services total nearly three times the number of all of the Department of Labor's federal employees for all functions.

The federal-state public employment offices have developed many of the basic tools of modern personnel practice. USES created the *Dictionary of Occupational Titles,* a "Bible" for personnel officers, which describes and classifies nearly twenty-two thousand jobs in the American economy. The federal-state employment system collects and disseminates labor market information, including current and anticipated employment. Its publications, such as the *Job Guide for Young Workers,* are best sellers and can be obtained from the Government Printing Office.

However, as is true in many partnerships, the partners in this federal-state operation do not always agree. There is general consent that state administrators can better respond to local needs. But some federal officials complain that state systems have too much autonomy, resist desirable change, and frustrate national purposes. By contrast, some state officials protest against impractical federal meddling.

Universal Service

In carrying out its mission, the local Employment Service office matches job seekers' qualifications with employers' requirements for available jobs. The Employment Service helps a worker find the best available job and an employer find the best available worker. In a sense, it becomes a service to employers by screening and referring to them the most qualified workers.

One major controversy has been over the issue of whether the Employment Service should provide "universal service," which means job seeking assistance to all, or whether it should concentrate on affording help to the "disadvantaged." The Wagner-Peyser Act, which provides the legal basis for USES, calls for "employment offices for men, women, and juniors." This supports the view that USES should help everyone who wants assistance. As explained by Robert Goodwin, a long-time director of USES, "this is a basic service that the government has decided should be available to all people."

In its early days, a poor public image handicapped USES in its effort to provide universal service. Providing applicants for work-relief programs during the Depression and finding work for the unemployed, many of whom were marginal workers, gave it a reputation as a labor exchange for low-level jobs and low-level applicants. Many employers and better-qualified workers shunned its services, even though they were free.

USES fought hard to upgrade its reputation. It improved its counseling activities and, as early as 1945, moved to establish a national counseling program. It became pre-eminent in the field of job-aptitude testing. The General Aptitude Test Battery (GATB) and the specific aptitude tests that it developed for about six hundred occupations were good predictors of success in an occupation. In large metropolitan areas, Employment Service operations in local offices were separated from unemployment insurance work and functional offices were established along occupational lines, with special attention to commercial, professional, and service occupations—all growing fields of work. A convention placement service helped people seeking work through their professional associations. New entrants found this service most useful. Also, national registries were established for librarians, economists, statisticians, philosophers, and other high-level professionals.

The policy of upgrading USES in these ways ignited a fiery controversy. A corollary of this policy was that those who got the most help were the better-qualified workers, that is, the workers who could most easily get jobs on their own. The seemingly objective selection process was less than helpful, in one respect, for it screened out the less qualified, who needed the most help. Strange bedfellows joined the attack on USES. Private fee-charging employment agencies, fighting for survival, blasted the concept of free, tax-supported government services to people who could pay their own way. At the same time, but for different reasons, poverty fighters also assailed USES as a middle-class operation, insensitive to the needs of the black, the poor, the chronically unemployed, and other disadvantaged Americans. USES was, according to the poverty fighters, a "passive accessory to discriminatory practices," which mirrored the attitudes of employers and alienated the groups that needed it most. In response, Malcolm R. Lovell, an assistant secretary of Labor for Manpower, caught in the crossfire, philosophically summarized, "Any institution at the cutting edge of social change can't be in an easy position."

Help for the Disadvantaged

During the 1960's, some policy-making officials at the Department of Labor tried to transform USES into a tool of national manpower policy with the major goal of upgrading the disadvantaged one-tenth of the population. Under pressure, USES moved away from the concept of the best worker for the job toward assistance to the hard-core unemployed. As explained by a former manpower administrator, "If (the Employment Service) must continue to provide service to all [given its limited resources], it cannot adequately serve the disadvantaged."

Three of the many examples of this reorientation toward the hard-core unemployed are the development of new types of testing, the adoption of the Outreach program, and increased emphasis on human resources development.

Although USES, since its inception, distinguished itself in testing, most of its tests called for reading and arithmetic skills. Such tests, it was realized later, may not reveal the real aptitudes of the culturally deprived unemployed. Much of the stimulus for a new approach came from outside testing groups, but USES on its own initiative adopted nonreading, alternative aptitude tests, as well as work-sample techniques that avoided the bias of standard written tests. It also developed tests in Spanish to remove the language barrier for capable Spanish-speaking applicants for jobs.

In 1971, the Supreme Court ruled that tests used for hiring or promotion must not discriminate against minorities and must have a demonstrable relation to the job. Chief Justice Warren E. Burger, in delivering the court's decision, told the fable of the fox offering the stork a dinner of milk in a shallow dish. The fox lapped up the milk, but the stork's long bill kept him from getting a single mouthful. He was as hungry at the end of the dinner as he had been at the start. Analogously, tests for employment or promotion may not provide equal opportunity. The tests, like the "vessel in which the milk is proffered," must be "one all seekers can use."

USES had previously validated its tests by checking them against records of occupational job success. After the ruling, it undertook to recheck the tests to make sure that they were not operating against minorities.

"Outreach" is just what the word implies. Because the unemployed may be too alienated to come to the Employment Service office, the staff reaches out to them. Outreach workers, paid out of manpower-training funds, who as far as possible come from the same economic and ethnic background as the people they are trying to reach, go to community groups and visit potential recruits in their homes. They are salespeople in the best sense of the word. Instead of selling merchandise, they offer people an opportunity to participate in manpower programs that may help prepare them for good jobs at decent pay.

Human resources development is a high-sounding title for a simple idea. Its intent is to give the disadvantaged potential worker all the help he needs to raise him to the level where he can be placed in a decent job. Local employment offices organize employment-development led by a counselor who works with a job-development specialist, a work-training specialist, a coach, and a clerk. The team guides the client through an individually tailored program of basic education, skill training, work experience, and whatever else he needs, until the client is placed in a suitable job. It should be noted that such five-member teams with limited case loads use up resources and may force reductions in other services to employers and applicants who do not need as much help and can be placed at lower cost.

These changes of direction—of which new testing techniques, Outreach, and human resources development programs are examples—were not unchallenged. A policy of too heavy a concentration on the disadvantaged could be self-defeating to the Employment Service.

Most jobs are in the private economy. In the real world of business, employers hire those they think will perform best. As it was crudely expressed by one employer, "I don't care if he's black or white. The color of money is green."

If the Employment Service recommends applicants who are less qualified than other candidates, the employer will make his arrangements elsewhere. Actually, most new hirings consist of workers already employed but moving to other jobs, while about 96 per cent of the Employment Service clientele are unemployed workers and new entrants into the labor market. Although it is a public service, Employment Service offices are also handicapped in finding job openings for so many less experienced workers. Although USES makes an impressive 3.5 million to 6.5 million nonagricultural job placements each year, those numbers are only about 10 to 15 per cent of the total of new hirings in the economy. If employers do not like the kinds of referrals they get from the Employment Service, they have alternative ways of finding the workers they need.

Matching People with Jobs

During the 1960's and early 1970's, the traditional operation of the federal-state employment system deteriorated. While budgets have multiplied and the labor force has grown, job placements have declined. In some years in the early 1970's, placements dropped below the 4 million a year level, about 3 million fewer than a decade earlier. One reason was an economic slump; another was employer dissatisfaction. In serving the disadvantaged, USES had paid less attention to employers.

USES is recovering ground lost because of its relative neglect of services to private employers in the last half of the 1960's; it is assisting employers in several ways and emphasizing cooperative relations in the hope that more business firms will refer to USES the additional job vacancies that it now needs.

As part of this program for expanding the job vacancies listed with USES, a Presidential order in 1971 called on federal contractors to list their openings with the Employment Service. The contractor is not obligated to hire applicants referred by the Employment Service, but at least its applicants have a chance. The mandatory listing is likely to help veterans most. As in the past, they are given priority in referrals.

USES is also striving to improve its service through computer technology. It is experimenting with wholly mechanical matching of the requirements of jobs with the qualifications of applicants by computer. Of more immediate use is the partly computerized "job bank," which provides job-placement interviewers in local offices with a daily list of all job orders in an extended geographical area. First tried in Baltimore in 1968, it now operates in almost all states and in more than a hundred cities. It covers a large proportion of the labor markets in the country.

This service is particularly helpful to the placement interviewer in a local USES office, who is on the firing line. In an office crowded with job seekers, the interviewer may examine a client's application while flipping the job-bank viewer for available openings and calling potential employers to arrange interviews.

A day in the life of an interviewer like Florence Hopson in the Indianapolis office might include interviews with a college graduate in biology, who decides he wants forestry work, and a twenty-year-old father, who is referred to an auto-parts dealer for a $2.50-an-hour stockroom job. It also might involve an attractive, barefoot young woman in blue jeans who says she was fired for resisting the amorous advances of a superior and asks for a job requiring shorthand, and a nine-teen-year-old girl in a skimpy dress dragging a sleepy male along for an interview. Calls by the interviewer to an insurance company could turn up a job interview for a thirty-three-year-old, laid-off keypunch operator. At an average of two or three applicants an hour, a busy day goes by for an interviewer with a varied succession of clients and employers. Work like this of matching jobs and people is one of USES's vital functions.

Universal Service plus Help for the Disadvantaged

The Employment Service is now re-emphasizing its regular activities. It recognizes that job placement for everyone seeking work is the lifeblood of the system and should be the objective toward which all other activities and programs are aimed.

This does not mean abandoning the disadvantaged. Work with the hard-core unemployed has made too deep an impression on USES programs to be forgotten. Contrary to claims of antipoverty warriors that USES cannot provide both universal service and intensive assistance to marginal workers, there may be a "golden mean" with adequate attention to both goals.

Even the Wagner-Peyser Act of 1933, at the same time as it mandated assistance for all, specified particular help to such groups as veterans and farm workers. USES continues to give priority to veterans. When a job comes up, the placement official will first check the salmon-colored applications indicating veterans' preferences.

Placing farm workers is a traditional government responsibility that antedates the present employment system. A bulletin posted throughout the country by the Department of Labor during World War I read in part, "Kansas—40,000 men needed; wages will range upward from $2 per day and board . . . from 90 to 120 days. Men can go direct to towns in wheat belt . . . or write to . . . free employment bureau, Topeka, Kansas, for directions."

Currently farm placement has become a controversial issue,

with criticism directed at USES both by farmers and by farm laborers. Migrant workers, who follow the crops, are in many cases poorly paid, often have large families, and their wives and children generally work with them in order to subsist. To be sure, the situation has improved since John Steinbeck's famous novel *The Grapes of Wrath* described migrants fleeing the dust bowl in the 1930's and the TV documentary "Harvest of Shame" pictured the shameful living conditions of migrant farm labor in 1960. In fact, USES will place migrant workers only where minimum wages are ensured and where there is housing having sufficient room and good water in or near living units, as well as toilets, sanitary facilities, and other basic requirements. In this situation, however, farm owners complain that USES interferes too much, while workers assail it because it does not do enough.

In the early 1970's, engineers, scientists, and technicians made up another special group receiving special help. Many of them had been laid off with the winding down of the war in Vietnam. A tragic paradox of modern society is that, along with the killing, war unleashes a demand for scientific and technical activities that the nation cannot seem to generate in peacetime. USES is trying to help these scientific professionals and technicians convert their skills to peacetime use through job-search grants, relocation aid, training, and job development.

Intensive service to the hard-core unemployed also fits into the pattern of aid to special groups. It faces the particularly difficult obstacle of employer resistance. "They want better qualified people," one local employment supervisor explained. "Who would you hire if you were in business?"

Such an obstacle, however, also provides an opportunity. Putting unqualified workers into jobs is a type of welfare reform. Upgrading an indigent worker's capabilities is obviously the best way of helping him.

Translated into operating goals, this means bringing some of the disadvantaged to the competitive starting line through programs of intensive training, subsidized work experience, supportive services, and antidiscrimination measures. Once they are ready for jobs, they may need extra motivation and help, but they are mostly on their own. Under such conditions, some of the hard-core may be screened into jobs by the normal job-matching process of finding the best workers for the best jobs.

This concept is being followed most intensively in what USES calls its comprehensive manpower agency experiment. Model public employment offices in ten cities and one rural area are experimenting with three levels of service in the same office:

1. A streamlined, self-help service for job-ready applicants
2. Help in planning a personal job search for applicants needing more assistance
3. Intensive counseling, placement, and supportive service for the most disadvantaged, who are assigned to employability teams with limited case loads

What the experimental program is trying to do in microcosm, USES as a whole hopes eventually to achieve in macrocosm. Its goal is universal service for all who need assistance, while special help is to be provided to those who need it most.

UNEMPLOYMENT INSURANCE

Employment service is one side of the coin; unemployment insurance is the other. Unemployment insurance was established during the Depression of the 1930's to take the place of the bread line as an honorable method of getting those who want work and are unable to find it through a slump period. From its beginnings in 1935 to the early 1970's, unemployment insurance has paid more than $60 billion to more than 60 million workers.

Unemployment insurance was launched as a partnership

between the federal government, which recommended standards, and the states, which passed their own laws and handled compensation claims. State practices vary widely, depending on attitudes toward provision of government help to individuals and on competition between some states to attract industry by offering the incentive of lower payroll taxes. Lower taxes are made possible by restricting eligibility for benefit payments and by establishing stingy benefit formulas.

Secretaries of Labor have led campaigns to update the unemployment insurance laws and establish firmer federal standards. As recently as 1968, Secretary of Labor Willard Wirtz reviewed his frustration. The laws were substantially the same as they had been thirty-five years earlier, he said, "and the barnacles on them have become rebukes to legislative and administrative responsibility." Action came two years later.

The New Amendments

In 1970, Congress passed a major bill entitled Employment Security Act Amendments, which set up stronger requirements for state systems of unemployment insurance. President Richard Nixon signed the bill at a ceremony in the Blue Room of the White House. Although the amendments fall short of the goals of the Department, they call for significant changes. All states revised their own laws to meet the new federal requirements.

A unique feature of the unemployment insurance system is that it is paid for by employers through a tax on payrolls. A small part of the tax goes to the federal government for administering employment services and unemployment compensation. Most of the tax goes to the states to pay benefits and to build up reserves (sometimes running to billions of dollars) for years of recession. Under a merit-rating system, employers with a record of providing workers with steady jobs pay lower taxes.

One advantage of this financing system is that, because benefits are paid from premiums, workers receive their benefits as a right they have earned rather than as relief. Another is that employers are encouraged to keep workers on the job in order to reduce tax costs. A serious drawback is that a pay-roll-related tax is an incentive to limit the scope and services of unemployment insurance.

The new admendments call for somewhat more generous financing. When unemployment insurance went into effect in the 1930's, it was supported by a tax on the first $3,000 of each worker's pay, which then in effect taxed more than 90 per cent of the wages paid. In 1970, most states still had the same $3,000 base, but at that time it represented only 50 per cent of the wages of covered workers. The retention of a low tax base created pressure to keep the benefit payments also at a low level, with the result that benefits fell far behind the continuing rise in wage level. In 1969, the average weekly un-employment benefit for the country as a whole was only $46, compared to $134 earned on an average each week by factory workers.

Congress did not go as far as the Administration had wanted, but it raised the taxable base to $4,200 a year. In addition, the Employment Security Amendments of 1970 brought unemployment insurance to 5 million of the 17 mil-lion workers not previously covered by this benefit. Most newly protected jobs were in nonprofit establishments, in the 700,000 small firms that had formerly been exempt because they had fewer than four employees, in state hospitals and institutions of higher education, and in additional categories such as agent-drivers and outside salesmen.

From the very start, unemployment insurance provided benefits only for temporary loss of work. In most states, the maximum period over which benefits could be paid was twenty-six weeks. Workers who did not find jobs during the twenty-six–week period faced personal tragedy.

During economic slumps in the late 1950's and in the 1960's, the federal government paid for extended benefits for additional weeks to those whose regular benefits had been used up. These extra payments not only alleviated suffering but also added "high velocity" dollars to the nation's purchasing power. Legislation providing for such extended benefits had always been temporary.

The new program established permanent extended benefits, paid half by the state and half by the federal government, which would be triggered when the insured unemployment rate reached specified levels. Workers who had exhausted their regular benefits would be automatically entitled to a 50 per cent extension, up to thirteen extra weeks (but not more than thirty-nine weeks of regular plus extended benefits). In fiscal 1972, extended benefits mitigated the hardship of unemployment for more than 1.5 million workers.

Level of Benefits

A major issue, over which there has been bitter controversy, is the level of benefits. The object is to provide the unemployed worker with enough to get by on, but not so much that unemployment compensation would be an inducement *not* to work.

Situations where idleness is more profitable than work, though not very common, occur when workers have sources of income supplementing their unemployment compensation. Generally, states ignored the relatively small portion of earnings that can be added to unemployment benefits. But, in some industries, strong unions have won for their members substantial Supplementary Unemployment Benefits (SUB). For example, during a bad slump in the steel industry in 1971, steelworkers could draw, in addition to state unemployment payments, up to another $88.50 weekly from their employers. One union official commented, "If you take what the average guy's making and subtract from that his taxes, what it costs to drive back and forth . . . and compare that with what he draws from the combination of compensation and SUB, sometimes he's ahead."

But most workers do not have other income, and unemployment benefits are usually very meager. Originally, the goal had been to help most workers cover 50 per cent of their wage loss. As a matter of fair play and to avoid bad publicity, a flat maximum was also established. This would prevent those with high wages from drawing seemingly excessive unemployment benefits. To take an extreme example, a movie actor in California during a 13-week period earned $1,000 weekly. If there were no maximums, under the California formula he would receive $500 weekly in state unemployment benefits. However, California law limits him to $75 weekly. In 1939, in all but two states, workers received 50 per cent or more of their average wage, with only 27 per cent of the workers affected by the ceiling. By 1970, as a result of inflation and lagging state adjustments, the flat maximum acted as a ceiling on payments to nearly half of all beneficiaries, and the overall ratio of insurance payments to normal wages was lower in many states than it had been thirty years earlier.

When efforts to establish national standards of unemployment benefits were decisively rejected in Congress in 1970, the President suggested that the states pass their own laws increasing benefits. He set as a goal an amount equal to two-thirds of the average weekly wage in the state. Many states increased their payments, but not nearly to the level the President had requested. In 1972, half the states had maximums below 50 per cent of the state's average wage, and in Alaska and Illinois the maximum was less than 30 per cent of the average wage.

Who Is Eligible?

Another important problem in unemployment insurance is determining eligibility. Unlike relief, where decisions are based on need, unemployment payments are a form of insurance to which covered workers are entitled. Every now and then, this is brought home by a spectacular case such as that of a millionaire collecting his insurance benefits, but most people who lose jobs genuinely need the benefits they receive.

Local unemployment officials must constantly determine

who is and who is not eligible to draw benefits. The general rule is that people are entitled to unemployment benefits when they lose their jobs and are looking for work. Three major causes for disqualification, at least for a period of time, are quitting a job voluntarily, dismissal for misconduct, and refusal to take suitable work without good cause. The definition of what is suitable work is a thorny issue. Rules, procedures, and interpretations vary widely among states. The successful operation of unemployment insurance, in large measure, depends on intelligent and impartial judgments by administrators.

There is a sharp difference of view on the part of observers and commentators about the character of workers on unemployment insurance. Advocates of the system draw a picture of the average beneficiary as a good worker thrown out of work because of circumstances beyond his control. He diligently looks for and, after a short time, finds another job. Critics of unemployment insurance, by contrast, depict a motley group of beneficiaries such as strikers, retirees, students, pregnant women, and people who quit work and do not wish to find another job as long as public funds are available. However, on balance, the claims of most beneficiaries appear to be proper and legitimate.

Currently, only about 12 million American workers are not protected by unemployment insurance. Of these, nearly 8 million work for state and local governments, where employment is moderately stable. The two largest groups still seriously exposed to the risk of unemployment without receiving benefits are domestic service workers and farm workers.

The Department of Labor is engaged in major research dealing with seasonal unemployment, the relationship between unemployment insurance and other social programs, and the extension of unemployment insurance to farm workers. Also, in accord with the goal of locating jobs for all who are able and willing to work, unemployment insurance officials are actively helping benefit claimants to find jobs.

Unemployment insurance is meeting some of the social and economic goals for which it was established by providing the first line of defense for the unemployed. Unemployment is a hazard to society, and its causes are usually beyond the worker's control. Benefits also sustain purchasing power and act as an automatic stabilizer of the economy, which helps to curtail further spread of unemployment. Payments provide income to workers and their families, who might otherwise suffer privation. Another value of the benefits is that they allow a laid-off worker to maintain a sense of dignity and personal worth while he is looking for another job.

VI

Special Manpower Development and Placement Activities

Historians find it difficult to review the current programs of any organization. What seems trivial now may become important later, and what seems important now may become trivial. The Department of Labor is no exception. In 1961, the Department's relatively minor role under the Area Redevelopment Act in retraining jobless workers in depressed areas foreshadowed a giant program to follow. About the same time, the possibility that automation would destroy the jobs of millions of workers turned out to be an idle fear. So in 1973, the sixtieth anniversary of the Department of Labor, it is difficult to prophesy with accuracy what current activities will turn out to be the most significant. The Department's manpower work, however, seems likely to loom large in any future perspective.

The Department of Labor has become primarily a manpower department. About 2 million Americans are enrolled in work and training programs directed by an assistant secretary of Labor for Manpower who supervises the crucially important Manpower Administration. This function of the Department stems from the Employment Act of 1946, in which the government declared its concern with opportunities for employment. President Harry S. Truman, in signing the Act, considered a proposed statement:

> Occasionally, as we pore through the pages of history, we are struck by the fact that some incident, little noted at the time, profoundly affects the whole subsequent course of events. I venture the prediction that history, someday, will so record the enactment of the Employment Act of 1946.

President Truman did not use this statement, and it appeared for a time that his decision not to use it was prophetic, for the Act lay dormant for many years. Then, with enactment of the Manpower Development and Training Act of 1962, the Employment Act of 1946 became the epochal symbol of the broadened role of the federal government in manpower policy.

THE MANPOWER DEVELOPMENT AND TRAINING ACT

The Area Redevelopment Act of 1961 was a pioneering step in American manpower development. Almost buried in the Act's broad range of government measures to help localities with unusually high unemployment was a provision for paying unemployed workers in depressed areas allowances for up to sixteen weeks while teaching them new skills.

From this seed blossomed the Manpower Development and Training Act of 1962 (MDTA). The MDTA carries the American tradition of free education a step farther. It pays people to learn. Its two main thrusts are institutional training and on-the-job-training.

The institutional program is administered jointly by the Department of Labor and the Department of Health, Education, and Welfare (HEW). It provides classes in public or private schools for people who are not expected to obtain decent jobs without such training. Enrollees are trained for hundreds of occupations, from typist to hospital worker to auto mechanic. When it turned out that many trainees failed to absorb the job instruction because they were not ready to benefit, courses were added in such basic subjects as reading and arithmetic. The original 16-week limit set by the Area Redevelopment Act was expanded at first to 52 weeks and in successive steps to 104 weeks. The MDTA provides that federal funds should pay for tuition, transportation, and living allowances.

The MDTA program for on-the-job-training, now known as the Jobs Optional Program (JOP), is administered by the states. It trains people at the place of employment. To trainees who did not like school, on-the-job-training has the psychological advantage of permitting them to hold an actual job in a real work atmosphere. Projects are concentrated on skilled and semiskilled occupations in manufacturing and construction. The government pays all training costs, while the employer pays the worker the prevailing wage for the industry in the area.

Originally, the MDTA program emphasized retraining those who had lost their jobs because of technological change. Automation, according to thinking then prevalent, benefits the nation as a whole but hurts some individuals whose jobs are wiped out. Although there were tragic cases of workers whose jobs were junked because of technology, the problem has turned out to be not nearly as widespread as had been thought.

The MDTA program continues to have as one of its goals the retraining of workers with outdated skills for jobs requiring skills that are in short supply. In addition, the program aims, as it has done since the beginning, to increase national industrial productivity by upgrading skills. But, with the passage of time, more emphasis was placed on helping the disadvantaged.

There seems to be a conflict of purposes in MDTA training because it seeks, on one hand, to increase productivity and reduce the inflationary pressures of skill shortages and, on the other hand, to draw into the work force people who lack skill, who work for low earnings, and who may be, even after training, marginal workers. In practice, only lip service is paid to the program's productivity and anti-inflation aspects. The primary objective has become helping people to escape poverty. Today, only 35 per cent of MDTA enrollees are selected on the basis of labor-market needs; the disadvantaged constitute the other 65 per cent.

The MDTA program has become a tremendous undertaking. Between March 15, 1962, and June 30, 1972, the federal government allocated about $2.5 billion to enroll 2 million trainees. Some 1.3 million people completed their training, and almost a million got jobs after training. Most of the trainees had been economically poor. Many of them were under twenty-two years of age or over forty-four; our industrial society sometimes considers people in these age categories either too young and inexperienced or too old and inflexible. Many blacks and high school dropouts also received MDTA assistance. An increasing proportion of trainees consists of people drawn from relief rolls and from among the handicapped.

Findings of a recent study showed that, a year or more after completing training, those who had participated in the MDTA institutional program averaged $1,800 more in earnings annually, and those trained on the job averaged $1,600 more. By no stretch of the imagination did most of the participants become affluent, but their annual incomes, which hovered around the $3,400 to $3,800 level, brought them from economic degradation to at least the edge of the mainstream of the American economy. Although standards for measuring the value of the MDTA program are hard to set, such results indicate that, if costs are balanced against the benefits, the MDTA program stands among the better federal social programs.

Research and Development

Since the enactment of the Manpower Development and Training Act in 1962, the Department of Labor has used

experimental and demonstration projects, along with a research program, to test the effectiveness of new solutions to
manpower problems and to improve the manpower program in
general. This research-and-development work conducted under the MDTA covers the gamut of manpower problems. Its
objective, stated broadly, is to develop ways of dealing with
problems that interfere with full and satisfying employment of
all American workers.

Among the more interesting aspects of this objective, which
has engaged a variety of Department projects, is the problem
of providing effective service to the "hard-to-employ." This
category of citizens includes some people who are so poor
that they are not counted in the census and who in an economic sense simply do not exist. The MDTA program generally has helped the more visible and easily reachable group
that is willing and able to work but lacks skill and opportunity.
It has seldom reached those who were so alienated as to live
totally beyond the reach of the Establishment. But it has tried
hard to do so and, in some cases, achieved notable success.

For example, after shocking riots in Detroit in the summer
of 1967, the big auto companies opened employment offices in
the slums, offering jobs to anyone who applied. Although
many of these specially employed people were not essentially
different from those normally hired, the president of the Chrysler Corporation noted that there were some who were too illiterate to sign their names, who could not read such words as
"in" and "out" on doors, and who did not know when to report
for work. The Chrysler Corporation experimented with a class
of 125 from the "backwaters of our society," and in three
months 50 of these had moved into jobs.

In this and many other ways, manpower specialists in the
Department of Labor delved into recruiting, counseling, training, and finding jobs for the hard-to-employ. They worked
with ghetto youth and other young people who had never had
a real chance in the competitive job market. They worked with
the aging, the illiterate, the mentally handicapped, and even

with drug addicts and convicts, who posed particularly baffling problems. Lessons learned from experimental projects have subsequently been applied on an expanded scale.

Thus, the findings of early tests in training convicts are now being applied more broadly. Criminals often find it almost impossible to "go straight." Few employers will hire former convicts, whose only practical choice, after repeated failures to land a job, appears to be committing new crimes. In 1971, there were sixty MDTA projects conducted in prisons, teaching offenders job skills. In at least one course, prisoners were so motivated that eight men refused discharge in order to finish their class. One of these prisoners served nine extra months.

One of the more important projects for reintegrating prisoners into the community is a two-year Department of Labor experiment with about five hundred inmates from Baltimore, Maryland. As they are released, these prisoners are placed at random in one of four groups. The first group receives money and help in getting jobs; the second group receives only financial assistance; the third group gets job help only; the fourth group, which gets little or no help of any kind, serves as a control group. The experimenters hope to show that former prisoners, if properly helped, can become useful citizens. The demonstration may provide information for a model program.

A descriptive account of the numerous MDTA projects could fill several fascinating books. In general, what the Department of Labor wants to find are successful training methods that can be applied more broadly. A small experiment in which disadvantaged high school students were put to work as tutors of elementary school children is now being widely used to improve youth literacy. A work-sample procedure was developed, tested, refined, and then applied more broadly for persons for whom normal paper-and-pencil tests of potential were inappropriate. A special "prepping" of minority youth for apprenticeship examinations has spread to about eighty cities.

PARTNERSHIP OF GOVERNMENT AND BUSINESS: JOBS

Because private enterprise employs most working Americans, an effective program to hire disadvantaged Americans depends on a partnership of government and business. Beginning in 1967, the federal government initiated several experiments that encouraged businesses to locate in slum areas and hire slum dwellers by offering government contracts, bonuses for hiring long-term jobless persons, and other financial inducements. Although many of these ventures were unsuccessful, they set the stage for a major program to create Job Opportunities in the Business Sector (the program was given the appropriate acronym JOBS). Following the recommendations of a White House task force to increase the involvement of private enterprise in training the disadvantaged, President Lyndon B. Johnson, in January, 1968, called for an alliance between government and business for the hiring of 500,000 men and women from the slums of fifty American cities.

Businessmen formed a National Alliance of Businessmen (NAB) for this purpose. The president of the Ford Motor Company headed the organization, and the president of the Coca-Cola Company was the vice-chairman. They set the precedent that influential businessmen would lead the effort. President Richard Nixon, shortly after he came into office, endorsed the NAB and appeared at a glamorous dinner at the Sheraton Park Hotel in Washington, D.C., held for the purpose of promoting the hiring of the disadvantaged. The dinner was attended by 350 prominent people representing over a trillion dollars in assets. The NAB agreed to work with the Department of Labor to hire and train the hard-core, the alienated, and the hard-to-reach and sometimes invisible unemployed.

The JOBS program is, in a very real sense, an expansion of MDTA on-the-job training. It assumes that the best way to learn a job is to work on the job. Employers commit themselves to hire the disadvantaged first—and then train them. The trainees are paid to learn and are motivated by the hope of getting a real job when they finish their training.

The program operates in two important ways. Some companies are paid by the government for extra training costs. Most companies, for a variety of motives ranging from a fear of government red tape to a desire to contribute to society, participate without reimbursement.

JOBS was launched with great enthusiasm, but, like many rapidly expanding programs, it suffered from growing pains. Companies occasionally made commitments that they could not keep. The program was sometimes "oversold." As is the case with many entry-level jobs in industry, the "quit rate" was very high.

But the major problem was that, though JOBS was inaugurated in a period of prosperity, its glowing hopes were dampened by business recession. One example was the Chrysler Corporation, which signed the largest single JOBS contract with the Department of Labor to train 4,500 disadvantaged unemployed to become auto production workers. Then auto sales lagged, profits dropped, and the price of Chrysler stock nose-dived from more than $70 a share to $16. Chrysler backed out of its contract and laid off 10,000 workers. Under the prevailing seniority policy of last-hired, first-fired, some of those laid off were formerly hard-core unemployed. One of the articles of faith of the JOBS program—that most training slots would turn into real jobs—had been shattered.

Yet, with all its misadventures, JOBS has had a good record of achievement. Economic slowdown hurt it, and some of the funds appropriated for it were shifted to other programs. But not all segments of the economy are as recession-prone as automobile manufacturing. Many firms continued to hire and train under the program even during the recession. Chrysler itself showed its good faith by developing several smaller programs to upgrade 4,000 disadvantaged workers already on the payroll and to hire and train 1,000 men as auto mechanics, body repairmen, and clerks for its auto dealers.

The JOBS program has the virtue of combining the efforts of government and business in locating and providing acceptable jobs that offer advancement after training. Moreover, JOBS helps with remedial education, counseling on personal problems, assistance with health and transportation, and, in some cases, child day care. In addition, JOBS now concerns itself not only with placing people in entry-level jobs but also with encouraging them to prepare for promotion to better-paying positions. Successful trainees generally have earned more than enough to raise themselves and their families out of poverty.

The JOBS program has been expanded from fifty original cities to a nationwide network. It has provided employment for more than 1.3 million people. Over half of them stayed at their jobs six months or longer. This performance is roughly comparable to the average job tenure of workers from the general population in similar age brackets. JOBS is a major program of government and business to give a chance to many Americans who in the normal course of events would never have had a chance.

Providing New Careers

One of the ironies of finding jobs for the disadvantaged is that, while some people are looking for work and failing to find it, some jobs, particularly in skilled and public service fields, go begging because people with the requisite skills are not available. One solution is to break down complex jobs into their simpler components. In this way, the easy parts of the jobs can be handled by the less skilled and the better trained can spend time more efficiently at the higher level of their skills.

During World War I, the Department of Labor had a Dilution Division to apply this idea, and, during World War II, the War Manpower Commission followed a similar program on a larger scale. In peacetime also, there is good reason for the highly trained to do the more complicated parts of a job—tasks for which there is a shortage of skilled people—while at the same time rewarding employment is created in the less specialized parts of the same job for those who need work.

In the mid-1960's, the government sponsored the New Careers Program, developing paraprofessional jobs for the disadvantaged that might alleviate the critical shortages of skilled and professional workers in schools, hospitals, welfare agencies, and other public institutions. For example, social workers were helped by people with less training who could relieve them of certain amounts of detail work. Although such helpers did not have diplomas, they often had firsthand experience and sensitivity, assets that are sometimes lacking among experts.

One success story that shows how the program works is the history of Leefay, a former domestic worker. She at first thought she could never get a decent job because she was uneducated. But she learned arts and crafts and related skills. She now helps a recreation director in Winston-Salem, North Carolina. "I work with children of all ages," she has said, "and I love the job."

The federal government not only paid most of the training bills for the New Careers Program but also hired people on its own, using the same principle of dividing a job into its professional and nonprofessional aspects. In 1966, Operation MUST (Maximum Utilization of Skills and Training) redesigned a number of types of government jobs to separate higher-level skills and create jobs requiring lower skills. In a similar program, about fifty thousand employees have been hired from a special worker-trainee examination for filling low-level entry jobs (low-level components of complex functions) in the federal government.

A Public Service Careers program, providing the disadvan-

taged not only with permanent government employment but
also with facilitated upgrading, has been called by some supporters a "moral revolution." It enables poor people to get a
firm grasp on the first rung of a career ladder and then climb
from low-level beginner's jobs to eventual professional status
in public service. The program has operated in federal, state,
and local government agencies. But difficulties have arisen.
Some agencies have hired aides for menial, dead-end jobs;
others have fired them when federal subsidies have ended. In
many agencies, including some in the federal government, the
Public Service Careers concept has come into direct conflict
with the merit system. The principle that the best qualified
should be hired creates barriers for those who are poorly educated and handicapped by their environment. Nevertheless,
there are cases where the New Careers idea of subdividing
higher-level jobs can make for greater efficiency in government agencies while at the same time creating work with a
future for some who might otherwise never have a chance. Although New Careers is being phased out, its purposes are being incorporated into over-all federal-government personnel
policies.

On Behalf of Youth

While teenage unemployment in general in the United
States is bad, it is worse for black teenagers. The 15 per cent
rate for jobless teenagers is four to five times that of adults
over twenty-five, and the more than 30 per cent unemployment
among black teenagers in the early 1970's is double the rate
for white youth. Many young people, particularly in slums, are
alienated and believe that getting a job is not possible for them.
When riots broke out in the summer of 1968 in many American inner cities, the spark that ignited the tinder was the assassination of Martin Luther King, Jr., but among the complex
causes of the riots were the frustration and joblessness of youth
in the slums.

The roots of youth unemployment in the late 1960's and the 1970's are complicated and numerous. The baby boom in the early 1950's had the effect, some fifteen to twenty years later, of increasing the proportion of youth to over-all population at the same time as technology was reducing the number of simple jobs. People on relief, forced to look for jobs, along with more working women, were competing strongly for the same kind of jobs that youngsters were seeking. Misunderstanding of child labor laws, unnecessary educational "requirements" for jobs, and preference of employers for older and more stable workers also added to this many-sided problem.

The challenge of what to do about jobless youth impinges on the field of education and other areas beyond the scope of the Department of Labor. But the Department carries a major responsibility in relation to this challenge. The Department conducts, in addition to its regular training programs that benefit many young people, programs designed specially for youth.

At the turn of the century, almost the entire teenage labor force was made up of out-of-school youth who had finished high school or were school dropouts. In 1947, this group still made up 75 per cent of working teenagers. By the early 1970's, however, the proportion had dropped to 44 per cent, while 56 per cent of the teenage jobholders continued in school. Although the trend continues for more and more students to work, out-of-school youth are still a significant part of the youth job market. The kind of job one has is usually more important to out-of-school young workers than it is to student workers. Those who are out of school eagerly desire jobs from which they can learn new skills and that will give them upward mobility.

Apprenticeship

For centuries upon centuries, one of the best ways to learn a skilled job has been through apprenticeship. In 1937, under the Federal Apprenticeship Act, the Department of Labor began promoting acceptance of standards for apprenticeship, primarily to prevent employers from exploiting young workers by paying them low wages. During World War II, the apprenticeship program was used to meet emergency shortages of skilled labor. Today the Bureau of Apprenticeship and Training in the Department encourages private enterprise to improve apprenticeship and other training in industry. There are in the United States about half a million apprentices, of whom about two-thirds are in registered programs in more than 350 skilled trades.

An apprentice normally trains on the job under an experienced craftsman. He also spends some time in a class, where he learns why things are done in certain ways on the job. His apprenticeship extends from two to six years, depending on the trade. The apprentice is paid, usually starting at about half the journeyman's pay, with an increase every six months until he reaches 90 per cent of the journeyman's rate, in the last six months of his training. In most trades in which there are apprentices, the pay is excellent.

Generally, the skilled trades limit the number of apprentices. Moreover, because it is a human tendency to keep a good thing among relatives, friends, and associates, restrictive entry into the trades through the avenue of apprenticeship has worked harshly against blacks and other minorities whose fathers, other relatives, and friends were not in a position to ease their entrance into apprenticeship. When a newspaper reporter asked George Meany, president of the AFL-CIO, whether many trades discriminated against blacks, he replied in his blunt fashion, "Hell, no! We discriminate against everybody." Lest this quotation be taken out of context, it should be pointed out that Meany has opposed racial discrimination. The point he was making was that the number of jobs was limited and that skilled workers preferred to maintain a scarcity of workers in their trade, making it easier for already established craftsmen to get new jobs, to win increases in wages, and to control work rules.

The Department of Labor in 1963 issued equal-opportunity regulations affecting entry into apprenticeship. Five years later, an agreement was worked out with the AFL-CIO Building Trades Department on a voluntary Apprentice Outreach Program, under which churches, civil rights groups, schools, and other organizations recruited minority youth and helped them to meet the requirements of apprenticeship. When the voluntary method of opening the way for minorities proved only marginally successful, the Department of Labor invoked statutory authority and called for affirmative action rather than mere passive acceptance of platitudes on nondiscrimination. By the early 1970's, Outreach had brought about 150,000 blacks into apprenticeship programs, and the proportion of minority youth entering apprenticeship more than doubled from the 6 per cent of the mid-1960's.

The Job Corps

Apprenticeship programs opened the way to the more energetic and ambitious out-of-school young worker. Other programs were developed to help some of the seriously disadvantaged and less motivated youth whose early failures might lead to self-destructive idleness and antisocial activities.

Of all the youth programs, the Job Corps was the most attractive in theory and the most troublesome in practice. What could be better than giving deprived youth a fresh start in wholesome camps conducted exclusively for young people? And who could run the camps better than the great American corporations, which proudly proclaimed that they would thus prove their social responsibility? Along with appropriate government agencies and nonprofit groups, corporations agreed to take these disadvantaged young men and women; give them clean clothes, good food, and supervised recreation; teach them job skills; and make them into responsible, employable, and productive citizens. In some cases, these glowing expectations were actually realized. At Camp Kilmer, New Jersey, for example, the International Telephone and Telegraph Company trained Corps members in shop work, auto repair, type-writer repair, building maintenance, cooking, and basic police work. About five thousand Kilmer graduates moved into pay-ing jobs.

In many cases, however, the lovely dream turned into a nightmare. Perhaps it was inevitable. The program enrolled many dropouts burdened with grave adjustment problems. When camps were established they proved frightfully expen-sive; the more than $8,000 cost per year per enrollee far exceeded costs at top universities. Even worse than the high cost was the fact that moving slum youth hundreds of miles for expensive special training failed to give them either the so-cial or the job skills that could help them when they returned home. A survey ordered by Congress reported in 1969 that the billion dollars spent on the program since 1964 had been largely wasted. About 40 per cent of the enrollees left during the first three months because of homesickness and failure to adjust. Only 36 per cent finished their training.

The Job Corps was administered initially by the Office of Economic Opportunity. During the Presidential election cam-paign in 1968, Richard Nixon attacked the Corps as a failure. After his election, the new President transferred the Job Corps to the Department of Labor, and the new Secretary of Labor phased out more than half of the 113 Job Corps training centers.

The cutbacks notwithstanding, the Department of Labor recognized the validity of Job Corps residential training for underprivileged youth. Unlike other manpower programs, the Job Corps provided round-the-clock training and supervision that could help young people coming from severely deprived backgrounds. Now limited in size, the Job Corps is improving. The facts that the centers are smaller and are located in metro-politan areas near the homes of enrollees make possible more individual attention and may reduce the number of dropouts.

The new Job Corps is trying to achieve a double advantage

over the old. First, because it no longer stands in isolation from other manpower services supervised by the Department of Labor, Corps members can more readily benefit from these services. Second, the Job Corps now, as a matter of policy, gives more help with health care, education, skill training, and finding jobs. Increasingly, the last phase of participation in the Job Corps is work in industry under close guidance. If the Corps member is deficient in this phase, he can return for further training. Early results show that about three-quarters of those who left the Job Corps in 1971 had jobs, were in school, or were serving in the armed forces. Considering the multiple handicaps of enrollees, this performance shows promising potential.

The Neighborhood Youth Corps

Numerically, the Neighborhood Youth Corps (NYC) is one of the largest of the government's manpower programs. Since its inception in the mid-1960's, several million young people have enrolled. The NYC has three major segments—an out-of-school program, a summer program, and an in-school program.

The out-of-school program has some activities that are like, and some that are unlike, the activities of the Job Corps. Like the Corps, it enrolls from a group including many school dropouts and long-term unemployed people; however, its activities are nonresidential, and it costs much less per enrollee than the Job Corps. Although the NYC found work for many enrollees, some of the jobs were at low levels and without a future. Like the Job Corps, the NYC out-of-school program has been criticized as an "aging vat" rather than a training program.

By the early 1970's, the NYC had reduced the number of out-of-school trainees. It encouraged some to return to school and transferred others, eighteen years and older, to other manpower programs. The out-of-school activity was then enriched for sixteen- and seventeen-year-olds by blending health services, remedial education, skill training, work experience, and counseling aimed at preparing the enrollees to compete in the job market.

The NYC's summer program takes cognizance of the fact that, of the approximately 7 million school-age youths who compete for summer employment, about 5 million succeed in finding vacation-time jobs, but youth unemployment swells to near the 2 million mark every summer. For some of these, their unemployment is more of an inconvenience than a tragedy. Their parents support them, they return to school, and all they have lost is a little spending money. Later successes usually wash away the impressions of their earlier incidental unemployment. For others, however, their failure to find summer jobs may mean the difference between going back to school and dropping out. These disadvantaged students, plus those who need part-time work during the school years, are helped by special federal programs that provide more than a million jobs a year.

By far the largest of these programs is that of the NYC, which each year finances summer work for more than 600,000 young people who are unemployed and poor. NYC projects try to steer these young people into useful jobs such as helping in hospitals, supervising younger children, cleaning vacant lots, and other work that is good for the community.

During the school year, an NYC in-school program provides part-time work, with on-the-job training, for dropout-prone students who need money to stay in school in the ninth through twelfth grades.

Naturally, large-scale activities such as those of the NYC, aimed at providing temporary paid work and training for young unskilled workers, are likely to have both faults and virtues. There is inevitably a good deal of waste, along with much useless work and a little outright fraud. When millions of dollars are dribbled out to hundreds of thousands of people, idealistic theory sometimes conflicts with the realities of local politics and human frailties. Such weaknesses, however, are more than offset by benefits. At the least, the NYC has given millions of youngsters a little earned income. They have been encouraged to stay in school. Some of them also have developed skills and learned something about the world of work.

In an inspirational comic book used by the NYC for recruiting, Pogo tells prospective enrollees that they will get "scratch, cash . . . bread . . . a job." He also tells them, "The government wants you to be a drop-in" at the NYC, and he confidently predicts, "You'll walk into a brighter future . . . where the chance to work will be bigger and better—the pay and your heart will be higher. Because then you'll be able to help others—just as the Neighborhood Youth Corps helps you now."

ON BEHALF OF OLDER WORKERS

Operation Mainstream does for older people in small towns and rural areas what the Neighborhood Youth Corps does for youth. In America, where it is sometimes considered almost a crime to be old, Mainstream pays needy senior citizens to improve the communities in which they live.

One of the first Mainstream projects was Green Thumb, a nonprofit organization for low-income retired farmers. Several hundred workers, mostly more than sixty-five years old, built and rehabilitated hundreds of parks and recreation areas and planted millions of trees. Green Thumb has been called the "most beautiful antipoverty program." Another Mainstream project, in the mining area of Trinidad, Colorado, retrained elderly coal miners, enabling them to build a city garage and a day-care center, as well as to refurbish or improve scores of public buildings in Trinidad.

A profile of Mainstream workers shows that almost half had fewer than eight years of school and another third had between nine and eleven years of school. Most of them had annual incomes below $2,000; many were on welfare and had been unemployed for more than a year. A large proportion were over forty-five years old, and many of them were much older.

Despite the fact that many Mainstream projects are located in areas of high unemployment and little industry, some of the Mainstream jobs led to permanent employment. Since its inception in 1967, Operation Mainstream has given a new purpose in life to thousands of older people who once faced bleak futures. As one senior citizen in Arkansas working on a Green Thumb project put it, "We create something for the coming generations to enjoy and remember us by. This program has changed our outlook on life."

Another program for older workers is the Community Senior Service Program, conducted in ten cities, which hires workers fifty-five years old and older for part-time paid jobs such as serving as teachers' aides, helping the elderly poor, and providing other community services. After a White House Conference on the Aging in 1971, the Department of Labor announced an expansion of its efforts to provide work opportunities for older people.

In the perspective of the total number of those who are old and needy, even the expanded programs for older workers will help relatively few people. Moreover, it is a hard fact that training a young person with a life ahead is a better economic investment of limited funds than training an oldtimer whose future is limited. Nevertheless, humanitarian motives impel society to make at least a moderate effort to mitigate the economic rigors endured by the aged, not only by providing means of economic relief such as Social Security benefits but also by providing assistance in finding suitable employment.

On Behalf of Veterans

Department of Labor activities for veterans are wide-ranging. They cut across many programs and projects. "This is an effort which I consider to be of the highest priority in Federal manpower and training programs," President Nixon wrote to Secretary James D. Hodgson in 1971. "Every available program should be used to the maximum."

The task presents a dilemma. On the one hand, a veterans' program is easier to conduct effectively than programs directed toward people who are difficult to employ. For the most part, veterans make good workers, and their difficulties are generally temporary. With a little help, most veterans can be trained and can find jobs.

On the other hand, the familiar scene of ex-GI's returning home and being greeted by crowds of well-wishers is rare today. The Vietnam conflict was not a popular war, and many Americans do not regard the veterans of that war as heroes. Furthermore, as a result of one of that war's unique problems, the veteran may come home to face an employer who is skeptical about his involvement with drugs, though less than 5 per cent of the personnel of the armed forces have had contact with hard drugs. Many employers also do not want to be bothered with veterans who have had little or no civilian work experience. And adding to the other difficulties is the fact that veterans are returning home at a time when jobs are scarce.

About 6 million Vietnam-era veterans have been separated from the armed forces. Many of them cannot find jobs. But, by the end of 1972, the tremendous government effort to train and find jobs for veterans resulted in a lower unemployment rate for veterans than for nonveterans.

President Nixon in 1972 recalled America's moral debt to the men who had fought for their country. "The nation may be weary of war," he said in his State of the Union message to Congress, "but we dare not grow weary of doing right by those who have borne its heaviest burdens." He called on private enterprise, through the National Alliance of Businessmen (NAB), and on the Department of Labor, to place unemployed Vietnam-era veterans in jobs or training.

Under the President's six-point Jobs for Veterans program,

in June, 1971, the NAB pledged to find 100,000 jobs in industry. The Department of Defense expanded Project Transition, which provides basic education and skill training to servicemen during their last six months in service to prepare them for civilian jobs. Veterans were encouraged to go to school under the GI Bill or to enroll in an appropriate manpower program. Federal agencies and government contractors were required to list all job openings with the U.S. Employment Service—which provided special help to veterans. All ex-servicemen who had drawn unemployment insurance for thirteen weeks received special help. When the Public Employment Program described below was established, veterans received preference; of the first four thousand people hired for city, county, and state jobs under this program, 41 per cent were Vietnam veterans. These efforts, in which the Department of Labor was a major participant, placed many Vietnam veterans in training or jobs, bringing the difference between veterans' and nonveterans' unemployment rates down to only seven-tenths of one per cent.

Here are some examples of how these programs work:

- Joe is a twenty-three-year-old ex-paratrooper. He has used drugs but was never an addict. He earned only $800 during his first year at home, but the NAB found a job for him as an offset-press operator in a blueprint firm, where he is doing well.
- Jefferson was blinded in Vietnam and discharged. He received some training with the Florida Blind Services and went to work for a telephone company, repairing telephones. Seeing him work, you would never believe he is blind.
- Lou, a young black, is the product of a broken home. To escape the street life, he joined the army, got into trouble, and was given a dishonorable discharge. The NAB placed him in a hospital as a laboratory assistant, where he works part time and goes to school part time.

Government programs help returning veterans through education, work training, and financial and medical assistance. Since 1969, payments under the GI Bill for education, disability compensation, and pension benefits have all been increased. Drug treatment programs are available. And, through manpower assistance, on-the-job-training, counseling, and apprenticeship programs, most veterans are able to find jobs with a bright future in the country for which they fought.

On Behalf of the Hard-Core Unemployed

As stated previously, several special programs are concerned with finding jobs for the hard-core unemployed. The resources of these programs are combined in the Concentrated Employment Program (CEP), which strives to place the hard-core unemployed, who reside in the worst slums, in decent jobs that pay a living wage. Before the CEP was instituted, federal manpower efforts usually operated independently. By contrast, the CEP coordinates (as do also the program for veterans described above and the Work Incentive Program for welfare clients described later) a variety of manpower activities aimed at providing a broad range of services to potential workers.

In March, 1967, President Lyndon Johnson, in his "Message on America's Unfinished Business: Urban and Rural Poverty," emphasized that neither general prosperity nor regular manpower programs reached the hard-core unemployed. He directed the Secretary of Labor and other officials to zero in with special help for those with the severest job problems in areas of high unemployment.

The CEP was established to carry out this directive. It developed no new programs but became an "umbrella delivery system" under which a single sponsor coordinated the efforts of other programs to provide effective help for the unemployed and underemployed in selected urban and rural slums. Usually the sponsor was a federally funded Community Action Agency, made up of local citizens, some of them beneficiaries of the various community improvement and self-help programs. The CEP arranged, through appropriate agencies, to provide these clients with counseling, training, work experience, job-placement services, and such social services as medical attention, child care, and legal aid.

The CEP areas were selected because of the amount of unemployment and poverty prevalent in them; the existence there of established manpower programs such as the MDTA programs, JOBS, and Public Careers; and the "climate" of the community—how it might affect the implementation of such a cooperative effort. The first local CEP unit was established in Cleveland in 1967. The number of units grew to sixty-nine in urban slums and thirteen in poor rural areas.

Individual examples of the results of CEP programs, though they run the danger of being atypical, are in some ways more revealing than statistics. Wallace B. dropped out of school in the tenth grade. In the previous four years, he had worked only seventeen months—at rotten jobs. He suffered from bad eyes and bad feet and lived on welfare with his foster mother. He came to the program with a belligerent attitude and refused the first job offered to him after the completion of a period of training, because he did not like the minimal wage that the job paid. His CEP coach found him more satisfactory work that promised regular pay increases. He was promoted, joined a union, and made plans to go to night school to learn machine operations.

The CEP is fighting an uphill battle to reshape the lives of potential workers who are difficult clients. A large proportion are very poor, and some are so discouraged about their prospects that they have given up looking for work. A few are hostile and suspicious. About 80 per cent of those who have been enrolled by the CEP are black or come from Spanish-speaking backgrounds. Although the dropout rate is high, a reasonable number fight their way out of poverty and qualify for decent jobs. The progress made by the CEP can be summarized: "We're walking, not running, but we're getting there."

THE PUBLIC EMPLOYMENT PROGRAM

Many manpower programs, as has been noted, focus on the needs of special groups—the young, the old, veterans, and the hard-core unemployed. One program, by contrast, concentrates on placing unemployed people of any category in a special kind of employment, namely, public employment, and paying their wages. This endeavor is carried out by the Public Employment Program (PEP), which tackles the problem of bringing together people looking for work with states and local communities that need services for which they cannot afford to pay. Although the problem is complicated, the logic is simple: Why not put the unemployed to work providing services to satisfy unmet public needs? Through PEP, the federal government gives money to state and local governments to enable them to hire the unemployed for public service jobs until these people find regular employment.

PEP provides a way of combating two tragedies of economic depression. The first results from the fact that, while the goal of federal manpower programs is to prepare people for jobs, the availability of jobs depends on a prosperous economy. During a recession, potentially valuable training or work experience may be followed by the shock of unemployment, which dashes the hopes of men and women fighting their way out of poverty. Second, though public service has been the source of as many as one out of every three new jobs during the 1960's, when times are bad communities receive insufficient revenue to meet the demand for public services. PEP can come to the rescue by helping the communities pay for job-producing projects in such areas as public works, transportation, education, law enforcement, fire protection, health services and hospital work, park maintenance, and recreation.

On July 12, 1971, President Nixon signed the Emergency Employment Act, providing a total of $2.25 billion to create nearly a quarter of a million public service jobs in state and local governments over a period of two years. As a counter-cyclical measure, PEP has pumped money into the economy during economic recessions. The President assigned to the Department of Labor a vast new array of responsibilities and charged it with putting jobless people to work as fast as possible. From a standing start in August, 1971, about $1 billion was allocated in six months to 650 "program agents," including states, counties, cities, and Indian intertribal councils.

Although PEP is a large program, it has not been able to help all of the unemployed. It has aimed at target groups. Among those who have received special attention are young people entering the labor force, older workers, veterans, graduates of manpower-training programs, those below the poverty level, welfare recipients, migrant farm workers, and workers hurt by defense cutbacks, technological change, or shifts in patterns of federal spending.

One of the most complex issues is that of "transitional" employment, that is, temporary work that is likely to lead to permanent work. To a greater degree than other manpower programs, PEP, instead of preparing participants for already existing permanent jobs, places people in temporary work that has been "created." President Nixon vetoed the first public employment bill because he disapproved of marginally useful, temporary make-work jobs and preferred real jobs that would be generated by the needs of the economy and would be permanent. When he accepted a revised bill, he stressed the point that the work created must be a bridge to permanent productive jobs and not a substitute for them. It is an understatement to say that the creation of hundreds of thousands of transitional jobs—which are meaningful, contribute to career advancement, and lead to good permanent jobs—is no easy task. The difficulties notwithstanding, hundreds of thousands of men and women have been placed by PEP in worthwhile jobs with relative speed.

It is still too early to evaluate PEP realistically. Studies are being made to yield information on the impact of the program. But here are some examples of what the program means to some individuals:

- A black World War II veteran with four dependents was thrown out of work when his employer moved from Chicago. PEP financed his employment as an assistant code-enforcement inspector in Chicago; he was one of fifty-six people hired to enforce local building codes.
- A bilingual high school graduate who could not find a job was employed to assist a public health nurse in making house calls among Mexican-American families.
- A Montana welfare mother of two with a disabled husband was hired to provide rural residents with information about government services.

In the intricate interplay of economic forces, it is difficult to predict future needs. Perhaps a growing economy will create sufficient jobs so that there will be no need for public employment programs. Because of reduced unemployment, by early 1973, the Administration had not requested extension of the Emergency Employment Act. But enough money remained from the 1973 appropriation to continue financing the program at about a $500 million level for 1974. Some additional money may also come from manpower funds to be distributed by the federal government to state and local governments.

But, if unemployment again becomes a stubborn problem, programs like PEP, whether operated directly by the federal government or through revenue-sharing programs, can subsidize transitional public service jobs. Such jobs can improve the skills of the labor force, are good for the localities, and help people to help themselves during periods of general unemployment.

WORK AND WELFARE

One of the curiosities of the English language is that "welfare" has become a dirty word. The Preamble of the Constitution of the United States enshrines the promotion of the "general welfare" as one of the goals of a "more perfect union." But in time, the word became associated with helping the poor. Then, as relief rolls grew, the word was downgraded so that today a kind of stigma is attached to this formerly noble noun.

In the 1960's, welfare rolls not only tripled but, for the first time in history, increased in times of prosperity as well as in times of high unemployment. In the early 1970's, the number of welfare clients again soared to reach about 15 million people. President Nixon called the welfare system a monumental failure that infuriated taxpayers and embittered people on relief. He proposed a system of welfare reform based on the dignity of work.

The idea that the able-bodied poor should work in return for government support goes back four hundred years to the "Poor Laws" of Queen Elizabeth of England. Beginning with the New Deal in the 1930's, the U.S. Government has attempted to reduce relief rolls by substituting, where possible, paid work for welfare. In the 1960's, Congress passed laws that provided special training and job assistance for relief recipients. Then, in 1967, a Senate-financed study concluded that stronger measures than existing work-training programs were needed to move able-bodied relief clients from welfare rolls to jobs.

The Work Incentive Program

The Social Security Amendments Act of 1967 planted the seeds of a system based on rehabilitation of welfare recipients who are potential workers rather than on their long-term maintenance on welfare. The landmark Work Incentive Program (WIN) concentrated on people supported by Aid to Families with Dependent Children (AFDC). Under this program, social workers referred welfare clients who were adults or out-of-school youth for work or training. Those who were too old, too sick, or had other disabilities were exempt. Mothers with children could volunteer for the program if child care could be arranged.

Although the compulsory features were mild, some opponents considered the program a form of slavery. They took the acronym for *W*ork *I*ncentive *P*rogram, "WIP," added an "H" to make it read "WHIP," and circulated a caricature of the program showing a black woman scrubbing a floor on her knees while a whip was held over her head. Government officials preferred to use "WIN" rather than "WIP."

In actuality, sanctions were seldom used. WIN clients were trained for "jobs with a future" not for domestic work or other jobs with a poor image. WIN took the view that many Americans wanted to work but, because of lack of skill, medical or social difficulties, or poor environment, could not earn enough to support a family. Their only practical choice was welfare. They needed a change of direction to bring them into the mainstream of American life. To bring about such a change, WIN combined a variety of social services, child care, training, and work-experience programs to prepare potentially employable persons to find and hold decent jobs.

A Department of Labor booklet, *Win for a Change,* describes how a loser can become a winner. As an example, it follows Mrs. Mary T. through a WIN program. Mrs. T.'s background and needs are similar to those of many other participants.

Mrs. T. felt trapped. She had once worked briefly as a part-time waitress but knew she could not get a job that would pay enough to support her three children. She volunteered for WIN. Her social worker found a day-care center for her preschool child, and a church in the neighborhood provided an after-school program foı her school-age children. She passed a medical examination at the welfare agency and was assigned to a WIN team. During a two-week orientation, she learned how to dress for work, how to talk to employers, and about different kinds of jobs. She decided she wanted to be an office worker. Her counselor suggested she aim high and become a medical secretary.

Mrs. T. and her counselor worked out a plan for reaching her goal. Because she had dropped out of school in the tenth grade, she first prepared for a High School Equivalency Diploma. "My mommy's going to school too," Mrs. T.'s fourth-grade child told her classmates. The work-training specialist then helped her enroll at a business school, where she learned typing, shorthand, office practice, and special subjects, such as medical terminology. When she graduated, her WIN team reviewed her record. Because she had been a good student, a job developer arranged an interview for her with a doctor, who hired her. As a medical secretary, Mrs. T. soon earned twice her welfare payment.

Mrs. T.'s training was long and costly, but it was a good investment. She continued to receive welfare payments, including an extra $30 a month, while training, as well as transportation, lunch, and other out-of-pocket costs. The government paid for day care, tuition, and social services. In return, the taxpayers saved the dollar value of subsequent welfare benefits, which might have lasted a lifetime. More important in a society that concerns itself with human values as well as cost, Mrs. T. gained self-respect and was proud to become a self-supporting American.

Unfortunately, though there are other success stories, most enrollees drop out before being placed in a job. Many WIN participants quit because of health problems or pregnancy. Fragile child-care arrangements often break down. Some participants simply disappear for no apparent reason. Only 20 to 25 per cent of those enrolled stay with WIN to the point of being placed and holding a job for at least ninety days. Moreover, while some of the jobs in which WIN enrollees are placed have a promising future, the over-all record shows how hard it is to locate satisfactory work for severely disadvantaged people.

In spite of these difficulties, WIN has genuine potential. A WIN demonstration project was taking place in 1972 in each of five sites in five states. A research and evaluation staff had begun to develop a body of knowledge on how the program could become more effective. WIN may provide highly useful information that can be applied to a welfare reform program.

Welfare Reform

Compared with the millions on welfare, those who are helped by WIN are only a drop in the bucket. Despite its small size, however, WIN is important as a forerunner of the welfare reform that President Nixon made his major domestic goal.

The President made it clear that Americans want to help those who are in need but do not want to support able-bodied loafers. He told a group of state governors, "I advocate a system that will encourage people to work, and that means whatever work is available." He added that he did not think that "certain kinds of work are demeaning—scrubbing floors, emptying bedpans. My mother used to do that." He pointed out that so-called dead-end jobs are useful to society and that an able-bodied person should find any kind of work that supported a family more dignified than going on relief.

If welfare reform of the kind that the President proposed (or anything resembling it) is passed, it will be the most important social legislation since the 1930's. Its goal would be to break the cycle of poverty. It would guarantee a minimum income, and for the first time it would include subsidies for the working poor.

Welfare reform would separate those who cannot work from those who can. The bill proposed by the President assigns to the Department of Labor the Opportunities for Families

Program (OFP), which would register those on welfare who are required by the bill to work or who volunteer for work or training. These potential workers would be on "workfare" rather than welfare.

Welfare reform faces a hard political battle. It is attacked by liberals, who claim its subsidies are too stingy and its work provisions too harsh. It is assailed by conservatives, who claim it is too extravagant and its work requirements are too lax. The current welfare reform proposal was first introduced in Congress in August, 1969. President Nixon has repeatedly urged action on it in his State of the Union messages. The House of Representatives has twice passed a welfare reform bill. But it remains the subject of fierce controversy.

It is logical to predict that the welfare system will be revised and in the future will be financed in large measure by the federal government. Because of the millions of families involved and the enormous amounts of money required, the initial steps may be in the form of trial-and-error projects to test the efficacy of various procedures.

Forecasting is difficult. Congress, in rejecting all alternatives under consideration in 1972, left the situation in an unsettled state. But it seems likely that welfare reform will be based on, first, outright subsidies to those who are unable to work and, second, incentives, along with an effective work requirement, for those who are employable.

JOBS FOR ALL

What is the essence of manpower programs? Shorn of complexities, the essence is simply equal opportunity for all people who are able to work.

The American dream is of a society where everyone can get ahead through his own effort. Unlike the case in class societies in many parts of the world, most poor immigrants to the United States overcame economic hardship, and they or their children now share in the affluence of American life.

But the dream has not come true for everyone. Back in 1890, a humanitarian journalist, Jacob Riis, wrote a heart-rending book about *How the Other Half Lives.* In 1962, Michael Harrington, in another notable book, again described *The Other America,* which had shrunk in size to one-tenth of the population. Although progress in this respect, especially in recent decades, has been significant, many families living in depressed areas, many older workers, and most blacks have never had a chance to make the American dream come true for themselves.

Why cannot government manpower programs train and find jobs for the "other Americans" who are able to work, so that they too can fight their way out of poverty? The question is disarmingly simple, but the answer is unbelievably complex. The gap between dreams and deeds is tremendous.

With the exception of the relatively few manpower activities that actually create jobs, manpower programs aim to train the unemployed for jobs assumed or found to exist in the economy. Some projects, despite careful planning, prepare participants for jobs that turn out to be nonexistent. Such projects raise false hopes and seem an exercise in deception. In addition, the onset and continuance of a recession doom some manpower programs from the start. Although full employment is one of the paramount goals of economic policy, manpower programs can make only a limited contribution to the realization of that goal.

Even with full employment, obstacles to earning a living remain. Hard-core unemployment is more than lack of a job. Unlike the immigrants of the past who looked upon their poverty as temporary, some of the unemployed of today accept their unemployment as permanent. They are dispirited and alienated, and their joblessness has deep social and psychological roots. They need more than job training to enable them to get and hold decent jobs.

The difficulty is compounded by the fact that manpower programs, unlike other forms of government aid that provide food and money, require effort and self-discipline on the part of the trainee. Many who start have neither the ability nor the staying power to finish. The dropout rate is high.

Difficulties pile on top of difficulties when those who finish their training cannot get jobs for which they have prepared. And it is ironic that, if a training graduate does get a job, he may be taking it way from someone who was about to make the grade on his own. The workers most hurt by this competition are those who, without federal help, are eking out an existence just above the poverty line.

This raises the question of whether the gains from manpower programs are worth their cost. The English social philosopher Jeremy Bentham, almost 200 years ago, proposed measuring the greatest good for the greatest number by means of a calculus of pleasure and pain. Current cost-benefit analysis is more sophisticated, but there are few control groups, and sound judgments are difficult to make. One devastating evaluation of the Job Corps concluded that Corps members made about the same gains as youth of similar backgrounds who did not participate and that their progress was simply part of the process of growing up. Other evaluations show mixed results. In general, the skimpy and inconclusive evidence available tends to show that, as a result of manpower activities, more people get jobs, and those who work earn more money and are more productive, than would have been the case if there were no federal manpower programs.

The Department of Labor is seeking to enhance the beneficial results through more efficient management. As the manpower programs grew from a small beginning in 1962 to activities involving millions of people in the 1970's, massive problems of administration developed. President Nixon in his manpower message to Congress in 1971 noted that, while "efforts (in the manpower field) proceed from the best intentions, they are overcentralized, bureaucratic," and remote from the people they serve. The President objected to the "Byzantine administrative tangles" involved and cited, as one of many examples, the burden of vocational school administrators who had to cope with a 930-page Department of Labor manual and other extensive materials to meet requirements of a single MDTA program. The President repeatedly asserted that manpower programs were *not* delivering the jobs or the training that the nation had the right to expect. It is hoped by some that the proposed unification of federal policy activities in the manpower field and the decentralization of operations to states, cities, and localities (see Chapter IV) will remedy the existing weaknesses in administration.

Aristophanes, in ancient Athens, poked fun at Socrates for stumbling into puddles on the road while keeping his eyes on the clouds. The analogy can be reversed with equal force and applied against those who never see the sky because they are always looking for puddles. There are many pitfalls in the path of pioneering federal manpower programs, but there is also a broad frontier with promising potential. Those in the business of manpower need to be both realists and idealists. They need both skepticism and faith.

VII

Labor-Management Relations

Collective bargaining seems to be one of the worst ways of keeping industrial peace—except for nearly every other way. Under collective bargaining, labor and capital sometimes engage in self-destructive economic warfare. Serious strikes seem to feed inflation and otherwise hurt the public. But what are the alternatives? Communism? Dictatorship? Nationalization of industry? Free collective bargaining has flaws that might not exist under an authoritarian system. But, because of the importance of liberty in the dominant American ideology, and because of the unparalleled magnitude of the output of American industry, the American collective bargaining process, in spite of its shortcomings, is the envy of civilized nations throughout the world.

When the Department of Labor was established, one of its most important missions was to promote industrial peace. This responsibility made the position of Secretary of Labor the least enviable in the Cabinet. Often, when a third party intervenes in a strike, neither side is satisfied. Both accept what, at best, is the least objectionable solution to avoid a greater catastrophe, and they tend to blame the peacemaker for the frustration of their real desires.

Although the first Secretary of Labor, in 1913, and nearly

every Secretary after him, proclaimed the doctrine of fairness, one side or the other often accuses the Department of being prejudiced. Usually, management charges the Department with being prounion. For example, Secretary of Labor Arthur Goldberg, through words and deeds, showed that he had been "brainwashed" of his earlier labor union ties; yet business accused him of being prolabor. By contrast, labor unions claimed, in spite of Secretary James D. Hodgson's record of fair play, that the Department was being run for the benefit of business.

Such charges have seriously damaged the Department's national image. The allegation of partiality on the part of the Department was a major reason why, in the 1930's, the National Labor Relations Board was created outside the Department and why, in the 1940's, the Federal Mediation and Conciliation Service was removed from the Department and made independent. Today, many agencies share with the Department of Labor the government's responsibilities bearing on labor-management relations.

Still, the Department remains a powerful force working for industrial peace. An assistant secretary of Labor heads the Department's Labor-Management Services Administration. The Department conducts research in labor relations; administers laws dealing with welfare and pension plans, fair play for union members, and the right of veterans to re-employment; supervises key aspects of labor relations for government employees; and plays an important role in national-emergency strikes.

In theory, the government should not intervene in strikes. Labor and management have a common interest in keeping an industry going. When a business closes down, the owners lose their revenue and the workers lose their wages. Fear of losses by both sides in an impending strike brings pressure on both labor and management to settle industrial disputes. As a general policy, workers and employers should resolve their differences between themselves through free collective bargaining.

Even when management and labor cannot agree and call for the intervention of an impartial third party, the Department of Labor tries to stay aloof. For example, in a longshoremen's strike, municipal and state labor agencies, officials of port cities, *ad hoc* boards and commissions, special committees, an array of mediators, emergency agencies of all types, and the Federal Mediation and Conciliation Service will probably all have a hand in fact-finding, development of creative recommendations, and almost every other imaginable means of trying to adjust differences. Only after other peacemaking efforts are exhausted will the Department of Labor make a last-ditch attempt to bring the parties together before the dispute goes to the President and Congress labeled as an "emergency."

It would seem that, with such a long process involving so many alternatives, the Department of Labor would have to intervene in very few disputes. Not so. As an example of the number of times that the Department is called upon, Secretary of Labor James D. Hodgson described his activities and those of Assistant Secretary W. J. Usery, Jr., one weekend in the summer of 1971:

> The United Transportation Union . . . was using the creeping paralysis strategy against the nation's railroad system. The United Steelworkers of America prepared to shut down the nation's steel mills on Saturday night. . . . We were on the verge of asking President Nixon to refer the whole discouraging mess to Congress. The President . . . asked us to make another try. . . .
>
> Assistant Secretary Usery took fresh soundings. Negotiators were grouped in four separate rooms and Bill moved from room to room. . . . By midnight some of the negotiators were so fatigued and discouraged they wanted to go home, which meant leaving town. Usery wouldn't let them.
>
> Meantime, steel negotiations were lurching to a crisis at the Shoreham Hotel. In the morning I breakfasted privately with R. Heath Larry, principal industry negotiator. . . . That after-

noon I met privately at my home with I. W. Abel, the Steel-workers' President. . . .

After talking with the President, who was flying into Washington on Air Force One at the time, I headed for the Shoreham and proposed that the parties give themselves more time—48 hours—and invited them to resume their negotiations at the White House. . . .

Usery allowed his railroad charges a breather for dinner Saturday but refused to listen to recess talk. . . . By Sunday morning a few things had fallen into place and Usery signalled a few hours bedrest, telling everybody to be back by 5:00 P.M. Sunday. . . . The steel talks were back on the tracks even if the railroads weren't. By 9:00 P.M. Sunday we knew that steel was settled. . . .

Usery redoubled his persistence . . . and eventually crashed through with an agreement on the big issue, the interdivisional run which required unnecessary crew changes on hauls over 100 miles.

Bill fell into bed about the time most people in the East were taking lunch. The telephone jangled him out of a sound sleep. It was the President. . . .

Bill managed a grin, and a "Thank you, Mr. President," and hit the sack once more.

This kind of strike participation is not a regular activity of the Department of Labor, but neither is it exceptional. Secretary of Labor Arthur Goldberg, a near genius in mediation, was constantly on the go, helping to settle disputes that ranged from a national "noninflationary" steel pact to a walkout at the Metropolitan Opera. During major disputes in the early 1960's, Secretary of Labor Willard Wirtz ruefully described his relation with emergency strikes as roughly the same as the relation of an egg to an egg beater.

Many Secretaries of Labor maintained a "hands-off" policy toward labor conflicts. Secretary Frances Perkins sought to keep the Department, and also the White House, from getting unnecessarily embroiled in labor disputes. Early in his Administration, Franklin Roosevelt good-humoredly allowed himself to be dragged into a minor labor conflict. He told the Secretary, "I must never do a thing like that again," and he teased her about his not being worth $3,600 a year, the salary that experienced conciliators were paid at that time. Secretary Perkins told him he might use his time more profitably being President. Later on, Roosevelt's participation became part of a staged dramatic climax that lubricated the acceptance of a compromise, with the Secretary prompting from backstage.

Whether a given Administration has an interventionist or a "hands-off" policy toward strikes, the fact is that most strikes are settled without government intervention. Of the almost 100,000 bargaining arrangements that expire each year, only a small number end in strikes, and, of the strikes that occur, only a minute proportion get to the Department of Labor, the President, and Congress.

Because strikes are spectacular, they make news. Yet industrial accidents cause more lost work time than strikes, and unemployment during a few years of recession results in more wasted manpower than have all the strikes that occurred in the twentieth century. Because of the drama of the moment, strike losses tend to be exaggerated. A Department of Labor study on the economic effects of national-emergency disputes shows that long-range damage is often minimal. The losses from the great steel strike of 1959 were not as great as appeared likely at the time. In serious longshore labor disputes, much of the damage is averted by rush shipments made before the strike deadline or is made up by extra activity after the strike is over.

MODERN STRIKE ISSUES

Although strike dangers may often have been magnified, it is important not to minimize them. Strikes are serious and may become more so in the future, as industrial society grows more interdependent and complex. A strike in one industry has widespread effects throughout the economy. So many prickly issues are involved in a confrontation between labor and management that one mediator humorously compared collective bargaining to two porcupines making love.

Not so long ago, disagreements that engendered strikes were limited mostly to wages and hours. Then, as the economy developed, holidays, vacations, shift premiums, and other fringe benefits became issues. Newer subjects of bargaining are income security, extended leaves or sabbaticals, and variations of welfare and pension plans. Effective bargaining requires many kinds of legal, accounting, and technical skills.

In recent years, many agreements have been hammered out with great difficulty by designated negotiators, only to be rejected in record number by rank and file union members. Today's new breed of young workers has different values and does not always agree with its leaders as to what are satisfactory settlements.

In addition to rebellion in traditional areas of union strength, strikes are spreading in places where they once were uncommon, such as agriculture and government. There is a certain novelty in the near-miraculous feat of Cesar Chavez in the early 1970's—unionizing grape orchard workers. Chavez had strong support from other unions, and his nonviolent idealism won liberal support for a boycott. Not eating grapes became a chic and easy liberalism, which provided sufficient economic pressure to win a favorable settlement for downtrodden Mexican and Filipino workers. Such labor disputes in agriculture pose unique problems for the Department of Labor because strikes at harvest time do irreparable damage if crops rot in the fields, while a policy of barring such strikes would leave farm workers at the mercy of their employers.

Strikes against the government also pose special problems. Traditionally, the thinking on this subject is that there should be no partisan labor-management conflict in government employment, because the government represents all the people. Supposedly nonstrike remedies should always bring about a fair settlement of government employees' grievances. A half a century ago, Governor Calvin Coolidge of Massachusetts virtually catapulted himself to the Presidency when he declared, during the Boston policemen's strike, "There is no right to strike against the public safety, anywhere, anytime." Even so liberal a President as Franklin Roosevelt, in the 1930's, unequivocally denied the right of federal workers to strike.

Times have changed. In recent years, there have been dramatic strikes against local governments and even against the federal government. Martin Luther King, Jr., was assassinated when he went to Memphis, Tennessee, to dramatize the plight of striking municipal garbage workers. At the request of President Lyndon Johnson, Under Secretary of Labor James Reynolds helped to settle that dispute.

In 1970, wildcat strikes broke out among postal workers. Pickets marched in front of buildings that bore Herodotus's accolade "Neither snow nor rain nor heat nor gloom of night stays these couriers from the swift completion of their appointed rounds." President Nixon declared a national emergency and authorized the use of troops to replace postal workers. Although the strikers ran the risk of dismissal, fines, and jail sentences, in the end Congress authorized higher pay for postal workers.

President John F. Kennedy pioneered with a new, sympathetic attitude toward government unions. Additional progress for these unions was made under President Richard M. Nixon. George Meany, president of the AFL-CIO, no friend of President Nixon's, admitted in his honest fashion that Nixon was "more liberal [on this issue] than any man in the White House before him, because he has come out for collective bargaining for government employees at every level." Executive Order 11491, issued in 1969, assures federal workers of the right to join or not to join a union without fear of reprisal. The Department of Labor determines appropriate bargaining units for groups of federal employees, supervises elections for bargaining representatives, and rules on complaints of unfair labor practices in the government. In 1972, there were, in addition to 600,000 fully organized postal workers, about a million federal nonpostal workers in unions.

Modern strikes of nongovernment workers sometimes involve the government's economic policy. For example, after a difficult longshoremen's strike in 1971 and 1972, when the parties finally agreed on a settlement, the government's Pay Board decided that the wage increases called for by the settlement were inflationary and trimmed them back. President Nixon at that time was in China on an unprecedented trip in the interest of world peace. He took time out, in the shadow of the Great Wall of China, to sign an emergency bill passed to prevent a renewal of the walkout.

Similar considerations affected the construction industry, where runaway costs of labor, land, materials, and interest had fueled inflationary pressures. Collective bargaining in the industry took place in an "Alice in Wonderland" situation. High demand was coupled with high unemployment. Local unions played leapfrog with wage increases, each craft seeking greater increases than the others had won. For a time, wages increased at a rate of 20 per cent a year. Secretary of Labor George Shultz called this a "formula for disaster" and helped create a Construction Industry Stabilization Committee, where management and labor cooperated with fair success in the difficult job of slowing down the rate of wage increases.

Perhaps the most difficult strikes of all are those in industries in which technological change makes some jobs obsolete. This is one of the reasons for the extraordinary stubbornness of both sides in railroad disputes. What to a railroad company is "featherbedding" is to union workers "job protection." As it is, the number of workers in railroad transportation has shrunk from more than 2 million in 1920 to fewer than 600,000 in the early 1970's.

Few people understood better than former Secretary of Labor Wirtz the cruel effect of technology on individual workers. From the standpoint of management's problem, however, even he, when he became a trustee of the bankrupt Pennsylvania Railroad, could not avoid reporting that costly work rules were at the root of the railroad's financial difficulties. Faced with rising costs, railroad management fights for greater productivity. But unions do not want to bargain over what is, for them, self-destruction. In railway labor disputes, the bargaining over wages is not easy, but the really tough battles develop over issues such as frequency of changing train crews, minimum size of train crews, maximum size of trains, use of walkie-talkies, the type of work that members of each union are allowed to do, and similar practices that to one side mean efficiency and to the other economic suicide.

One of the greatest conflicts caused by technology's effects on railway labor has been the third-of-a-century battle for continuing the jobs of firemen, who originally tended coal-burning engines. When oil-burning diesel engines came into use, firemen's duties were greatly reduced. President Kennedy ordered arbitration of a dispute over this issue and asked Congress to prevent a threatening railroad strike. Nearly a decade later, President Nixon called an emergency board into being to deal with renewed strife over this issue. The board recommended keeping on the job the remaining 17,500 firemen, hiring no new firemen, and combining the duties of firemen and brakemen on diesel engines. Finally, in 1972, the United Transportation Union and railroad management agreed that firemen on freight trains would remain until all present firemen are promoted to engineers, resign, die, or retire, with compulsory retirement age set at sixty-five.

THE PUBLIC INTEREST

The federal government faces the problem of when to intervene and when not to intervene in strikes. Setting the general policy is easy; making specific decisions is difficult. In general, the government intervenes to protect the public interest. As far back as 1921, Secretary of Labor James Davis explained that, in a labor dispute, "employer and employee both have one great boss—the people."

What is the public interest? The question is debatable. At least in part, the public interest is made up of a combination of private interests that sometimes conflict. In a democratic society, individual freedom, the right to strike, and free collective bargaining are as much a part of the public interest as is the right of the people to an uninterrupted flow of goods and services.

Before intervening in a strike, the government must weigh the costs and benefits to several interest groups. Care should be taken to distinguish between transient inconvenience and permanent damage, between a public nuisance and a public menace. In the last analysis, the President, the Secretary of Labor (as his representative), and Congress bear the burden of deciding—often on an *ad hoc* basis—which labor disputes truly threaten the public interest.

In 1902, when a coal strike imperiled the health of millions of people, President Theodore Roosevelt put pressure on the coal companies to submit the dispute to arbitration. In two world wars, the government created national war labor boards to prevent strikes from disrupting war production. The Railway Labor Act of 1926, covering one industry, and the Taft-Hartley Act of 1947 covering industry in general, established procedures to deal with national-emergency strikes.

Ironically, some laws intended to prevent strikes have had just the opposite effect. One side or the other, in labor contract bargaining, often does not bargain until it has exploited the prearranged procedures for its own strategic advantage. The experience of the War Labor Board in World War II showed that contestants did not bargain in good faith if they were assured of arbitration. In the coal mine dispute of 1950, mine operators dawdled for nine months in the expectation that, if an impasse developed, President Harry S. Truman would prohibit a strike during the eighty-day "cooling off period" provided by the Taft-Hartley Act. Union president John L. Lewis outguessed the mine owners and created a situation in which the President asked Congress for authority to seize the mines. Two days later, miners and mine owners reached an agreement.

In recent years, threatened transportation strikes have most seriously affected the public interest. Too often, the expectation of government action became an inducement not to settle. Both sides used the procedures set forth in the Railway Labor Act in a way designed to force Congress to act as the arbitrator.

The crucial question now in public service disputes is "Why bargain?" At one time, both labor and management feared a settlement imposed by Congress. Now, based on experience, they know that Congress sometimes provides wage increases for workers and loans, subsidies, or rate increases for management. Both sides may gain. And, if the settlement turns sour, the negotiators can blame the government.

For more than a decade, the Department of Labor has considered, and at times advocated, legislation that provides a wide choice of antistrike weapons. Secretary of Labor Goldberg, experienced as both a partisan bargainer and an impartial mediator, was one of those who argued that antagonists should not be able to base their strike strategy on fixed government procedures. Flexibility, he and others have felt, is needed particularly in transportation disputes, where Presidents have again and again been impelled to ask Congress to stop nationwide walkouts.

The Nixon Administration, shortly after it came into office, favored bringing the transportation industry under the Taft-Hartley Act, which in recent years has had a little better success than the Railway Labor Act. One bill introduced in Congress to increase the President's options under the Act included an innovative proposal, suggesting "final offer selection" under which each side would submit a "final offer" and a board had to accept one proposal or another in its entirety. In normal arbitration procedures, both parties tend to make excessive demands in the expectation that the arbitrator will seek the middle ground. However, under the new proposal, parties might be motivated to make reasonable offers, because the board would be likely to reject extreme positions. But unions and management alike opposed this procedure and the Administration withdrew its support from the idea before the 1972 Presidential election.

In general, when public service strikes flare up dangerously, everyone thinks that something should be done right away. When the danger is over, however, the urgency of the call for action fades away. So far, repeated efforts by the Department of Labor to persuade Congress to establish permanent procedures for dealing with public service strikes have been in vain, despite the dramatic warning of one senator that inaction on this problem leaves the nation "hanging on the edge of a precipice," waiting for the next crisis.

SPECIAL LEGISLATION ADMINISTERED BY THE DEPARTMENT

Included among the responsibilities of the Department of Labor bearing on labor relations is the task of administering one law passed in 1959 and another passed in 1958 and amended in 1962.

Labor-Management Reporting and Disclosure Act

In 1957, a Senate committee, with John McClellan as chairman and Robert Kennedy as chief counsel, revealed misdeeds and abuse of power in several labor unions. Although most unions were free from corruption, there had been enough cases of racketeering and violations of members' rights to induce Congress in 1959 to pass the Labor-Management Reporting and Disclosure Act (LMRDA), designed to eliminate improper activities not only by unions but also by business firms in management-labor relations.

The Act provided a "bill of rights" for union members, required the filing of reports on organization practices and financial dealings, and established safeguards for democracy in union elections. Approximately fifty thousand labor organizations now report to the Department of Labor each year, pursuant to this legislation, disclosing basic information about their operations.

The Department administers the LMRDA under the premise that the vast majority of those affected by the law want to comply. The Department publishes pamphlets, prepares kits, and holds workshops. Its officials make personal visits to help management, as well as union members and leaders, to understand their rights and responsibilities under the law. The overwhelming majority of violations of the law that come to light are settled by voluntary acceptance on the part of offending companies or unions of arrangements for future compliance.

However, the courts are used when necessary. An example of judicial defense of a union member's rights is the case of *Robins* v. *Schonfeld,* involving a union member who was blacklisted for protesting certain union procedures. A federal district court awarded the member not only pension credits and damages for lost income but attorney's fees as well. Other victories in the Department's war on labor-related crime were the jailing of a union official for embezzling $16,700 from a potters' union and the indictment of union officials and a labor consultant in Newark, New Jersey, charged with extortion involving a payoff by an employer of $10,000.

A major aspect of the LMRDA is the safeguarding of honest union elections. Most cases that arise in this area are closed because of either lack of evidence or voluntary compliance. In a few instances, the Secretary of Labor intervenes. In an important election in 1965 in the International Union of Electrical, Radio, and Machine Workers, long-time president James B. Carey allegedly defeated his challenger Paul Jennings by a vote of 67,897 to 65,704. Jennings charged the election was rigged. The Department of Labor supervised a recount, with observers from both sides, and announced that

Jennings had won by 20,000 instead of losing by 2,000. Carey turned over the presidency to Jennings. Another election case, involving the National Maritime Union, went farther than a recount. The court ordered a new election on the basis of the Department of Labor's complaint. In the rerun, Joseph Curran, the union's founder and sole president for thirty-two years, again swamped his opposition.

Undoubtedly, the most spectacular case of all was Joseph ("Jock") Yablonski's challenge of W. A. ("Tony") Boyle for the presidency of the United Mine Workers (UMW). Yablonski complained of rigging, intimidation, partisan use of union funds, and many other violations. On December 9, 1969, Boyle defeated Yablonski by a wide margin. Yablonski vowed he would work to have the election set aside.

In the early morning of December 31, 1969, three hired assassins murdered Yablonski, his wife, and his daughter in their beds in their Clarksville, Pennsylvania, farmhouse. One killer who helped the prosecution was sentenced to life imprisonment; the other two were sentenced to death.

Boyle and other UMW officials were indicted in this case but denied complicity. Boyle charged that he and his union had been made victims of scandalous false charges. Secretary of Labor Shultz advised a Senate subcommittee that the Department had no evidence linking Yablonski's murder to the election. But the subsequent conviction of a UMW official for murder indicates a possible link between union management and the Yablonski killings.

In a painstaking investigation of the conduct of the election, the Department had gathered information on widespread violations of the LMRDA and asked that Boyle's re-election be set aside. A federal court ordered a new election under supervision by the Department. Thereafter, the Department monitored the UMW so closely that, were it not for the unusual provocation, the principle of freedom of labor unions might be at issue. Meanwhile, after a trial, Boyle was sentenced to five years in prison for using union funds improperly for political purposes. Three years after murder had made a martyr of Yablonski, Arnold Miller, running on a "Miners for Democracy" slate, decisively defeated Boyle for the UMW presidency.

The LMRDA is a hard law to administer. Organized labor originally opposed it bitterly as a massive intrusion by government into internal union affairs. A recitation of cases that were investigated under the law may make it seem that unions are filled with criminals, but the truth is that, considering that it has nearly 20 million members, the American labor movement compares favorably with most other institutions.

Enforcers win few friends. On one hand, some people, such as Senator Robert Griffin of Michigan, who was one of the sponsors of the law, claim that all Secretaries of Labor since the enactment of the law have been timid in carrying out their responsibility under it; on the other hand, the Department has won at least the grudging cooperation of unions in living with a law they dislike.

Welfare and Pension Plans Disclosure Act

Employee welfare and pension plans in American industry originated in the nineteenth century but were relatively unimportant for many years. They started to grow rapidly during World War II, when such plans provided indirect pay boosts used to circumvent wage controls. The Inland Steel court case in 1949 gave further impetus by making welfare and pension plans legitimate subjects for collective bargaining. Furthermore, corporate contributions to such funds are tax-deductible, the plans can have a perpetual life, and the pension funds pay no taxes on the money they earn.

Under such a convergence of favorable circumstances, welfare and pension funds mushroomed. By the early 1970's, there were nearly 200,000 active private plans. About one-fourth of the plans covered retirement payments to more than 20 million workers. Other plans provide for health, hospital, death, unemployment, or other benefits for about 50 million people. Including families and other beneficiaries, welfare and pension plans affect more than half the population of the United States. They take in and spend billions of dollars each year. Their more than $125 billion in assets is the fastest-growing pool of private capital in the United States.

Such vast amounts of money tempt racketeers and wrongdoers. Welfare and pension plans, though fewer than today, were already numerous and rich in 1958, when the Welfare and Pension Plans Disclosure Act (WPPDA) was passed. The law had grown out of investigations of thievery and corruption in this field. A Senate subcommittee reported in 1956 that, though most plans were honestly administered, some grave abuses, both by business and by labor, needed to be corrected by legislation.

The WPPDA, as enacted in 1958 and slightly strengthened in 1962, depends primarily on reporting and disclosure to prevent dishonesty in, and to improve the management of, welfare and pension plans. Under the law, the administrators of each private plan of this kind are required to file a complete description of the plan, and annual financial reports on its operations, with the Secretary of Labor. They also must provide information to the participants in the plan, who bear most of the burden of policing against wrongdoing.

The Secretary of Labor is given the authority to investigate, if he has reason to believe the law has been violated. Most often, he tries to win voluntary compliance. In a few instances, he forwards to the Department of Justice information that may warrant criminal prosecution. Whenever specific examples of crooked dealings in this field are cited, they leave an impression of widespread misconduct, which is simply not a true picture. But there are some horrible cases. In one instance, trustees of a welfare fund were among those convicted for murdering two union officers who were aware of embezzlements of $120,000 from the fund. In another incident, people were charged with taking "kickbacks" for arranging loans from the $25 million barbers' pension fund.

Operation of employees' welfare and pension plans has given rise to a new problem more intangible and elusive, and also more significant, than dishonesty and mismanagement. This new problem concerns fulfillment of the expectations of participants in welfare and pension plans.

Rising expectations put pressure on plans for greater benefits. Beneficiaries demand better health and welfare services. On retiring, they want a level of living close to what they had before retirement. People retire earlier and live longer than formerly. Welfare and pension plans must strain to meet the costs.

Some plans have gone bankrupt, and others are unable to pay for all the benefits expected. In many cases, an employee who has worked for years on a job is disappointed to find, when he leaves, that he has lost the valuable credits he had built up for the pleasant and secure retirement about which he dreamed. Millions of people face such future disappointment.

The private welfare and pension system is a largely neglected giant, except for surveillance for possible corruption. The major obstacle to fulfillment of its potential is the high cost of meeting the anticipations of beneficiaries. But it is a challenging field that already has brought, and bids fair to continue to bring, enormous benefits to American working people.

VIII

Occupational Safety and Health

Among the great emerging responsibilities of the Department of Labor are safety and health at the place of work. Working people have always been concerned about jobs, training, and decent wages. But, as their standard of living has improved, American workers have become more concerned, especially since the growth of concern about the environment, with the safety and quality of the job environment. Every year more Americans are killed on the job than died in action during the peak year of the Vietnam war (1968), when 12,629 were killed. Many more man-days are lost because of accidents at work and occupational disease than are lost because of strikes. To remedy this situation, the landmark Williams-Steiger Occupational Safety and Health Act was passed in 1970, creating an Occupational Safety and Health Administration in the Department of Labor.

ORIGIN OF GOVERNMENT CONCERN

The role of the Department in making the work environment safer and healthier started small, and it started late. The Industrial Revolution was well under way before the federal government did anything about hazardous working conditions. State labor departments acted first. They collected accident data, did some research, and started inspecting factories. Before 1913, the federal government merely conducted a little research and published some reports on what the states' labor departments were doing.

When the Department of Labor was created in 1913, it adopted a policy of encouraging voluntary steps toward job safety and health. It wanted to encourage, but not compel, betterment of the work environment. The early work of the Department was mainly collecting and reporting accident statistics—the idea being that, once employers were made aware of bad conditions, they would take it upon themselves to improve them. The Department made a thorough study of accidents in the iron and steel industry, but otherwise its accident statistics were incomplete. Often the state departments, on which the Department depended for much of its data, collected very poor statistics.

In 1926, the Department took unusual direct action to solve a problem. In 1925, the Bureau of Labor Statistics published a study of phosphorus necrosis in the fireworks and phosphorus industries. This painful and disfiguring disease, also known as "phossy jaw," was widespread among workers in these industries. It attacked the mouth and in the worst cases completely destroyed the jawbone. The Department contacted all manufacturers using white phosphorus, the cause of "phossy jaw," and persuaded them to sign a voluntary agreement to stop using it.

The Department also began to help formulate safety codes, working with the management-oriented standards-setting organizations. It did research on special topics in industrial health and attempted to be an information clearing-house for inquiries on specific problems. However, from 1913 until about 1933, the Department's safety and health work was seriously hampered by a chronic lack of money.

There was a marked upswing in 1933, when Frances Perkins became Secretary of Labor. She believed that the federal

government should promote minimum safety and health standards for the work place, and she created a new bureau to do
this: the Bureau of Labor Standards, abbreviated as LSB to
distinguish it from the Bureau of Labor Statistics (BLS).

The main function of this bureau was to serve state labor
departments. It encouraged better labor laws by preparing
model drafts of legislation and holding conferences on labor
law. In 1936, it gave its first two-week training class for state
factory inspectors at Johns Hopkins University. There was a
great demand for these classes, and they soon became a major
part of the Department's safety program. In 1938, the LSB
published a manual on factory inspection to help states improve their inspection systems. The Bureau gathered data on
health hazards, suggested ways of preventing occupational disease, and participated in research on industrial hygiene. In
1940, it published a major study on the rayon industry, written by Alice Hamilton, a pioneer in industrial hygiene. This
study showed that exposure of workers to carbon disulphide
caused illness and sometimes even led to insanity.

The Gauley Bridge disaster in West Virginia in the early
1930's dramatized another occupational disease: silicosis. This
disease results in scarring of the lung tissues due to excessive
inhalation of dust containing free silica. Victims suffer from
shortness of breath, wheezing, and reduced capacity for work.
At Gauley Bridge silicosis reached epidemic proportions when
a tunnel for a hydroelectric power plant was being dug
through rock with a high silica content. The dust in the tunnel
was so thick at times that it was hard to see more than ten
feet ahead. Workers dropped like flies from the deadly dust.
Ultimately, some 476 men died from silicosis at Gauley
Bridge and another 1,500 were disabled. Appalled by this
disaster, Secretary Perkins called a National Conference on
Silicosis in 1936 to stimulate research and action to eliminate
this disease.

In that same year, the Department was given responsibility
over a much broader area of the job environment when the

Walsh-Healey Public Contracts Act was passed. Designed to prevent sweatshop conditions resulting from excessive competition for government supply contracts, the Act contained a clause requiring that government contract work be done under safe and healthful working conditions. The Department of Labor was given the authority to set and enforce standards in this area, and, in 1942, it published a "green book" of safety regulations by which contractors were expected to abide.

When World War II began, production of war supplies was stepped up tremendously. Inevitably there was a tendency to cut corners and reduce working standards. Aware of this problem, the Department made maintenance of standards its first priority during the war. Secretary Perkins wrote in the 1941 *Annual Report,* "It is generally agreed that national security depends . . . upon the health and safety . . . of our people."

The Department worked in a number of ways to conserve manpower by reducing accidents. It began War Safety Training, a program of college courses in industrial safety for factory supervisors. The LSB helped develop safety instruction in the apprentice-training programs. Even the Children's Bureau pitched in by investigating jobs hazardous to minors. The Department helped stem the rising tide of accidents, and by 1945 the accident rate was declining.

After World War II, several factors combined to generate pressure for a greater federal role in job safety and health. The experience on the job front during the war brought about a greater awareness of the need for better protection of life, limb, and health on the job. The accomplishments of the Department of Labor in World War II showed labor, management, and the general public that the federal government had a contribution to make. A special impetus was given when industrial injury rates shot upward after wartime safety programs were discontinued.

A program that grew out of the wartime experience was

the Special Industry Drives. These were concentrated accident-reduction programs administered by a given state and directed at a specific high-hazard industry for one year. Technicians from the Department did the initial research and worked out a recommended program for the state to use. Results were often dramatic. In the South Carolina woodworking industry, accidents were reduced by 34 per cent in just four months.

The Department stepped up its development and promotion of safety codes. It persuaded the standards-setting groups to use an "informational method" of presenting completed codes. Previously, the codes, which were often highly technical, were simply handed down with no explanation, leaving employers and others to try to figure them out. Under the new method, explanations of the rules and necessary background information were given out with the code itself. As more codes were adopted by the states, there was little uniformity in their quality or quantity. In 1960, the LSB began comparing state codes with national standards and with each other and publishing the results to prod lagging states to raise their standards.

There were several groups of workers for whom the Department had a special responsibility. Among them were longshoremen and harbor workers, who had extremely high injury rates and were generally beyond state jurisdictions. The Department of Labor, working with employers and unions in major ports, developed an extensive safety program, and eventually accident rates were reduced by more than 50 per cent. Another group consisted of young workers who were protected by the Fair Labor Standards Act. The Secretary of Labor was given the authority under this Act to prohibit the employment of minors under eighteen in occupations that were, in his judgment, too dangerous. The federal employee was not neglected either. The Department had the prime responsibility for making the federal work place safer and healthier.

The Department also became involved in improvement of working conditions in foreign countries. The LSB gave safety training to personnel from foreign labor departments and supplied other countries with technical information on safety and health problems. A number of LSB safety engineers and administrators were sent abroad to help set up safety programs.

Impressive as the Department's achievements were in making the work place less hazardous by the 1960's, it was using a piecemeal approach to a problem that required a comprehensive solution. The vast majority of workers were still covered only by often inadequate state programs. In the late 1960's, pressure for a federal law that would protect all workers began to mount, and the government took several actions that built up the momentum toward passage of a comprehensive federal job safety and health law.

One thrust was given by Secretary of Labor Willard Wirtz's bold use of his authority under the Walsh-Healey Act. The Secretary, reacting to horrifying projections of the incidence of lung cancer among uranium miners, threw his weight behind remedial measures. Uranium mining had become a boom industry in 1948, when the U.S. Atomic Energy Commission had begun buying uranium. An unfortunate side effect was the damage of radon and its by-products to the health of uranium miners. Recommended standards of the Public Health Service were not translated into programs that protected the miners. State laws varied and were generally inadequate. Differences of scientific opinion and problems of economic costs prevented the Federal Radiation Council from taking action.

Because the Atomic Energy Commission was the purchaser of uranium, the Department of Labor was able to invoke the Walsh-Healey Public Contracts Act. The Department issued standards that specified maximum exposure of uranium miners to radon and its by-products. Because of strong opposition from other government agencies and from mine owners, the proposal was watered down, but even the diluted standards published in 1967 were indicative of progress. The Department of Labor intervention spurred industry, the states, and other federal agencies to take action and stimulated research, changes in mining techniques, and new protective programs. The Department no longer has authority over uranium mining; new legislation places this function under the Bureau of Mines in the Department of the Interior.

Another special impetus to the passage of the Occupational Safety and Health Act grew out of the campaign for safety in one of the most hazardous of all occupations—coal mining. It took a series of major disasters in that field of work to awaken the American people to the danger. More than 120,000 coal miners have died in mine accidents in the hundred years during which partial records have been kept. In the earliest recorded mine accident in the United States, which occurred in 1839 in the Black Heath pit near Richmond, Virginia, 52 men died. The worst disaster of this kind occurred in 1908 in a mine in West Virginia, in which 362 men perished. A Bureau of Mines was created in the Department of the Interior in 1910, but it had little power to impose safety requirements. Successive tragedies brought increasingly strong safety laws until the Federal Coal Mine Health and Safety Act of 1969 was passed. That act assigned a primary role to the Bureau of Mines and a participatory role to the Department of Labor in ensuring occupational safety and health for those who go under the surface of the earth to dig coal.

President Richard Nixon termed the bill a "historic advance in industrial practices." Under the new law, the federal government for the first time became directly involved in safety and health standards for work done in the nation's 3,600 coal mines.

One of the more important goals of the law was preventing "black lung" disease, by limiting the concentration of respirable dust in mines. Because state laws do not adequately cover conditions conducive to black lung, the Secretary of Labor issues regulations on the subject. The Secretary also compares state workmen's compensation systems in coal-mining states with the standards deemed adequate. The assignment of these responsibilities to the Department of Labor rather than to the Bureau of Mines in the Department of the Interior shows recognition of the role of the former in championing safety and health in industry. Some critics of federal policy in this field have asked that additional powers be transferred to the Department of Labor, which they believe is more safety-minded than the Bureau of Mines.

Providing a safe workplace for America's coal miners is but one aspect of a greater goal—safety in the work place for all Americans. Annually, about fifteen thousand workers are killed on the job, and more than 2 million are disabled. After the passage of the Federal Coal Mine Health and Safety Act, legislators debated a job-safety bill that would cover all workers.

THE OCCUPATIONAL SAFETY AND HEALTH ACT

The goal of job safety and health is widely endorsed. The *Wall Street Journal* once commented that, like motherhood and apple pie, it is approved by all. Everyone has decried the grisly statistics on deaths and disability incurred at the work place. But unanimity evaporated over such questions as who should set and enforce safety standards and where the line should be drawn between costs and benefits.

Secretary of Labor Wirtz, in 1968, proposed a strong bill, placing authority for establishing safety codes for all industry in the hands of the Department of Labor. Industry objected, and Congress turned the bill down. President Nixon also endorsed a job-safety bill, but, instead of proposing to vest enforcement authority in the Secretary of Labor, he asked Congress to establish a new federal agency that would exercise safety and health responsibility for American industry under a five-member board.

A battle erupted between organized labor, on one side, and the Administration and business, on the other, over who should be responsible for establishing and enforcing occupational safety and health standards under the law. Business generally favored the Administration proposal of a special board appointed by the President. Unions wanted the Department of Labor to have the responsibility. George Meany, president of the AFL-CIO, said that "no bill" would be better than the Administration proposal.

Congress compromised in the historic Occupational Safety and Health Act, establishing federal supervision over working conditions, an area that had previously been mainly the responsibility of the states. The Act declared that its purpose was "to assure so far as possible every working man and woman in the Nation safe and healthful working conditions." Upon signing it on December 29, 1970, President Nixon called it "one of the most important pieces of legislation to pass in this Congress." Secretary of Labor James Hodgson stated, "From this day forward, the occupational safety and health of the American worker becomes a top priority objective for us."

As demanded by unions, primary responsibility was vested by the law in the Secretary of Labor. To assure business of fair play, an Occupational Safety and Health Review Commission, a quasi-judicial board of three members appointed by the President, was established. The Act requires the Secretary of Labor to set safety and health standards and conduct investigations to determine whether the standards are being met.

To allay fears of arbitrary action, the Act provides that, where violations are specified, the employer is allowed a reasonable period to correct the violation or contest the Secretary's findings. Violators can be fined up to $10,000, but they can carry their case to a federal court of appeals. A court order is required before safety inspectors can close down a business.

Unlike most new social legislation, this law contains few exemptions. Its coverage is broad. Under it, more than 60 million workers in approximately 5 million large and small establishments are protected. Starting big was both an advantage and a disadvantage. A plus factor is that future difficulties in expanding coverage are averted. On the minus side, so large a responsibility for a new agency creates a sort of administrative indigestion, and the inclusion of so many small business firms arouses a hurricane of opposition.

Within the Department of Labor, the law created a new position of assistant secretary to head the Occupational Safety and Health Administration (OSHA). This officer also heads the National Safety Advisory Commission, made up of eminent public, labor, and management members who help implement the new law.

After the law became effective in April, 1971, OSHA zeroed in on three key items: utilization of state safety programs, setting of uniform standards, and securing of compliance with state and federal standards. OSHA granted federal money to the states to pay 90 per cent of the costs of developing plans to set and enforce their own standards. These plans are submitted to the Secretary of Labor, who yields his jurisdiction to states that establish programs at least as effective as that of the federal government.

The first "standards package" was published in the *Federal Register* of May 31, 1971. It took up 250 pages. In general, the standards are rules for avoiding hazards that have been proved by research and experience to be harmful to safety and health. The first package contained three main sections: construction standards, maritime standards, and industry standards. Among the many thousands of published standards, a typical one requires that in any operation, such as shipping, drilling, or grinding, that creates flying particles, molten metal, or chemicals hazardous to the eyes, workers must wear suitable face shields or goggles. Business was given a ninety-day period to familiarize itself with the new standards. The heart of the Act lay in the requirement for each employer to furnish a work place "free from recognized hazards that are likely to cause death or serious physical harm to his employees."

Compliance has been one of the most controversial issues in the administration of the Occupational Safety and Health Act. On one hand, some employers feared that rigid enforcement would cripple their businesses and claimed that several proposed standards were inconvenient, costly, and irrelevant. On the other hand, criticism of an opposite kind came not so much from labor as from consumer advocates, who attacked with impartial vehemence vacillating federal bureaucrats, greedy corporations, and even some unions that, in negotiating contracts, put safety and health clauses after coffee breaks in importance.

The policy of the Labor Department is to encourage voluntary compliance with the new law to the maximum extent possible and to emphasize the "do's" rather than the "don't's." The initial effort was to inform and motivate employers and workers alike. The earliest inspections were made on a "worst first" basis in work places likely to be unsafe in industries with high injury rates.

During the first six months after the law went into effect, federal inspectors found violations in 80 per cent of the 9,300 work places inspected and found that 75 per cent of the violations were serious enough to warrant issuance of citations against employers. Fines were imposed against thousands of establishments.

"Guesstimates" of the Occupational Safety and Health Act's cost to industry run into many billions of dollars. The reason for so high a global cost is that the law applies to virtually every interstate business not already covered by existing laws; it sets some twenty-two thousand standards in such areas as unguarded machinery, excessive noise, hazardous materials, and worker safety devices; and the safety base that the law seeks to raise was deplorably low. Many businesses, large and small, are experiencing the pains of the cost of safety. General Motors said that, because of the new law, it would permanently close a Detroit tool-and-die plant, putting a thousand people out of work.

The cost to industry could run even higher if the recommendations of a federal commission on workmen's compensation are followed. The commission, appointed by President Nixon in 1971 under the Occupational Safety and Health Act, reported that between 10 million and 15 million workers are not covered by workmen's compensation and that "in most states maximum weekly benefits for a nonfarm family of four are below the poverty level." The commission has recommended that the states pass laws providing higher benefits and broader coverage, and it suggested that, if the states do not do so, Congress should force them to improve their programs by setting minimum *national* workmen's compensation standards.

In addition to industry recalcitrance, another problem is the difficulty of getting workers to use safety equipment, particularly when they are paid on a piecework basis. Workers think that guards on power tools may slow their production rates and cut their paychecks. At Detroit's Regal Stamping Company, installation of new guards on metal stamping machines allegedly reduced productivity 10 to 15 per cent.

With the prevalent high rates of deaths and disabling injuries, most companies agree that safety pays. The nongovernmental National Safety Council estimates that injuries on the job cost employees and employers approximately $10 billion a year. This includes losses to employees of wages and losses to employers in insurance, administrative costs, medical and hospital payments, wages and other compensation paid to injured employees, and fire losses. The number of deaths and disabilities caused by work-related illness is harder to gauge, because the effects may not appear for years. Lamp-factory workers of the 1940's are still dying from berylliosis, a lung disease brought on by exposure to beryllium, a lightweight metal used for coating fluorescent lights. Forty per cent of today's thirty-six thousand insulation installers may die of cancer and asbestos-related illnesses. These are just a few of the job-related health hazards to which workers are exposed daily.

Thus, it is easy to understand why safeguarding of safety and health, no matter how great the cost, is imperative for today's workers. The Department of Labor is leading the crusade. It is hoped that in the long run the Occupational Safety and Health Act will not only save lives and reduce injuries but also facilitate achievement of increased efficiency and productivity by promoting the operation of safer and healthier work places.

IX

Employment Standards

The Employment Standards Administration in the Department of Labor consolidates, for purposes of administration, a variety of activities concerning rights and protection of workers. Although enumerating these activities may make dull reading, behind them lie the struggles, hopes, and achievements of tens of millions of workers.

This chapter will describe a representative sample of programs such as those of the Women's Bureau; activities on behalf of older workers; administration of a floor on wages, a ceiling on hours of work, and premium overtime pay; wage garnishment; and workmen's compensation, which provides benefits for employees killed or injured on the job. Further on (see Chapter X) is an examination of the use of government contracts as instruments to abolish child labor, require the payment of prevailing wages, and promote equal job opportunities for minorities. Such activities represent the ethical gains of nearly a century of legislation.

THE WOMEN'S BUREAU AND CONCERN FOR WOMEN WORKERS

The creation of the Women's Bureau in 1920 reflected belated recognition of the role of working women in the labor force. Observers in the late eighteenth century told tragic stories of how the Industrial Revolution forced working women from their rural environment to work long hours in industrial settings at pitifully low wages. This is one side of the story. On the other side, jobs in factories attracted women and allowed them at least to earn something, whereas before they could earn nothing at all or, at best, receive a meager pittance as domestic servants or agricultural laborers.

The Working Girl in 1883

The Industrial Revolution opened new horizons, but it also brought problems for women who worked. Just before he began his career as the first federal Commissioner of Labor in 1884, Carroll Wright tried to determine the facts about women in the labor force and published his findings in a study of *The Working Girls of Boston*. His staff interviewed more than 1,000 female employees in the Boston area, plus 170 prostitutes in brothels known to the Boston police. Wright summarized:

> There are 20,000 working girls in the city of Boston, exclusive of domestics; of these 68.7 percent are living at home. . . .
>
> The single constitute 88.9 percent of the whole; the married, 6.7 percent; the widowed, 4.4 percent. . . .
>
> The present average age of the working girls is 24.81 years, while the average age they began work was 16.81. . . . 8.9 percent work more than 10 hours per day, and 8.6 percent more than 60 hours per week. . . . 76.2 percent of the whole number employed are in good health. . . . the average weekly earnings for the average time employed, 42.95 weeks, was $6.01, *and the average weekly earnings* of the working girls of Boston for a whole year are $4.91.
>
> Of the total average yearly expenses . . . 88+ percent of the total expenses for subsistence and clothing, leaving but 11+ percent . . . for all other wants of living.

Treading in an area where few modern labor statisticians would dare to venture, Wright analyzed the prevailing belief that low wages forced working girls to become immoral. His investigation disproved the charge that employers made "the honor of the girls they employ the price of a position." Most women in "houses of ill repute," Wright reported, became prostitutes because they were seduced or because they liked the easy life. Only 15 per cent said they were driven to prostitution by poor pay and hard work. The report concluded, "The working girls of Boston, as a class, are honest, industrious, virtuous, and are making an heroic struggle . . . to maintain reputable lives."

Early History of the Women's Bureau

The emancipation of women has been a centuries-long process. Women, instead of being, as formerly, merely the property of men, are gradually gaining equality with men. The Department of Labor is participating in the economic part of this movement through its effort to provide equal job opportunities for working women. During World War I, when women's work was needed for war industries, the Department established a Woman in Industry Service to "insure the effective employment of women while conserving their health and welfare."

After the war, in 1920, Congress established the Women's Bureau in the Department of Labor. Although not as climactic a victory as the Nineteenth Amendment to the Constitution, ratified that same year, which gave women the right to vote, the creation of the Women's Bureau also symbolized a notable achievement. Congress gave the new bureau a mandate to "formulate standards and policies which shall promote the welfare of wage-earning women, improve their working conditions, increase their efficiency, and advance their opportunities for profitable employment."

During its first decade, with a staff ranging in size from 17 to 47 employees, and an annual budget of between $40,000 and $108,000, the Bureau administratively was a "lightweight." But, led by Mary Anderson, who headed the Bureau for a quarter of a century, and supported by prominent women's groups throughout the country, it was a policy "heavyweight," which influenced many states to pass laws protecting working women.

The Bureau almost won a fantastic public relations victory when it seemed in 1930 that President Herbert Hoover would appoint Mary Anderson, the Bureau's chief, as Secretary of Labor. The appointment did not materialize. Nevertheless, some years later, President Roosevelt selected Frances Perkins for this post. Her appointment symbolized growing recognition of the ability of women to hold even the highest positions in society. The idea of a woman Cabinet member was so unusual, however, that it invoked the question of whether Miss Perkins found it a disadvantage to be a woman. When asked this question, she answered, "Only in climbing trees."

During the 1930's, the hardships of the Depression may have fallen more heavily on working women than on men. Women often were the first to be fired. Married women, in particular, had to overcome strong prejudices because of the feeling that they should not take jobs away from men; instead, they should let their husbands support them. The situation was reversed during World War II, when millions of women helped make America the "arsenal of democracy." Some women at that time moved into traditionally male occupations, and "Rosie the Riveter" became a celebrated figure. Although many women left the labor market after the war, others remained. The female labor force began to take on some of its present characteristics—a higher proportion of working women than formerly, a higher average age, and more married women.

The Female Labor Force: Present and Past

Today, women are a more important part of the work force than ever before. More than 32 million working women make up about 40 per cent of the American labor force, compared with 18 per cent at the turn of the twentieth century. About

45 per cent of all women over fifteen years of age work, compared with about 80 per cent for men.

The characteristics of the female work force have changed over the years. It is intriguing to make some comparisons with figures given by Carroll Wright in his report on Boston working girls in 1883.

The female labor force today is older, on the average. Of the total number of women now working, nearly 40 per cent are over forty-five years old, compared with 3 per cent in Boston in 1883.

The social stigma attached to married women who work has mostly, though not entirely, disappeared. About 60 per cent of working women are married now, compared with 6.7 per cent then. Many women who stop work now begin again when widowed, separated, or divorced; they comprise 20 per cent of the female work force now, compared with 4.4 per cent widowed in the 1883 report, which does not even mention divorce or separation. About a third of working women today are mothers with children under eighteen years of age. Such a category was not even listed in the 1883 investigation.

Esther Peterson, a director of the Women's Bureau during the 1960's, observed that formerly:

> The young woman who entered the work force seldom had any intention of remaining long. As soon as "Mr. Right" came along she handed in her resignation, put the finishing touches on her hope chest, and made plans for the wedding. . . . Only the tragedy of penniless widowhood or a broken marriage could drive her back into the labor market.

Many years earlier, in 1888, the Commissioner of Labor drew a similar conclusion and commented that female workers were "entitled to their popular designation of 'working girls.' " Today, such a term applied to women workers would be tongue-in-cheek gallantry.

Why is the picture changing? Why do women work? What accounts for their greater labor-force participation?

First, more jobs are available. Technology has opened new fields to women. Much of the heavy manual work has disappeared. Women have better educations and are able to meet higher employment standards.

Second, the "pill" and other improved techniques of birth control, along with labor-saving devices in the home, have given women more freedom to take jobs.

Third, social attitudes held by and toward women who work are changing.

And, perhaps most important of all, women want and need the money. Today the "good life" is easier to attain when both husband and wife are wage earners. In about 40 per cent of the husband-wife families, the wife is working. There are also more situations in which women need jobs because they are heads of families. In the early 1970's, about 6 million families were headed by women.

Laws That Help Women Workers

The Women's Bureau seeks social justice for women in many ways. It promotes enactment of laws providing equal pay for equal work and equal employment opportunities for women, as well as protective legislation. In most instances, these objectives support each other, but in some cases they are in conflict and create paradoxes.

Some women work in the same positions as men and are paid less for the same job. Women have fought long and hard for equal pay for equal work on the same job. One of their first victories was the Federal Government Classification Act of 1923, establishing the present system under which government salaries are determined according to the duties of the job.

An even more important milestone was the equal pay law enacted in 1963, which applied to about 70 per cent of the women working in private enterprise. Under this law, the Department has collected millions of dollars for thousands of workers who were paid less than men for doing the same work.

The courts have interpreted the law broadly. For example, jobs need not be identical. They merely must be similar and involve equal skill, effort, and responsibility. Thus, a court in Dallas, Texas, found that the all-female job of nurse's aide was equal to the all-male job of hospital orderly, and both were entitled to the same pay.

Probably the most controversial law involving the economic emancipation of women is Title VII of the Civil Rights Act of 1964, which prohibits discrimination in private employment based on *sex,* race, color, religion, or national origin. This law goes beyond equal pay. It applies also to hiring, promotion, and all other aspects of employment. It is based on complete equality of opportunity.

The law has occasionally been challenged. In one instance, a strike in 1970 closed down a company's division that had five hundred employees. The strikers were quoted as saying that, if women "can take our jobs, they sure as hell can go fight in Vietnam."

Another issue arises over the provision of the law that hiring can be confined to one sex if such a restriction is reasonably necessary to the normal operation of a business. For example, women are prohibited from working in mines in Utah, and in some states only masseurs may serve men and only masseuses may serve women. The tendency of those who enforce or interpret the law is to limit such exceptions, because most previously accepted special requirements are no longer relevant.

In 1967, President Lyndon Johnson issued guidelines that barred various types of discrimination. They included prohibitions against help-wanted advertisements labeled "male" and "female," job promotions or seniority based on sex, and different retirement rules for men and women. Women's groups demanded even more comprehensive regulations and still stronger enforcement. By the end of 1971, the Department of Labor required businessmen working on government contracts to take positive action to end discrimination against women.

In its efforts to accelerate the snail-like progress toward equality of the sexes in jobs, the Women's Bureau faces one of the most perplexing and paradoxical social questions of our age: What should be done about laws limiting the hours women work, the weights they lift, night work for women, and minimum wages for women? Do these laws protect women, or do they discriminate against them?

Humane political leaders once pointed with pride to their great victory in 1908, when Louis Brandeis, later a Supreme Court justice, presented a "sociological brief" in *Muller* v. *Oregon* that induced the Supreme Court to find that a woman's "physical structure . . . justif[ies] special legislation restricting or qualifying the conditions under which she should be permitted to toil." On this basis, almost every state and the District of Columbia limited maximum weekly or daily hours of work to protect the "health and morals" of women.

Minimum-wage laws did not at first fare as well. All laws passed between 1912 and 1922 setting minimum wages for women were declared unconstitutional because they interfered with freedom of contract for women who wanted to work for less. The Supreme Court reversed itself on this issue in 1937 in *West Coast Hotel Co.* v. *Parrish,* and many states thereafter passed minimum-wage laws that applied to women. Other states have other protective laws for the benefit of women.

The question now is: How can these hard-won laws be reconciled with the Civil Rights Act? Their provisions prohibiting employment of women in certain occupations, limiting women's hours of work, and providing other protective features for working women may be unlawful. It would seem that, if women are to be truly equal, job restrictions that apply to women should be ended, and some privileges that exist only for women must be granted to men.

George Meany, president of the AFL-CIO, bluntly expressed his disagreement with these conclusions. He did not "buy" the attitude of professional feminists, "If you give us protection, we are not equal." He did not accept the claim that laws protecting working women denied them their freedom. Some states have tried to meet the problem through comprehensive social programs covering men and women alike. But the problem has not yet been resolved.

Why Women Are Paid Less than Men

Women earn far less than men. Currently the median wage for full-time women workers is a little more than $5,000 a year, or about 60 per cent of the median full-time earnings of men. Why?

More than seventy-five years ago, Commissioner of Labor Wright addressed himself to this problem. He concluded that the difference in pay for men and women doing the same work was not large. Men earned more than women, he said, because of the kind of work they did.

The same conclusions could be reached today. The gap has probably narrowed. Many women hold important positions. But most women earn less than men because they are concentrated most heavily in low-paying industries, and many are in temporary jobs.

Society still has powerful conceptions of what is a masculine and what a feminine job. In 250 occupations covered by the current census, half the women are in twenty-five occupations, and 25 per cent are in five fields: secretary-stenographer, household worker, bookkeeper, elementary school teacher, and waitress. Males are more widely dispersed, with 50 per cent of them in sixty-five occupations.

In order to help women improve the occupational structure under which they work, the Women's Bureau is trying to combat the prevalent assumptions that every male worker is the head of a family and that every female who does not have a husband to support her is a failure. But, in spite of progress in erasing these stereotypes, the activities of many female workers are still dictated by the needs of husbands and families. As a result, many trained and skilled women work below the level of their ability. Convenience of location, suitability of hours, and availability of childcare are often more important to them than higher pay or promotions.

Many employers reinforce the pattern by their hesitancy to hire and train women for responsible jobs. They are not opposed to women in higher-paying positions, but they think of how much it costs them if their prospective employee should get married, become pregnant, move because of her husband's career, or for any other reason leave her job.

The effort to improve conditions for working women has come a long way. Most women no longer work long hours for low wages under poor working conditions. Capable women do get ahead and have greater job opportunities than ever before. But, by and large, women do not have the equality that is theoretically guaranteed them by law.

Opinions about the future differ. On one hand, there are those who believe that "anatomy is destiny." These prophets contend that, while women will have more opportunities and will be better protected against exploitation on the job, most will continue to work at less responsible and lower-paying jobs than men. On the other hand, others are convinced that the long sweep of historical trends will inevitably bring true equality between men and women in the job market. Time, they feel, is on the side of women workers.

OLDER WORKERS

While time is on the side of women workers, the same cannot be said of older workers. The poet who once said, "Nothing to look backward to with pride, nothing to look forward to with hope," could certainly be speaking of the plight of many older workers in America today.

Department of Labor statistics use age forty-five as the breakoff point for older workers. More than 30 million workers forty-five years old and over make up 38 per cent of the total labor force. When these older workers lose their jobs, it is often difficult for them to find new employment.

Older workers encounter various types of discrimination when seeking employment. The most frequent explanations for not hiring older workers are physical incapability of the applicants, a policy of promotion from within, ability to hire younger workers for less money, cost of pension plans, cost of health and life insurance, limited period of productivity on the job, and lack of skill, experience, or education.

Specific age limits for hiring are the form of discrimination most commonly used. Age limitations are most frequent for clerical jobs, semiskilled and unskilled work, and "outside" sales positions. Retail stores, hotels, medical service industries, and government agencies hire a higher percentage of older workers.

Department of Labor studies show that older workers perform as well as younger workers. Where physical effort is involved, as in factory production, productivity does decrease slightly after age forty-five, but this decrease is not substantial until age sixty. Where little physical effort is involved, as in office work, little decline occurs before age sixty.

The government has prohibited age discrimination in federal employment for a long time. Its policy is to hire on merit regardless of age. In 1964, a Presidential order extended the federal policy against age discrimination to federal contractors and subcontractors.

The Age Discrimination in Employment Act, passed in 1967, prohibits arbitrary age discrimination in employment. The Act is administered by the Secretary of Labor. With some exceptions, the law forbids employers, employment agencies, and labor unions to discriminate against workers forty to sixty-five years old.

The Secretary of Labor also carries out a program of education and research to reduce obstacles barring older workers from employment. Under the Age Discrimination in Employment Act and also the Manpower Development and Training Act (see Chapter VI), the Department of Labor has designed programs specifically for older workers who are seeking jobs. In the early 1970's, the Department's efforts were eliminating age restrictions from about a million jobs a year.

FAIR LABOR STANDARDS

The Fair Labor Standards Act (FLSA) of 1938 broke new ground with its concern for poorly paid workers (see page 45). Yet, even for that period, the minimum pay of 25 cents an hour was low, and the 12.5 million workers in interstate commerce who were protected were only a small part of the work force. As a pioneer law, the FLSA was a high point in American history. But it needed development in two basic ways to meet the challenge of change.

The Law's Impact

One type of change raised the floor under wages. The 1938 law provided for yearly increments until the minimum reached 40 cents. Subsequent amendments in 1949, 1955, 1961, and 1966 raised the floor gradually to $1.60 an hour for most workers. Proposals for a further increase made headway in the early 1970's. Although part of such increases is offset by inflation, there has been a real gain in buying power. When the $1.60-an-hour rate was set in 1966, many full-time workers could earn, on that basis, only slightly more than the poverty-level income. Future increases will probably keep the minimum wage above the poverty line.

A second type of change is an increase in coverage to protect more workers. Between 1938 and 1960, increased coverage was limited to the increase in the number of industrial workers in interstate commerce. Since 1961, coverage has been broadened by several methods.

One way of bringing more workers under the FLSA umbrella has been through broadening the concept of coverage.

For example, an "enterprise" standard introduced in 1961 provided that, if a firm with more than $1 million in annual sales volume had some workers in interstate commerce, all workers were covered. The "enterprise" test was subsequently reduced so that, by 1969, firms with $250,000 in sales had to comply with the Act. Another means of increasing coverage was to define "employer" and other terms in such a way as to include more workers.

More direct ways of protecting additional workers were by expanding coverage to new fields and by reducing exemptions. The important FLSA amendments of 1966 covered hospitals, nursing homes, schools, large hotels, and laundries, and even made a beginning in agriculture by protecting certain workers on large farms. Thus, by a variety of means, the number of workers protected by the FLSA increased from about 11 million in 1938 to about 30 million in 1964 and almost 50 million in the early 1970's.

Additional workers are covered by state laws that take care of about one-third of all employees in private enterprise not protected by the FLSA. Many of these laws apply to workers in retail trade and the service industries. Some of the levels set by state laws are below the FLSA minimum, some are the same, and a few states have even higher floors than those set by federal standards.

Overtime

The FLSA defines overtime pay as one and a half times the regular pay rate for hours worked in excess of forty hours in one work week. Thus, a worker who receives $2 an hour base pay would be paid $3 an hour for all hours worked in excess of forty in any one week. There are some exceptions. Because hospitals need flexibility in this regard, overtime rates in hospital employment may be paid for time exceeding eight hours a day or eighty hours in a two-week period. In some instances, overtime pay does not begin until after forty-eight hours of work in a week. In a few categories, there are no requirements for premium overtime pay.

The theory behind overtime premiums is that too much work is bad for a worker's health and does not leave enough time for recreation and self-development. If overtime work is really necessary, the employer can get the extra work time, provided he is willing to pay a bonus.

Actually, the principle of premium pay for overtime work is partly an effort to spread work and partly an indirect increase in wages. During the Depression, a campaign for the thirty-hour week was mounted to provide more jobs for unemployed workers. In the recession during the early 1960's, the Department of Labor discussed double pay for overtime instead of time-and-a-half pay, with the purpose of reducing unemployment by distributing available work more widely.

Although circumstances vary from person to person, most workers like the overtime premium because it means more money. One cause of the great strike wave after World War II was the loss of overtime pay. The eight hours extra each week that employees worked during the war years meant a 30 per cent increase in pay. When unions such as the electricians' union in New York City win a work week of twenty-five hours, it means not that their members will work only twenty-five hours but, rather, that they will receive premiums for all time worked in excess of twenty-five hours in any week.

The time-and-a-half provisions of the FLSA apply to poor workers receiving low wages. They do not apply to executive, administrative, or professional employees. A major controversy arises over who is exempt from overtime provisions. Critics of the idea of paying overtime rates to higher-paid employees say that people seldom become rich or famous or do anything worthwhile if they work only a forty-hour week. Compelling an employer to pay overtime to a semiexecutive climbing a career ladder, they argue, is a far cry from preventing exploitation of "sweated" workers.

The Department of Labor has repeatedly asserted that its aim in this regard is to help the lowest-paid workers. Now, as formerly, about 60 per cent of the Department's investigations of alleged pay abuses, and collections of back wages, are for cases involving premiums for overtime work. A considerable part of the "overtime" collections is for the benefit of low-paid workers.

Enforcement

From the start, the Department of Labor emphasized that its aim in enforcement of fair labor standards legislation was educational rather than punitive. The Department has an intensive wage-hour information program. It distributes millions of pamphlets and circulars on laws regulating wages and hours. For educational and other functions, it maintains wage-hour field offices in one hundred large cities and field stations in three hundred communities.

The Department uses a wide variety of methods to help achieve voluntary compliance. A method of the utmost importance, supplementing the information programs, is investigation of reported violations. Today, as in the past, most of the money for fair labor standards work is spent for investigation. On the basis of investigations, the Department in the early 1970's has been revealing about $100 million a year owed to about 500,000 workers for underpayment of back wages. This estimate is slightly misleading because, for purposes of efficiency, the FLSA enforcement work is combined with enforcement of other wage laws, such as the Public Contracts Act (see page 211) and the Service Contract Act (see page 213). But the overwhelming bulk of collections is made under the FLSA.

Periodically, the Department of Labor conducts sample surveys to determine the degree of nationwide compliance with wage-hour laws. Such a survey, in 1965, estimated that, if all establishments were investigated in a single year, about 1.8

million workers would be owed about $300 million in additional pay.

The Department has run into some opposition in collecting back wages for underpaid workers. Enforcing almost anything is an unpopular task. The easiest collections are those made from schools, hospitals, and other local and state tax-supported institutions. Large companies sometimes dispute claims, but most pay voluntarily when they lose. A few small businessmen fight to the bitter end.

Some employers resent the idea of a government investigator's coming to their place of business to examine their payroll. In a rather unusual incident, one small businessman from Georgia, forced to pay back wages and penalties under a public contracts wage law, went to the fantastic extreme of trying to block the appointment of former Secretary of Labor Arthur Goldberg to the Supreme Court. He held Goldberg responsible for actions of wage-hour investigators who, he alleged, ruined him and other small businessmen. An increasing number of physical assaults by irate employers on wage investigators led the Department of Labor, in the early 1970's, to propose a law making it a crime to interfere with agents enforcing the FLSA wage floor.

In 1971, an employer was sentenced to six months in jail for violating the FLSA and defying a court order to pay $19,000 in back wages and court costs. Such cases are rare. Although there are from 50,000 to 75,000 wage-hour investigations a year, this was the first case in twenty years involving a prison sentence.

Effect of the Minimum-Wage Law

Are minimum-wage laws good or bad for the economy? The answer depends on whom you ask. Some economists are convinced that minimum-wage laws are bad for the economy. They point to the plight of young people as an example. When the FLSA was passed during the Depression, it was hoped that setting of minimum wages would cause employers to hire adults and encourage teenagers to go back to school. Today, however, teenage joblessness is a serious problem. A study by the Bureau of Labor Statistics showed teenage unemployment rising five times faster than the adult rate.

According to other opponents of minimum-wage laws, the difficulty goes beyond wage standards causing adults to take jobs from teenagers. They argue that the total number of jobs is reduced by the minimum-wage laws, partly because some activities worth doing at lower pay rates are no longer feasible at higher rates, and partly because employers shy away from marginal workers who are not worth their cost at the minimum wage.

Most Department of Labor studies show contrary results. Their findings indicate that minimum-wage laws raise the standard of living and spur economic growth. For example, the 1966 amendments to the FLSA added billions of dollars to the income of low-paid workers. Poor people generally spend the money they earn on goods and services they need and thus stimulate other segments of the economy. Their spending creates more and better-paying jobs.

The FLSA is now approaching its original goals of increasing earning power and, at the same time, putting an end to low pay and poor working conditions. Yet, by an ironic twist, changing times and a new government outlook may have downgraded what at one time seemed a most important instrument of social change. Today, a host of government welfare and manpower services compete in a war against poverty. The prolific range of government strategies in this war reduces the comparative role of fair labor standards. Laws on minimum wages and maximum hours of work do not, by themselves, give enough help to the working poor with large families. They mean nothing to workers who are unemployed or who are too young, too old, or too sick to work.

Nevertheless, it would be a mistake to underrate the achievements of the concept. The FLSA has helped more people than any other program. Cumulatively, it has added many billions of dollars to the wages of millions of people. One of the goals of American domestic policy is to move people from welfare rolls to payrolls. If this is to be done, the incentive should be work at decent jobs. Fair labor standards provide a measure of assurance that available jobs will provide the working poor with a chance to earn their way out of poverty.

GARNISHMENT

Garnishment, the legal procedure through which a person's earnings can be withheld for the payment of debt, is an ancient practice. In Roman law, a debtor, his family, and his personal effects were subject to forfeit. Today, men are not thrown into prison or left homeless because they cannot pay a debt; yet garnishment has pushed some people into poverty and caused others to lose their jobs.

American economic growth depends to a great extent on credit selling. As installment credit surged, some workers borrowed well beyond their means. One method for a creditor to recover his due has been to attach the wages of the debtor through a garnishment order. The order, issued by a court, directs the debtor's employer to pay all or part of his wages, up to the amount of the debt, to the court officer, who in turn pays the creditor.

Until 1970, the states decided the proportion of wages that could be garnished. Some states prohibited garnishment completely, but most allowed for some garnishment. In some instances, garnishment caused extreme hardship. For example, Robert B., father of two children, was enticed by easy credit and ran up a bill of $900 at a credit clothing store. He could not keep up payments on his $100-a-week salary as an office clerk. The merchant got a court order requiring the employer to deduct $40 from Robert B.'s weekly salary and pay the deduction to the merchant. Robert B. did not have enough to live on and started to look for another job. In the meantime, his work deteriorated. His employer, exasperated by legal proceedings not of his own making, and angry at the poor work performance, fired him.

The Department of Labor has long been interested in the problems of wage garnishment. In 1967, the Department prepared a federal wage-garnishment bill and urged its enactment by Congress. Such a proposal was finally passed as part of the Consumer Credit Protection Act. Title III of that Act concerns garnishment. It is enforced by the Department of Labor.

Title III limits the amount of an employee's disposable earnings that may be made subject to garnishment. Disposable earnings are those that remain after tax deductions and other withholding deductions. The law assures the worker of keeping 75 per cent of his disposable earnings or thirty times the existing federal minimum hourly wage (currently $1.60 an hour or $48 a week), whichever is greater.

Another feature of the law prohibits an employer from discharging any employee because his earnings are subject to garnishment for any one indebtedness. Employers often felt it was simpler to fire the worker rather than be harassed by creditors or served with a garnishment order. In addition, where state laws provide at least as much protection against garnishment as the federal law, the state law applies.

In effect, then, garnishment remains a recognized method of liquidating certain debts. But the methods by which a creditor can attach wages and the amounts he can garnish are now restricted. Federal law has made it a national policy that workers must be protected against excessive penalties for debt.

WORKMEN'S COMPENSATION

Workmen's compensation is so generally accepted that it is hard to realize that it is America's oldest social insurance program and that it once was a burning issue among progressive Americans. In the early years of the twentieth century, many workers were killed or crippled on their jobs, and they or their families were most often left destitute. Most industrial towns supported large numbers of maimed workers and their families through public charity.

Workmen's compensation supports, in part, the dependents and survivors of men killed or injured while at work. It was first tried on Prussian railroads in 1838. Bismarck, in 1884, established a nationwide workmen's compensation plan as part of an effort to undermine the growing German socialist movement. In the next quarter of a century, almost every European country adopted some sort of workmen's compensation.

About 1907, industrial accidents in the United States neared a peak. Nearly five thousand workers were killed in railroading alone. President Theodore Roosevelt mounted a campaign that culminated in the first national workmen's compensation law in the United States. Although limited in scope and crudely drawn, it stimulated states to enact their own laws providing for compensation to workers and their families in industrial accident cases.

Because of its gradual introduction on a state-by-state basis, and because of the technical and legal nature of its provisions, the system for workmen's compensation lacks glamour, and its importance tends to be overlooked. Most workers do not have the faintest idea of what their benefits would be if they were injured on the job. Some employees do not even know whether they are covered.

More than 80 per cent of all American workers are protected by workmen's compensation. It is a multibillion-dollar business, which provides a major source of income to thousands of doctors, lawyers, insurance-company employees, and others. It operates in every state, and there is litigation at every judicial level. Most important, workmen's compensation is a source of livelihood for the survivors of tens of thousands of workers killed on the job, and hundreds of thousands of employees and their dependents draw regular benefits because of work-related injuries.

Most workers in the United States are covered by state laws on workmen's compensation. The quality of the state systems varies from good to woefully deficient. Weaknesses in state systems include loopholes that leave a large part of the work force without any protection at all; benefits that have not kept up with inflation and are, in any case, much too low (sometimes paying less than half of the worker's normal salary); and inadequate attention to rehabilitating injured employees.

The Department of Labor constantly works with the states to improve their laws and administration in this area. But, traditionally, its role is limited to giving advice. It is working on proposals to remedy defects of the state workmen's compensation programs through establishing federal standards coupled with federal support.

The federal government has a workmen's compensation law, which covers two types of workers—people who work for private enterprise but for some reason are not covered by state systems, and people who work for the federal government itself. Federal coverage of the first category grew out of a 1917 Supreme Court decision barring longshoremen from state coverage for workmen's compensation. A decade later, in 1927, the federal government established workmen's compensation for longshoremen and harbor workers. This covered about fifty thousand longshoremen who

> . . . do dangerous rigging, crack open hatches, climb down dungeonlike holds, sling bulky treacherous loads, run winches, handle hatchbeams, gangways, and maneuver cargo of all kinds. . . . Their workplace changes from ship to ship. Inclement weather and ever changing work conditions add to the hazards. Frequency, severity, and cost of such injuries run high.

Over the years, the federal government has covered additional categories of workers in private enterprise. The Department of Labor administers programs for private-industry employees in the District of Columbia, employees of U.S. Government contractors at defense bases outside the United

States, workers on the outer continental shelf exploring for natural resources, and workers in other special circumstances who need protection. An estimated million workers come under this type of workmen's compensation.

The most important group that benefits from the federal law consists of approximately 3 million employees of the U.S. Government. In 1916, an inadequate 1908 law on this subject was replaced by a more comprehensive, though frequently amended, law that is still the basic Federal Employees' Compensation Act of today. The law was administered by an independent commission for thirty years, until 1946. After a four-year interim under another federal agency, the employees' compensation function was transferred to the Department of Labor in 1950. This function at present is carried out by the Department's Office of Federal Employees' Compensation.

Most people assume that work in the federal government is relatively safe. While this is true for many federal jobs, it is easy to forget that hundreds of thousands of government workers are engaged in construction, foundry work, warehousing, maintenance, postal services, work in munitions factories, fire fighting, and other occupations more hazardous than office work. Each year, numbers of people in these occupations suffer agonizing and crippling work injuries that sometimes end in death. They make up the bulk of federal compensation cases. Over 100,000 work injuries occur yearly. By the early 1970's, new claims for compensation were running at about 25,000 a year, and benefits paid were approaching an annual level of nearly $200 million.

The Federal Employees' Compensation Act is among the more advanced workmen's compensation laws in the world and is far ahead of state systems in the United States. Its provisions, which are hard for the average person to comprehend, include such items as compensation rates up to 75 per cent of the top step of the salary of a grade 15 employee and not less than 75 per cent of a grade 2 employee's pay, re-employment rights, payments to beneficiaries who are students (until they reach age twenty-three or marry), lump-sum terminal payments to widows who remarry equal to twenty-four times their monthly compensation benefits, cost-of-living increases, and many other features. Such seemingly dull and complicated details are, of course, not at all dull to dependents or survivors of those killed or injured.

Federal employees who are not satisfied with the decisions of Department of Labor compensation officials can appeal to an Employees' Compensation Appeals Board. This board, established in 1946, is an independent, quasi-judicial body of three experts appointed by the Secretary of Labor. It is distinct from the Department's other compensation operations, and its jurisdiction extends to questions of fact as well as law. Its decision is final and not subject to court review.

Illustrative of the board's work is a case decided in November, 1968. A personnel clerk in a Midwest post office claimed compensation for a disabling nervous condition. The board determined that pressure and harassment by her supervisors had aggravated a pre-existing emotional condition, causing disability, and ordered the Office of Federal Employees' Compensation to pay her benefits accordingly. The Post Office Department objected to the decision, and the Postmaster General asked that the Secretary of Labor personally review the case. The Secretary denied the request on the ground that the board's decision was final and not subject to review or intervention by him. Cases such as this illustrate not only the finality and independence of the Employees' Compensation Appeals Board but also the humanitarian purposes that underlie the whole concept of workmen's compensation.

X

Government Contracts as Instruments of Social Policy

The government, as a purchaser, has enormous economic power. At one time, the prevailing view was that the public interest was best served when the government bought goods or services from the responsible bidder who offered the best quality at the lowest price. Today, the more commonly accepted view is that, while price and quality are still considered, the government should use the economic power inherent in its contracts for a variety of special purposes such as promoting small business, favoring American firms over foreign competitors, and similar goals.

The goal of promoting the well-being of working people through the labor provisions in government contracts has become increasingly important. It involves raising wages, providing employment for minorities, assisting handicapped workers, preventing child labor, and helping workers in depressed areas. Government contracts now have many clauses related more to achieving social goals than to merely efficient buying of goods and services.

It is often said, mistakenly, that labor provisions in government contracts were developed during the Presidency of Franklin D. Roosevelt. Actually, they go back much farther.

During World War I, war-production agencies inserted several such provisions in their contracts. One of the earliest was the clause limiting child labor in war industries.

CHILD LABOR

In 1906, John Spargo, in his book *The Bitter Cry of the Children,* wrote, "There is no more terrible page in history than that which records the enslavement of mere babies by the industrial revolution. . . . Not even the crucifixion of twenty thousand slaves along the highways by Scipio excels it in horror."

Although some children still labor, particularly among migrant farm workers, oppressive child labor is one social disease that has largely been wiped out. At one time, all workers over ten years of age were counted as part of the labor force. Now, labor-force statistics start with workers over sixteen years old. Many individuals and organizations have had a hand in the remedy. It is a credit to the Department of Labor that child labor is one field in which, with the help of others, the Department's work has almost eliminated what was once one of its major responsibilities.

The Children's Bureau, established in 1912, was one of the four original bureaus transferred to the Department in 1913. It dealt with all matters pertaining to child welfare, including child labor and its effects.

During World War I, the Children's Bureau studied how European nations had lowered their child-labor standard to speed war production. The bureau determined to prevent a similar tragedy in the United States. Congress seemed to have made the job easier by passing a Child Labor Act in 1916. But the Supreme Court held the law unconstitutional because, though it was based on the power to regulate interstate commerce, it had as its purpose the regulation of child labor, a function reserved to the states.

Julia Lathrop, the fighting social worker who headed the

Children's Bureau, refused to accept defeat. She persuaded the War Industries Board to incorporate the child-labor standards of the invalidated law into government contracts for war production. Beginning July 12, 1918, a month after the Supreme Court had declared the child-labor law unconstitutional, the Children's Bureau, with funds provided by the President, began enforcing restrictions on child labor. Federal government contracts for war production included the following statement:

> . . . the contractor shall not directly or indirectly employ in the performance of this contract any minor under the age of 14 years, or permit any minor between the ages of 14 and 16 years to work more than eight hours in any one day, more than six days in any one week, or before 6 A.M. or after 7 P.M.

This clause was one of the earliest and most effective uses of government contracts as an instrument of social policy. (See Chapter I for a description of their first use.)

The Children's Bureau remained in the Department of Labor until after World War II. The Bureau dealt with all aspects of childhood, including maternity services, child care, family welfare, and other child-related social problems. It printed several million copies of such publications as *Prenatal Care* and *The Child from One to Six* and, by 1937, had distributed 8 million copies of its best seller, *Infant Care*. It had become obvious that child labor was no longer one of the Bureau's most important functions. In 1946, therefore, the Children's Bureau was transferred to an agency that ultimately became the Department of Health, Education, and Welfare. Only the sections dealing with children in industry and the application of the Fair Labor Standards Act (FLSA) to children remained in the Department of Labor.

Although by no means on a scale comparable with its activities of earlier decades, the Department still works with child-labor problems. The FLSA requires that minors employed during school hours be at least sixteen years of age.

The minimum age for occupations declared hazardous by the Secretary of Labor is eighteen. In its constant efforts to improve compliance with the law, the Department of Labor, during the early 1970's, uncovered between ten thousand and twenty thousand child-labor violations a year—a relatively small number, considering the former size of the problem. With the possible exception of work done by children of migrant laborers, even these violations are different in kind from those of earlier generations. For example, common infractions today involve youngsters working in retail stores or youth under eighteen driving motor vehicles on the job.

The use of government contracts by the Department of Labor to discourage child labor has been a single phase of a vast effort, and its importance should not be exaggerated. Yet it has been particularly significant for two reasons. First, it helped eliminate exploitation of children as a way of doing business in the American economy. Second, it showed that government purchasing power could be used for social ends. Because of such efforts, the kind of child labor that once enslaved children may soon be as outmoded as the horse and buggy and other historical-museum antiquities.

THE DAVIS-BACON ACT: PREVAILING WAGE IN CONSTRUCTION

The Davis-Bacon Act of 1931 is another example of the use of government contracts to correct abuses of labor in American society. Today, there may be some dispute over its social utility, and there are arguments on both sides. But, certainly, at the time it originated, the setting of a prevailing wage on government construction protected building workers from vicious exploitation.

President Herbert Hoover signed the Davis-Bacon Act in March, 1931. The story began in 1926, when New York State contractors, basing their bid on New York wages, lost to an Alabama firm a major contract for building a veterans' hospital in New York. This firm brought in thousands of Southern workers, who lived in shanties, received low wages, and upset community standards. Representative Robert Bacon, from the injured New York district, introduced his first bill in 1926 to establish local wage scales in federal contracts. The bill did not pass.

Herbert Hoover, while still Secretary of Commerce, supported Bacon because he felt that the federal government should "set the example as a good employer." Later, as President, Hoover tried to handle the problem internally by including local wage scales in specifications for public buildings. The comptroller general rejected administrative remedies, however, because they violated the principle of free, competitive bidding and increased the cost to the government without improving the product. If remedies were needed, it became clear, Congress would have to take action.

Senator James J. Davis, formerly Secretary of Labor, joined with Representative Bacon and introduced the Davis-Bacon Act. President Hoover, about to start a series of major public works to combat the Depression, determined to defend existing wage scales. Overcoming charges that this "pernicious bill" made advertising for the "lowest responsible bid" a farce, Hoover pushed the Davis-Bacon bill through Congress in 1931. It was a Depression measure to prevent awards of government building contracts on the basis of wage cuts.

The first Davis-Bacon Act provided that workers would not be paid less than the prevailing wage in a locality. Workers and contractors would bargain over that wage, and, in case of dispute, the Secretary of Labor would decide. Secretary of Labor William N. Doak did not think he would be called upon to make the decision often. He was mistaken. Unions held consistently that the prevailing wage was the union scale. Contractors did not agree. Numerous conflicts developed, and Congress amended the law so that the Secretary of Labor would "predetermine" the prevailing wages that all bidders would have to pay.

Over the years, the Davis-Bacon Act grew in importance as a major lever to raise wages. Davis-Bacon determinations were expanded to include federally funded emergency construction during the Depression and World War II construction work. Its jurisdiction has been broadened more recently to cover new types of construction, such as public airports, low-rent projects, schools in federally affected areas, and federally aided highways. Today, more than fifty laws dealing with many kinds of federal construction call for Davis-Bacon prevailing wages. In addition, most states have their own "little Davis-Bacon Act" for state construction. The field is continually growing, as new grant, loan, and insured programs of construction are added. Many billions of dollars of construction a year are affected by Davis-Bacon prevailing wage standards.

The law has been further expanded to include fringe benefits. When the Davis-Bacon Act was first passed, workers received primarily cash wages. Fringe benefits have since become important. Because the basic purpose of the law was to make contractors bid on the basis of efficiency rather than their ability to depress wages, unions protested that contractors who skimp on fringe benefits can thereby win contracts. In 1964, Congress added pensions, vacations, holiday pay, apprenticeship training, and "other bona fide fringe benefits" as part of the prevailing wage.

The prevailing wages under the Davis-Bacon provisions are usually higher than the minimum wages set by the Fair Labor Standards Act. Rates differ with location, type of work, the strength of the union, and other factors. For example, in the early 1970's, skilled craftsmen belonging to a strong union in high-wage localities could command $10 or more an hour.

The Davis-Bacon Act is still controversial, and the Department of Labor is caught in the middle. Opponents charge that the law has added billions of dollars to the cost of government construction, that it is an engine of inflation, that unions have too much influence, and that the Department is often irresponsible in determining wages. Some congressmen propose that decisions of the Secretary of Labor should be subject to ju-

dicial review. Defenders insist that the Act still meets its original purpose. It was designed to provide for competitive bidding while protecting living standards of workers and safeguarding the welfare of the local community, and that, they
say, is what it does.

Controversy over the Davis-Bacon Act flared anew when
President Richard Nixon tried to curb the inflation growing
out of the Vietnam war. Construction costs rose faster than
costs in other industries. Although higher land prices and
higher interest rates were partly to blame, most complaints
were directed against wage rates, which had gone up nearly
20 per cent in 1970. When the unions failed to respond to
Secretary of Labor James Hodgson's appeals for restraint,
President Nixon, in February, 1971, suspended the Davis-
Bacon Act.

The suspension eliminated the prevailing-wage principle,
with the consequence that nonunion contractors could win
most bids for government work by paying lower wages. Rather
than get involved in a wage-cutting contest, unions agreed to
cooperate with contractors in a construction-industry stabilization program that might end the rocket-like trajectory of
building wages. Guidelines called for collective bargaining
with pay increases in line with changes in the cost of living
and productivity. Such guidelines would mean increases of
about 6 per cent yearly for most union workers. President
Nixon then restored the Davis-Bacon prevailing-wage system.

Suspension of the Davis-Bacon Act had been used to compel unions to moderate their demands for increased wages.
The unions agreed because of the threat of growing nonunion
construction contractors. In the meantime, the basic question
remains: Is the Davis-Bacon Act in the public interest?

THE WALSH-HEALEY AND SERVICE CONTRACTS ACTS

The Walsh-Healey Public Contract Act of 1936 tried to do
for government supply contracts what the Davis-Bacon Act
had done for construction contracts. When the only qualifica-

tions for bidding were price and the ability to perform, the contracts almost inevitably went to cut-rate operators. The government became the unwilling collaborator with firms that cut wages most.

As in the case of the Davis-Bacon Act, the key to the Walsh-Healey Act, and the subject of fierce controversy, was the *prevailing* wage. The law provided that people employed by contractors for government supply contracts of more than $10,000 should be paid

> . . . not less than the minimum wages as determined by the Secretary of Labor to be the prevailing minimum wages for persons employed on similar work . . . in the locality in which the materials, supplies, articles, or equipment are to be manufactured or furnished under said contract.

In addition, the Act provided for the eight-hour day and the forty-hour work week, plus time and a half for overtime. It also banned use of convict labor, hiring of boys under eighteen or girls under sixteen years of age, and work done under "working conditions which are unsanitary or hazardous or dangerous to the health and safety of employees." The Secretary of Labor could punish violators by placing them on a blacklist, which would prevent them from working on government supply contracts for three years.

Employers often opposed the administration of the Act because they objected to the way in which the Department of Labor set the prevailing wage. Historically, the Department tried various approaches on this matter. It finally tried defining the prevailing wage as the minimum wage paid by the majority of establishments in an industry. This minimum wage was derived from data collected by the Bureau of Labor Statistics (BLS).

One of the opponents of this method of determining the prevailing wage was Senator J. W. Fulbright of Arkansas—a low-wage state. Under the original provisions of the Walsh-Healey Act, the rulings of the Secretary of Labor were final.

During the 1950's, the Fulbright amendment to the Defense Production Act was passed. The amendment provided that "any interested person shall have the right of judicial review" on questions arising from wage determinations. On the basis of this amendment, a dispute over wage determinations for the production of motors and generators was submitted to the U.S. District Court of Appeals for the District of Columbia in 1964.

In that case, the industry challenged findings based on data collected by the BLS. The BLS refused to make its sources public, on the grounds that the information had been given in confidence and that, if it violated confidentiality, its work in the future would be seriously hampered. On the other hand, it was not fair to the plaintiff that he could not see the data that were the basis of the decision he was protesting. The court, therefore, overturned the wage determination. The decision of the court made the prevailing-wage provision of the Walsh-Healey Act meaningless, and no determinations of prevailing wages have been made since. The safety and health provisions of the Act, however, remained in force.

The Service Contracts Act of 1965 also deals with the question of bidders' winning contract awards from the federal government because they pay the lowest possible wage. In this Act, Congress provided that all employees working for contractors who sell services to the government must be paid at least the minimum wage provided by the Fair Labor Standards Act. On contracts for more that $2,500, employees must be paid the higher of either the minimum wage or the prevailing wage as determined by the Secretary of Labor. This law has prevented contractors' exploitation of low-paid workers such as janitors and cleaning women.

NONDISCRIMINATION

One of the more recent and spectacular uses of the purchasing power of the federal government to accomplish social goals has been the campaign of the Department's Office of Federal Contract Compliance (OFCC) to prevent job discrimination in government contracts. Under earlier contract provisions, aimed at preventing child labor or payment of substandard wages, the employer was ordered *not* to do something that society believed to be harmful. Such prohibitions, while better than nothing, were not effective in achieving equal employment opportunities for minority and women workers. To deal with discrimination, a new technique based on a positive action by the employer was added.

Equal employment opportunity is a major national objective. The Council of Economic Advisers has estimated that $2 billion a month is wasted because of job discrimination. But the issue goes beyond money. It is a matter of social ethics. Not so long ago, refusing to hire a person because of race, color, or religion was accepted as normal. Today, such business practices offend our sense of justice. Most Americans have come to accept the fact that those hired should be the best qualified.

Although the controversy over jobs for blacks has simmered for a long time, it first became a major issue during World War II. To prevent a threatened "March on Washington," President Franklin Roosevelt, on June 25, 1941, issued an executive order that made it illegal for government agencies or defense industries to discriminate in hiring on account of race, creed, color, or national origin. Racial discrimination was the most important of these prohibitions. The appeal to a nation at war was based on the theme that the more black faces there were on the production line, the fewer white crosses there would be on the battle line.

Today, the war against discrimination rages on many fronts. More than 22 million blacks, the largest minority in the United States, have the most to win or lose. Probably there was no previous case in history in which an established majority tried so hard to raise the disadvantaged minority into a position of economic equality.

Affirmative Action

The struggle over minority hiring has been going on with varying degrees of intensity ever since, after World War II, Congress unceremoniously dismantled the Fair Employment Practices Committee without even giving it a chance to write a final report. But the conflict reached a new crescendo in the 1960's. Executive Order 11245, issued in 1965 and since amended, is the sixth of a series of Presidential edicts on this subject. This order goes beyond prohibiting discrimination. It requires a government contractor "to take *affirmative action*" so that applicants are employed and employees are treated "without regard to their race, color, religion, sex, or national origin." The Secretary of Labor makes rules and regulations to achieve these purposes. In 1970, the rules were tightened by requiring goals and timetables for hiring wherever it seemed that minorities did not get their fair share of jobs and promotions. A similar rule for affirmative action is being applied on behalf of women workers.

The OFCC supervises government contracts in the war against job discrimination. Contractors or subcontractors run the risk of losing government business if they show bias in employment. The approximately 225,000 contractors involved control about one-third of all jobs in the United States.

Civil rights advocates protest that the staff of the OFCC is much too small to monitor so many government contractors effectively. But a large staff may not be necessary, because most government contracts are awarded by individual government agencies, such as the Atomic Energy Commission, the Department of Agriculture, and the Department of Defense. These agencies also carry out procurement policies and conduct many thousands of compliance reviews each year. The OFCC recommends policies, makes broad industry and area studies of employment, and encourages the government contracting agencies to enforce more vigorously the rules that open up jobs to all on an equal basis.

Generally, government procurement officials cooperate with

the OFCC. But their main business is to buy goods and services. Very few purchasing officials oppose the social objectives that are incorporated into contracts, but they sometimes look upon them as nuisances that interfere with procurement. When problems arise, they sometimes look in the other direction or seek to solve them through mediation, compromise, and persuasion.

Many civil rights leaders oppose such conciliatory administration of equal-opportunity measures. They believe long experience shows that gentle tactics seldom end discrimination. They call for stronger action, and some have taunted the OFCC with the fact that, in spite of a great deal of talk, very few contracts are ever actually canceled on account of discrimination.

One example of a controversy over conciliatory solutions arose in the late 1960's, when the Department of Defense awarded contracts to three large Southern textile mills with records of past discrimination. These firms worked out an *oral* agreement with Deputy Secretary of Defense David Packard. Civil rights leaders charged a "sellout" because government policy required a commitment *in writing* before a contract is awarded.

Over the objections of the OFCC, the Defense Department stuck to its award to the three textile companies. Deputy Secretary Packard defended his action before Congress with the claim that his agreement had broken a two-year deadlock over textile hiring practices and would bring more jobs to blacks. A study made a year later showed that major textile firms were hiring more blacks and had even promoted some of them. Secretary of Labor James Hodgson acknowledged the improvement but warned that "much more remains to be done."

Fighting Discrimination in Construction

The struggle of blacks for better jobs in the construction industry shows how hard it is to eradicate discrimination.

Jobs in construction are usually hard, dirty, casual, intermittent, and seasonal, with constant shifts of workers from job site to job site and from employer to employer. Such conditions usually lead to job insecurity and low pay. Yet most craftsmen in construction unions control jobs and limit the entry of new workers into the trade.

The construction unions are referral unions. Contractors normally do not have workers on their payroll. They may employ an appraiser, an accountant, or other overhead staff, but they get the men they need for on-site construction from the union, which maintains a pool of workers. At the request of an employer, the union business agent will send men to a job on terms that have been established by a bargaining contract. The union tries to limit the supply of workers so that it can more easily command high wages and provide steady work for its members.

On this basis of operation, construction unions often restrict membership. New members tend to be selected from among relatives, friends, and friends of friends of existing members. Deeply rooted traditions make it difficult for any outsider to get in. For a black outsider, becoming a union member is almost, but not quite, impossible.

Over the years, blacks have gained a toehold in some unions, particularly in the "trowel trades." In 1970, about 10 to 15 per cent of union bricklayers, plasterers, and roofers were black. In the miscellaneous trades employing carpenters, operating engineers, and painters, blacks made up about 3 per cent of union membership. In the mechanical trades involving electricians, plumbers, ironworkers, and so on, blacks averaged only about 1.5 per cent.

A *New York Times* reporter described the efforts of a black civil rights worker in Boston, who was a skilled carpenter, to get a job. He applied at five federally financed building sites reportedly having a shortage of skilled workers and was turned down at every one. In another instance in Boston, all the skilled workers on housing projects in a black area were white because, allegedly, no blacks were available. A complaint to the Boston Housing Authority was referred to the Department of Commerce, which had funded the project. That department referred it to the Urban Renewal Agency in the Department of Housing and Development, which referred it back to the Boston Housing Authority, which had received the complaint in the first place.

In the late 1960's, many blacks took to the picket lines and demanded better jobs in construction. "If black men can't work, nobody works," some pickets shouted. On "Black Mondays," Negro demonstrators blocked work on major projects in Cleveland, Chicago, Pittsburgh, and other cities.

The federal government then launched an offensive against job bias in construction. The industry made a good target because it had become the symbol of uncontrolled inflation. Adding minority craftsmen to the number of construction workers might serve the twin goals of curbing inflation and reducing discrimination.

The unions resisted the federal government's antidiscrimination efforts. Racial discrimination, it appeared, was only a surface manifestation. Construction workers felt they were the "whipping boys" of upper-class liberals who, at no cost to themselves, were gratifying their social consciences, while workers ran the risk of job insecurity and lower wages.

The Philadelphia Plan. Philadelphia became the first battlefield. In the fall of 1967, the Department of Labor had sponsored the Philadelphia Plan, which established goals for black employment in federal construction in Philadelphia. The comptroller general, who is the "watchdog" over federal contracts, rejected the plan because no specific hiring standards were included in the invitations to bid. Further, contractors could be faced with added costs to meet the stated goals, the comptroller general said. This might, in turn, raise the cost to the government.

Department of Labor officials revised their regulations to meet the legal objections. They set standards for minority hiring in six highly paid Philadelphia building trades that had very few black craftsmen. These trades were those of iron-workers, electricians, sheetmetal workers, plumbers, elevator constructors, and steamfitters. To avoid quotas, which might raise legal issues, goals were set in the form of ranges of per-centages. These percentages, increasing over a period of years, varied from trade to trade on the basis of labor market factors. Under the plan, contractors who did not meet their goals would have a chance to show they had made reasonable efforts in good faith. Such provisions made enforcement more diffi-cult, but the basic objective of giving blacks the right to suc-ceed remained. After four years, it was expected that the Philadelphia Plan would bring blacks up to about 20 per cent of the labor force on federal contracts in the Philadelphia area.

The Philadelphia Plan was in the "eye of the storm." The comptroller general suggested that he might not authorize payments to contractors under it. Some congressmen attached anti–Philadelphia Plan riders to appropriation bills and threat-ened to cut off enforcement funds. Employers claimed that the scarcity of black workers was not their fault, because they did not hire workers—the unions did. Union leaders called the plan a stupid, bureaucratic concoction that discriminated against white workers. One union leader in Philadelphia defied the Department of Labor and announced that, contrary to its edict, he would not turn over the next three hundred vacancies in his union to blacks to equalize employment.

The OFCC held fast. Assistant Secretary of Labor Arthur Fletcher observed that in the previous years the six Philadel-phia unions involved had hired only thirty-seven blacks, and, at the rate they were going, it would take a century to reach their goals. Federal inspectors stepped up their investigation of building sites to see whether there was sufficient evidence of bias to debar some contractors who did not cooperate. One sheetmetal contractor was barred from further federal work because he failed to comply with the hiring standards of the plan.

Employers brought legal action, but the courts upheld the Philadelphia Plan. Secretary of Labor Hodgson noted with satisfaction that the court of appeals had agreed that "affirmative action," with goals and timetables, was a proper method for the federal government to use in order to broaden job opportunities for minorities.

But you cannot build buildings with court orders. The President's orders, the Department of Labor's regulations, and court decisions should not be underestimated. To apply the old parable, they brought the horse to water, and they even made him take a sip, but he really did not drink much. For example, numerous black youth were attracted by the $6 an hour (now higher) steamfitters' pay. After difficult training and tests, they went to personal interviews that lasted less than one minute a man. One black out of twenty was admitted into the union. Or take the case of Clarence W., one of the few blacks who made it in the building trades. He was pulled off private jobs where there were no racial goals and switched to federal work where inspectors would see him. And there were also the "motorcycle blacks," who were shifted from job to job in anticipation of federal inspectors' next spot check.

Loopholes notwithstanding, significant numbers of blacks were hired. At the end of the second year of a four-year schedule, five of six trades had met or exceeded their minimum goals under the Philadelphia Plan, with the sixth trade only 1 per cent behind. Although the task is not easy, hiring of blacks in construction trades may gradually turn from a trickle into a torrent.

Hometown Plans. George Meany, president of the AFL-CIO, was among the bluntest critics of the Philadelphia Plan. He argued that building craftsmen worked hard and had a high degree of skill. Plumbing, for example, required mastery of nine hundred different techniques. You did not make a craftsman, he said, by establishing a "phony" goal. He added that the Philadelphia Plan was misconceived because it was limited to federal jobs, that union members could be persuaded to accept minorities if they did not endanger their own jobs, and that the only real solution of the problem was a gradual process of training blacks and then bringing them into an area-wide work force as part of the area's pool of skilled labor. To achieve these goals, voluntary "hometown" agreements might be more effective than the Philadelphia Plan.

The Department of Labor did not disagree. No one formula was paramount. "There are many roads to Rome." The federal government was willing to work with unions and civil rights groups to upgrade skills through such avenues as training programs and the apprenticeship Outreach Program. (See Chapter V). In general, the Department of Labor preferred area-wide agreements, and in Philadelphia it moved in that direction by calling on federal contractors to expand their goals to cover both their federal and other contracts. The big questions about hometown solutions were whether promising agreements could be reached and, if reached, whether they would be effective.

The Department of Labor likes "voluntary plans," explained Richard Gruenwald, assistant secretary of Labor in charge of employment standards. "They have the strength that comes from voluntary support . . . and are tailored to meet the specific needs of the community. But if we run into a situation where a hometown solution is not succeeding," Gruenwald added, "we have authority to impose goals and timetables—and we do not hesitate to do so."

Early in 1970, the Department of Labor launched a program for equal opportunity through hometown agreements. As a start, the Department selected nineteen large cities from all sections of the country, including Los Angeles, Seattle, Detroit, Atlanta, Boston, and Newark. Other cities were added later. Cities were chosen because of labor shortages, the size and degree of organization of minorities, the availability of minority craftsmen, and similar labor market factors.

Experienced negotiators from other units of the Department joined the OFCC to work out hometown solutions. Although the Department encouraged negotiation of hometown agreements, it would not dilute requirements. In Cleveland, for example, the low bidder on a heating and air-conditioning contract for the community college lost the contract because he failed to provide manning tables that would show how many blacks he would hire. Many obstacles to this approach were encountered, and agreements were hard to reach, but more than fifty cities negotiated hometown solutions.

Some voluntary agreements, such as the one in Boston, seem, as of the present, to be working. Others, like one in Chicago, have encountered problems. The Chicago agreement was drafted in January, 1970, without specific goals for each craft and without penalties. Although the OFCC did not approve the plan, it was endorsed by city officials, employers, unions, and some minority groups. It was hailed as a step toward opening 30 per cent of skilled craft jobs in Chicago to blacks within five years. Eighteen months later, very few blacks were at work. The plan was dead. It was a mistake, one observer commented, to expect that the wrongdoer himself would effectively remedy past misdeeds.

In addition to hometown plans that did not meet expectations, many cities failed to reach any agreements at all. In Washington, D.C., San Francisco, Atlanta, Saint Louis, and Newark, when negotiations broke down, the Department of Labor imposed a "Philadelphia" type of plan. In Seattle, Washington, at the request of the Department of Labor, the Department of Justice took the parties to court. When the case had been heard, the court ordered five unions to admit ninety more black apprentices.

It is difficult to appraise results during the heat of battle. One problem, it is hoped, will be temporary. The drive for more jobs for blacks in the "hard hat" trades was initiated when business was booming. Later, inflation and the building slump brought unemployment in the building trades. Unions that have been reluctant to set aside future openings for blacks fight even harder when the jobs of members seem in jeopardy. With decreased unemployment, the situation may be eased.

An interim judgment indicates some progress in opening up construction jobs to minorities. But the level of hiring has been low. There is still a long distance to travel. Civil rights leaders have criticized the OFCC for failure to open up enough jobs. A former OFCC director heatedly replied that his goals were the same as those of the civil rights groups, but the OFCC was in there "fighting it alone, and we have done it damn near single-handed." Instead of standing on the outside criticizing, he said, everyone working for equal opportunity should support ongoing efforts.

Good News and Bad News

Almost every report on employment of blacks points out that the news is both positive and negative. On the bleak side, the fact remains incontrovertible that there is a large gap between whites and blacks in almost every field. The proportion of blacks in professional, technical, and management jobs is far below their proportion of the population. Even where blacks are a large part of the work force, they hold only a small share of the better jobs, and their participation in craft jobs is also small. Almost every employment-oriented comparison shows sharp differences between whites and blacks, and in every case the advantage is on the side of the whites. The black tenth of the population has nowhere near one-tenth of the things that make up the "good life" for Americans.

Yet everything is relative. In the famous Webster-Hayne debates in 1830, Senator Robert Hayne observed:

> Sir, there does not exist on the face of the whole earth a population so poor, so wretched, so vile, so loathsome, so utterly destitute of all comforts, conveniences and decencies of life as the unfortunate blacks of Philadelphia, New York and Boston. . . . I have seen this unhappy race, naked and houseless, almost starving in the streets, and abandoned by all the world.

Conditions improved over the next century. Yet in 1942, Gunnar Myrdal, in his book *An American Dilemma* noted:

> The economic situation of the Negroes in America is pathological. Except for a small minority enjoying upper or middle class status, the masses of American Negroes . . . are destitute. They own little property; even their household goods are mostly inadequate and dilapidated. Their incomes are not only low but irregular. They thus live from day to day and have scant security for the future.

Since the great Depression, the economic progress of blacks has been significant. They are earning more money. In 1939, when reasonable statistics first became available, the black median of income from wages and salaries was only 37 per cent of the white median. Although the statistics are not exactly comparable, the 1954 mean black family income was 56 per cent of the white mean, which indicated a rising trend. After hovering on a plateau for more than a decade, the ratio again rose so that by 1970 it was 61 per cent. Perhaps it is not a good statistical procedure to select from the Bureau of the Census *Current Population Reports* the almost 95 per cent black-to-white median-income ratio for husband-wife families between twenty-five and thirty-four years of age outside the South. But, in spite of the limitations on the validity of this statistic, the 95 per cent ratio showing black progress may be a promise of things to come.

In the field of employment, the old saying that blacks are the "last hired and first fired" may no longer apply. Since the early 1950's, the black unemployment rate has been more than double that of whites. But, as blacks are moving into more stable jobs, this statistical rule of thumb may also be changing. In the early 1970's, black unemployment dropped below the two-to-one ratio. This change may forecast a further narrowing of the gap between white and black unemployment.

Blacks are also climbing the occupational ladder. In the

federal government, where many jobs are not menial, more than one-fifth of all employees are from minorities. The Department of Labor leads all the Cabinet departments both in the percentage of minorities employed and in the proportion of minorities in higher grades. What is true in government is also true in professional and technical occupations. In the 1960's, over-all employment went up 22 per cent, while the number of blacks in these higher-paying occupations doubled. The number of blacks in managerial positions, skilled work, and sales also rose.

In 1972, the Bureau of Labor Statistics published a study entitled *Black Americans: A Decade of Occupational Change,* which documents the solid occupational progress of blacks. They are moving into better jobs with higher pay. Young and better-educated blacks are likely to keep moving up. Some obstacles loom ahead, but improvements in educational levels, training, and economic opportunities indicate that blacks should continue to move into better jobs.

Social and economic disabilities are hard to eradicate. However, the task is not impossible. Earlier in this chapter, the near abolition of exploited child labor was noted. The use of government contracts was one important element that helped remove that blight from the American economic landscape.

Job bias is another stubborn disease. The OFCC use of government contracts with affirmative action plans is only a single weapon in a vast arsenal deployed against discrimination in employment. From the short-term point of view, progress is painfully slow. Yet in the sweep of history, the forward movement is unmistakable. With many initiatives coming from the Department of Labor, the United States has made and is continuing to make progress toward equal job opportunities for all.

XI

The Mesh of Things

Relations with the President, Congress, and Other Government Agencies

When President Harry S. Truman left office, he sympathized with his successor, President Dwight Eisenhower. "Poor Ike," Truman is reputed to have said, "He'll sit right here and he'll say, 'do this,' 'do that' and nothing will happen. . . . It won't be a bit like the Army. He'll find it very frustrating."

President Truman's remark, though relating to the power of the President, highlights the importance of intergovernmental relations. Good relations with other parts of the government are essential in order to make the gigantic federal machinery move. The Department of Labor's relationships with other parts of the government are extensive, and important. They extend outward to the Congress and upward to the President as well as to parts of the Executive Office of the President, such as the Council of Economic Advisers and the Office of Management and Budget. The relations also extend laterally to other federal labor and social agencies and to other Cabinet departments. Certainly among the Department's vital associations are those that run down the government pyramid to states, cities, and other local governments. Planning, care, and intelligence in the conduct of these relations may make the difference between success and failure for departmental programs and objectives. The way interagency relations are handled may either "mesh" or "mess" government operations.

RELATIONS WITH THE PRESIDENT

When the President catches cold, his Cabinet members sneeze. A Cabinet member is principally the President's representative in his field of jurisdiction. He carries out the policy of the President. A Cabinet member has a hard job because, along with his primary responsibility to the President, he administers a department containing experienced officials who advocate activities and programs that are not always in line with the President's views (and who almost always differ with the President on priorities).

The federal bureaucracy is so vast and is so much in control of the administrative machinery that it is usually difficult for the President to be sure that his policy will filter down to operating levels. A good Cabinet member tries to bridge this chasm between the President and his bureaucracy. He is influenced by the advice of his career employees, and, in turn, he advises the President about the work of his department, fights for priority for his programs, and, in the end, bends his department slowly but firmly to the decisions of his boss, the President.

The first Secretary of Labor, William B. Wilson, during most of his eight years in office, got along well with President Woodrow Wilson. The President threw the prestige of his office behind his Secretary of Labor. He generally stayed aloof from specific issues, but, whenever Secretary Wilson worked out a strike settlement, President Wilson supported him.

Toward the end of Woodrow Wilson's Presidency, the previously close relations between the two Wilsons became strained, and the Secretary's influence declined. Secretary Wilson tried to help labor during the period of rampant postwar inflation, but the Presidential policy held labor to minute pay increases, on the ground that inflation had to be brought under control. Other factors widening the split were the preoccupation of President Wilson with the League of Nations and his physical collapse, which made him almost inaccessible to his Secretary of Labor.

James J. Davis served under three Republican Presidents— Warren Harding, Calvin Coolidge, and Herbert Hoover. Davis got along wonderfully well with Harding because both knew little about labor issues but were friendly to labor in a general way. Relations with Coolidge and Hoover were less cordial, and Davis survived only because he was an amiable fellow with a flair for personal relations.

William N. Doak, who succeeded Davis, had actively supported Hoover in his campaign for the Presidency. As Secretary, he loyally defended all of Hoover's policies. Doak, like Hoover, continued prematurely to predict the end of the Depression. With the deepening crisis, the rising anger against Hoover was aimed also at the men who supported him, and Doak became one of the most disliked Secretaries of Labor.

Franklin Roosevelt's Secretary of Labor, Frances Perkins, tried to advise him on all aspects of labor policy. She wanted to give labor leaders access to the President without his becoming embroiled in controversies or involved in details on labor questions, and she saw herself as Roosevelt's chief assistant on labor matters. In actuality, this was not the case. Roosevelt dealt directly with many people on labor affairs. Particularly during World War II, he repeatedly bypassed his Secretary of Labor. Sidney Hillman, Isador Lubin, and other Presidential advisers provided a "back door" to the White House.

President Truman had two Secretaries of Labor. Although his personal relations with them were good, neither was able to be really effective, because Truman emulated Roosevelt's habit of bypassing the Secretary of Labor. John R. Steelman of the White House Staff, who was sometimes called the assistant president, was the real power in labor matters.

Two Secretaries of Labor served in the next Administration. President Dwight Eisenhower hoped that the selection of Martin P. Durkin, president of the plumbers' union, might bring him some labor support. But Durkin had little direct contact with the President and resigned after less than eight months in office.

By contrast, James P. Mitchell got along well with Eisenhower. Secretary Mitchell's term brought an end to the Roosevelt-Truman tradition of resorting to major labor advisers other than the Secretary of Labor. Mitchell barred the "back door" to the White House and remained Eisenhower's man on labor questions. Although the formal, routinized method of operation that the President preferred made it difficult for Mitchell to have free and intimate dealings with him, the relationship was one of genuine confidence and smooth cooperation, which brought prestige and influence to the Department.

When Arthur J. Goldberg became Secretary of Labor under President John Kennedy, the Department of Labor entered a golden age. Goldberg had a nearly perfect relationship with President Kennedy. He had easy access to the President, and Kennedy had confidence in Goldberg's ability as well as in his political sense.

Secretary Willard Wirtz, Goldberg's successor, continued the excellent relationship of his predecessor with the White House. Wirtz was sensitive to human needs. This attribute was especially helpful in his relations with President Lyndon Johnson, who made sensitivity to human needs the hallmark of his domestic policy. Unfortunately, on the eve of the 1968 Presidential campaign, differences in opinion over how to bring about peace in Vietnam destroyed the previously smooth relationship between the President and his Secretary. (See page 81.)

George P. Shultz followed Wirtz as Secretary of Labor. Shultz's relationship with President Richard Nixon was remarkable. He spoke in a low key, which Nixon liked. He was among the best-educated aides to the President and seems to have influenced him extensively, for he became a member of the powerful group that advised him on economic policy.

The relations of a Secretary of Labor with the President range from close and cooperative to distant and even antagonistic. They vary greatly between Secretaries and sometimes change drastically during one Secretary's incumbency. Many factors affect this relationship, such as how well the two men get along personally and how compatible their "styles" are. But, even if the President and the Secretary "hit it off," success is not guaranteed. Lack of Presidential support may alienate and weaken the Secretary, as will the President's bypassing him in favor of preferred Presidential advisers. Conflicts over policy can kill the relationship and even result in the resignation of a Secretary of Labor. Too much independence on the Secretary's part may turn the President against him. Even the state of the President's health can influence the relationship, because a President in poor health is likely to be less accessible to the Secretary.

Obviously, the mix of such factors determines the effectiveness of the relationship between the Secretary of Labor and the President. This relationship is crucial, because it affects not only the personal power of the Secretary but also the status of the Department itself and the viability of its programs. Even more important, this relationship is often a critical factor in determining whether or not a President can achieve his goals.

The Office of Management and Budget and Director Shultz

President Nixon wished to orchestrate the programs of the departments and agencies into a unified government. In March, 1970, he strengthened the Bureau of the Budget and made it into the Office of Management and Budget (OMB). The President chose George Shultz to direct OMB because he felt that Shultz was one of the best administrators in the executive branch. He had been more than a Secretary of Labor. He had been Nixon's most used and useful homefront troubleshooter. He not only was called upon to head the committees a Secretary of Labor ordinarily heads, but he also sat on the Urban Affairs Council, the Cabinet Committee for Economic Policy, and even committees unrelated to labor, such as the Task Force on Oil Imports.

In his new capacity as OMB director, Shultz reviewed and coordinated the budgets and programs of other departments. Because he had been Secretary of Labor and his under secretary had succeeded him as Secretary, the Department of Labor sought Shultz's advice more than other departments did. Shultz, even more than the Secretary of Labor, was the key to the relations of the Administration with the labor movement. The "unflappable" Shultz, who retained his ability for critical analysis under pressure and combined a keen intellect with the tireless energy of a man of action, wielded great influence throughout all branches of the federal government. Later, when President Nixon selected him as Secretary of Treasury, Shultz continued, and perhaps even extended, his role as the coordinator of the President's domestic programs and policies.

RELATIONS WITH CONGRESS

The success of all departments of government, in large measure, depends on their relations with Congress; yet the Constitution, with its insistence on separation of powers, generates friction between the branches of government. Several Presidents have failed to achieve their goals because they failed to win congressional support. But Presidents who carefully cultivate Congress often overcome the obstacles created by the separation of powers. Presidents John F. Kennedy, Lyndon B. Johnson, and Richard M. Nixon had all served in Congress, and they understood the importance of congressional relations. They tried to work with Congress and encouraged their Cabinet secretaries to follow their lead.

The Department of Labor has a more difficult time than some government departments in achieving harmonious relations with Congress, because it deals with highly controversial affairs. The Department of Labor proposes legislation involving minimum wages, maximum hours of work, equal job opportunities for minorities, safety and health regulations on the job, unemployment insurance, welfare and pension plans, manpower training, strikes, and other social and economic issues. Some congressmen favor almost anything the Department of Labor does, while others are automatically against it.

Although every congressman is important, the Department of Labor pays special attention to the chairmen and members of special committees whose dealings affect the Department. The most important of these are the House Committee on Education and Labor, the Senate Committee on Labor and Public Welfare, and the appropriations subcommittees that provide the Department's funds. These committees have life-and-death power over every activity of the Department.

In 1867, the House of Representatives established a Committee on Labor. This was the first time the federal government considered labor important enough to warrant special recognition. In 1911, Congressman William B. Wilson, a former official of the United Mineworkers' Union, became chairman of the Committee. From this position, he managed the bill, signed in 1913, that created the Department of Labor, of which he became the first Secretary.

The Committee on Labor subsequently merged with the Committee on Education to form the present House Committee on Education and Labor. This committee rates somewhere in the middle on the prestige scale as far as congressmen are concerned. Membership on it is not sought as ardently as are posts on more powerful committees, such as the Ways and Means Committee or the appropriations committees, but many congressmen, especially those from urban areas, consider membership on the House Committee on Education and Labor desirable.

On the Senate side, the Committee on Education and Labor

was established in 1870. The functions of the committee have been revamped from time to time. Today it is the Committee on Labor and Public Welfare. This committee, has shaped much of the social legislation of the last generation.

The appropriations subcommittees are vital to the Department because, even when legislation is passed, nothing happens until money is provided. As picturesquely explained by a straight-talking legislative assistant, "If you don't get the bullets, beans and bandages, you can't operate." Many officials in the Department of Labor tell stories of how members of the Appropriations Committee killed some of their most desired projects.

Other committees also influence Department of Labor activities. For example, the Senate Committee on Government Operations made labor history in the late 1950's, when its chairman, Senator John McClellan of Arkansas, conducted a dramatic investigation of racketeering and corruption in labor unions. This investigation led to the Landrum-Griffin Labor-Management Reporting Act, under which unions now operate.

Although today the relationship between the Department of Labor and Congress is excellent, over the span of its history the nature of the Department's activities has been a source of difficulties with Congress. The punishment that Secretary Frances Perkins absorbed from Congress has already been described. (See Chapter II.) When Secretary of Labor Lewis Schwellenbach followed her after World War II, it seemed the situation might improve because Schwellenbach had been a U.S. Senator and knew his way around Capitol Hill. But he became a target of the conservative Eightieth Congress. Some succeeding Secretaries of Labor fared better, but not until after Arthur Goldberg became Secretary in 1961 did relations with Congress really improve.

Shortly after Goldberg assumed office, a dramatic fiasco focused attention on the Department's congressional relations. One of Goldberg's first battles occurred over increasing the minimum wage from $1.00 to $1.25 an hour. A mistake in coordination nearly turned into a disaster. The Department of Labor minimum-wage bill came up for a vote in the House of Representatives on a Thursday, when many liberal congressmen who lived near Washington went back to their home districts for a long weekend. The opposition substituted a bill that reduced the minimum wage, and this bill was passed by a vote of 186 to 185.

When President Kennedy learned the news, his legislative assistant recalled, he muttered, "One vote," and in frustration plunged a letter opener into the top of his desk. Later, the Senate passed a more liberal bill, and the House-Senate conference committee reported a measure more to the liking of the Administration. A new vote saved the $1.25-an-hour minimum wage. This victory, snatched from the jaws of defeat, brought a strengthened system of legislative relations.

A folklore has grown up around the work of legislative liaison. "The fanciful picture," noted one skilled practitioner, "features exchanging federal largess in the form of bridges, dams, post offices, and other projects for votes." He continued, "Such a picture, I believe, fulfills the all-too-human need of simple answers for complicated problems. The simple fact, however, is that such a picture is entirely incorrect. There is no effort to 'buy' votes through a kind of horsetrading process."

One of the most important tools of congressional liaison is reliable information as a major vote nears. The "head count" is of great significance. Politicians normally do not attach themselves to lost causes. Information on whether a bill is likely to carry, or on changes needed to make it carry, is a most important element of congressional relations.

The telephone poll is a useful device. Selected departmental officials call certain congressmen and ask them how they expect to vote on upcoming legislation. This information then serves as the basis of action in the executive branch. Practitioners of legislative liaison quickly learn that there is no substitute for "leg work." The best approach is usually to walk into the congressman's office and ask to see him, discuss the problem, exchange information, find out if he can be of help, and then get out.

Most congressmen appreciate receiving factual material. Slanted explanations can be disastrous, for they destroy the liaison officer's most important asset—credibility.

Congressmen also call on liaison officers for help with government business. When a constituent wants to straighten out a bureaucratic snarl or to get information about certain programs, the congressman may turn to the liaison officer for help. In this way, the liaison function serves the congressman, the Department, and the public.

One of the most difficult and delicate problems of congressional relations has to do with government jobs. Particularly when there is a change in Administration, the party coming into power wants people in key positions to carry out its policies. But the job hunt goes farther because congressmen want as many jobs for their constituents as possible. The problem is further complicated because White House staff members and other Administration officials also make requests, and unions, women's organizations, minorities, and other groups want their share of jobs too. Although the vast majority of the jobs come under the civil service merit system, there are some positions to which appointments are discretionary.

The Secretary of Labor and his principal assistants, for example, are appointed by the President and confirmed by the Senate. In addition, there are certain "super-grade" positions that are exempt from the competitive civil service because of their policy-making or confidential nature. The Secretary of Labor also has at his disposal about fifty "Schedule C" positions that are outside the civil service system. Chairmen of congressional committees are sometimes consulted about appointments to these positions.

In practice, job assignments do not always fit the patterns described above. Some seemingly political jobs are filled by career people risking job security to gain a higher grade, whereas some positions in the career service are occupied by political appointees who meet minimum merit standards. In general, government service has come a long way since President James A. Garfield was assassinated in 1881 by a disappointed office seeker. Most federal government positions are filled on the premise that the best-qualified person should get the job. In some cases, it helps a qualified applicant if he also has the backing of his congressman.

The Department often tries to influence the course of legislation through its expert testimony on bills being studied by congressional committees. Secretaries of Labor often appear before congressional committees to explain the budget or proposed legislation. In recent years, most Secretaries have been excellent witnesses. Other officials of the Department also participate in hearings from time to time.

The primary purpose of congressional relations is to carry forward the President's legislative program. Every week, each government agency sends political reports to the White House outlining the status of legislation in which the President is interested. If there is a chance of success, efforts are made to single out those congressmen with the "swing" votes and then to determine how to persuade them. A particular congressman may be more prone to listen to someone from his own state. He might be more easily influenced by an educator, a union official, a scientist, or someone with whom he has a common interest. What goes on, explained a former White House aide,

. . . is a delicate searching out of what can be done by an individual Congressman, how far he can extend himself without endangering his standing with his constituents, how much we can convince him that he and his home District really do have a stake in a particular piece of legislation, and how we can compromise without sacrificing principle or substance.

Congressional relations become more complex when the President in office does not have a majority in Congress. Democratic Presidents often need Republican votes for social legislation. The process is reversed when a Republican President tries to find the necessary Democratic votes to carry out his program. Labor Department officials and legislative liaison officers participate in a careful low-pressure campaign to win the needed marginal votes.

Good relations with Congress lubricate the political machinery. They can contribute to the success of almost every activity. Sometimes the cards are stacked so that, no matter what the Department of Labor does, it cannot make headway. But, at other times, an effective legislative-relations program spans the gap between Congress and the Department and furthers the goal of the Department in fostering the welfare of the workers of the United States.

RELATIONS WITH OTHER GOVERNMENT AGENCIES

The relations of the Department of Labor with other federal departments are ambivalent. They are a mixture of attraction and repulsion. Some activities bring about good working relationships. Others cause rivalry and conflict.

Those activities in which the Department provides services to other agencies, though not entirely trouble-free, tend to be harmonious. Just as the Postal Service routinely delivers mail to all branches of the government, so too the Department of Labor regularly deals with claims on behalf of government employees killed or injured on the job, supervises safety programs throughout the government, coordinates government management-labor relations, and monitors government-wide labor requirements. More controversial aspects of the Department's intragovernmental relations range from carrying out national employment policies affecting other government departments to dealing with disputes over which agency is responsible for which functions.

An example of the Department's interdepartmental relations based on national policy is found in the area of nondiscrimination in employment. Government agencies buy billions of dollars' worth of goods and services each year. Their contracts forbid contractors to discriminate because of sex, race, color, creed, or national origin. On the one hand, the agency letting the contract, whether it is buying books for a library or building a hospital, is most interested in its specific mission and sometimes considers the issue of nondiscrimination irrelevant. On the other hand, the Department of Labor places a higher priority on preventing prejudice in employment. In promoting the national goal of equal job opportunity, the Department of Labor works with every major government agency.

The issue that creates the most conflict is the determination of which agency can best handle which functions. There is nothing sacred about a particular program's being performed by a particular department. Tradition tends to fix certain activities in certain organizations, and this gives government departments an appearance of permanence, which really does not exist. The growth of the federal budget to hundreds of billions of dollars annually, together with the fantastic multiplication of government activities, magnifies the issue of who does what. Growing federal activities arouse the predatory instincts of some bureaucratic empire-builders, but, in general, public servants are stirred to work in harmony in order to make a program succeed.

Some basic ways of assigning functions to organizations are creating new agencies for new functions, reorganizing old agencies, placing new functions in existing institutions, and calling for joint responsibility. All these methods generate a tremendous and complicated amount of interdepartmental activity, and the strands in this interagency web take many forms and extend in many directions. There are interagency committees on every level, along with formal agreements, official delegations of authority, informal arrangements, and contacts in person or by telephone.

Labor Agencies

The Department of Labor works closely with other federal labor agencies, some of which were at one time part of the Department. The Federal Mediation and Conciliation Service grew out of the Department of Labor's original mandate in 1913 to mediate strikes. After World War II, that function was taken away from the Department, supposedly because a separate service would be more impartial. Today, the Department of Labor leaves federal intervention in strikes, as far as possible, to the Mediation and Conciliation Service. But, when a strike is important and serious, the Department is often called in.

Impartiality was also the motive, in the 1930's, for rejecting the Secretary of Labor's efforts to bring the National Labor Relations Board under the Department of Labor's administration. The board protects the rights of workers to organize, and it defines unfair labor practices. Secretaries of Labor have recommended changes in the law in this area, and the President may consult them in selecting members of the board. The two agencies work together in data collection and research and in other areas of common interest. But the board retains its judicial independence.

The work of the Equal Employment Opportunities Commission (EEOC) touches on many aspects of the Department of Labor's activities. The Manpower Administration, the solicitor's office, and the labor-standards officials in the Department work constantly with the EEOC. In the jurisdictional wars between government agencies, the proposal has been made that the Office of Federal Contract Compliance (OFCC) be transferred out of the Department of Labor to the EEOC. So far, such efforts have been turned back.

Cabinet Departments

The relations between the Department of Labor and other Cabinet departments are many and varied. The departments of Labor and Commerce have a long history of bitter-sweet association. For ten years, starting in 1903, they were joined together in an unhappy marriage. Since 1913, proposals for a merger have from time to time been resurrected and rejected. During the early history of the two departments, the Department of Commerce was the more affluent and the more influential, and at times the Secretary of Commerce determined policies for the Department of Labor.

Since 1953, the relationship has been that of equal partners who work well together. Both the Department of Labor and the Department of Commerce promote employment opportunities in private enterprise. In addition, the Census Bureau in Commerce and the Bureau of Labor Statistics often work together. For example, the Census Bureau collects labor-force data that the Bureau of Labor Statistics uses in its monthly reports on employment and unemployment. In international affairs, both Labor and Commerce work with the State Department in representing the United States in their special fields, and both try to gain for employers and workers the benefits of foreign commerce while softening the blows from foreign competition.

The Labor Department supports the Department of State in labor aspects of foreign affairs. Department of Labor officials go to international meetings and participate in the International Labor Organization. They also study the effects of imports and exports on American labor and make recommendations on trade and tariff policy.

The Department of Labor and the Department of Justice likewise work together in many fields. One of their first joint responsibilities was in immigration, which was the Labor Department's most important activity during the first quarter-century of its history.* Some Department of Labor respon-

* Before World War I, 92 per cent of the Department's employees were in the Bureau of Immigration and Naturalization. Because most of the millions of foreigners who came to the United States needed work, immigration was primarily a labor problem. (See Chapter I.)

After World War I, the nature of the immigration function changed. Attorney General A. Mitchell Palmer, tried to parlay a campaign against

sibilities for immigration remain. Many foreigners who come to the United States to work need first a certificate from the Department of Labor attesting that no Americans are available for the job. Often foreigners work illegally, and Department of Justice agents sometimes swoop down on a restaurant, janitorial service, or other business establishment and apprehend waiters, dishwashers, janitors, or others who are committing the crime of working illegally. The decision as to which foreigners may work in America involves coordination between the departments of Justice and Labor.

Labor Department activities involve other contacts with the Department of Justice, which in essence is a law firm handling federal business. The two departments work together on enforcement of the Fair Labor Standards Act, the Age Discrimination in Employment Act, the Civil Rights Act, and other legislation relating to discrimination in employment. Similarly, the two departments share responsibility for combating labor racketeering, preventing labor corruption, and in general policing a code of ethics prescribed by law for labor unions and welfare and pension funds.

At one time, the Department of Labor had closer relations with the Department of Agriculture than today. There had been conflicts between farmers who wanted cheap labor and workers who wanted more money and better working conditions. In the 1960's, the Department of Labor rallied support for a law to end the importation of braceros, Mexican laborers who worked in the fields, because they depressed wages for American workers. In earlier years, the Department of Agriculture might have used its influence to block such legislation. But in the social climate of the 1960's, the Department of

---

the "red terror" into the Democratic nomination for the Presidency. But Assistant Secretary of Labor Louis Post blocked Palmer's efforts for mass deportation of aliens. Although the Bolshevik scare abated, the new immigration quota laws transformed the immigration function into police-type work, involving such activities as ferreting out "illegal" aliens and deporting them. In 1940, most immigration responsibilities were transferred to the Department of Justice.

Agriculture's opposition changed to acquiescence when the law was passed. Most Department of Labor and Department of Agriculture contacts today involve research programs, statistics on farm labor, and work to attract better-qualified workers to farms, to train and upgrade rural labor, and to abolish rural poverty.

In no area do Labor Department interests converge more critically with those of other government agencies than in the broad domain encompassed by the Department of Health, Education, and Welfare (HEW). At times, the functions of the two departments overlap, and, depending on the results of jurisdictional warfare, some bureaus have shuttled back and forth between Labor and HEW. Sometimes both departments have lost out. As a result of a tug of war in the 1960's between the departments over the antipoverty program, the President assigned this responsibility to a new agency, the Office of Economic Opportunity (OEO).

Since then, the bureaucratic war between the Department of Labor and HEW seems to have abated. The OEO is being dismantled. Programs that failed are being abolished, and other activities have been reassigned and divided between Labor and HEW. The two departments may be embarking on a course of cooperation that is so unusual that one government official described it as "defying the laws of public administration just as much as an apple falling from the ground up to the tree would defy the law of gravity." Jurisdictional rivalry may yet corrode this cooperation, but at least in their objective the two departments are working together in the inextricably intertwined relationships between poverty, work, education, and welfare.

One of the earliest roots of this cooperation was an agreement of 1950 between the Department of Labor and the Office of Education to help high school students who were not going to college to select vocations and find jobs. The two units have broadened their interest to include the entire school-job relationship. They have harnessed their efforts together to solve the difficult problems of transition from school to work.

The greatest demand for cooperation grows out of the need to mesh manpower-training and welfare services. Under the Manpower Development and Training Act of 1962 (see Chapter VI), the Department of Labor determined what kind of training was needed, selected the trainees, and helped them find jobs after training. HEW supervised the actual classroom teaching.

As a result of the campaign to make the able-bodied poor self-supporting, Congress created a Work Incentive Program (WIN), which called on welfare agencies to refer people suitable for training to the Department of Labor, which was responsible for both the training and job placement. (See Chapter VI.) In the meantime, HEW provided a wide variety of social services, of which expanded child care was one of the most critical. Although WIN is a big program, it is puny compared in size to the problem of welfare. Proposed welfare reform based on "workfare" rather than welfare for the able-bodied poor foreshadows the closest working relationship between the Department of Labor and the Department of Health, Education, and Welfare. One department would provide social services and income, while the other would train and find jobs for suitable welfare clients who would move from relief rolls to payrolls.

RELATIONS WITH STATES, CITIES, AND OTHER LOCAL GOVERNMENTS

One of the gnawing frustrations for many Americans is the fact that bureaucrats in Washington are too distant from the people. To overcome this feeling, the federal government has sponsored a government-wide effort to bring its services closer to the people. The Department of Labor has traditionally based most of its activities on the federal-state relationship.

The state employees who deal with employment services and unemployment insurance outnumber federal Department of Labor employees by more than six to one.

In participating in this effort toward decentralization, the Department of Labor is expanding its front-line service to the states and localities to other areas besides employment services and unemployment insurance. As far as possible, the Department limits its role to coordinating and setting national policies and goals, while states and local agencies deliver the services. Most Department programs are being decentralized among ten standard federal regions authorized by the President, and many major activities have been delegated to the field.

The Labor Department decentralization extends beyond Department relations with field offices and local governments involved with its own labor-related activities. As do the sub-agencies of all the major Cabinet departments, the Labor Department also cooperates at the local level. When there has been interaction between Labor and HEW in education and welfare, the actual work has been done by the state vocational agencies, the state welfare agencies, and the state employment services. A Federal Assistance Review Program (FAR) has a broad vision of government providing a total integrated service rather than a disjointed series of services by particular agencies and bureaus. "The Department of Labor and its sub-agencies," a departmental report comments, "conceive of their roles to be a part of a total Federal, State and local government service system."

The U.S. federal government is the biggest and most complicated business in the world. It is almost impossible to catalogue all its activities spread among a dozen Cabinet departments, more than two score major independent agencies, and a multitude of other bureaus, boards, commissions, and committees.*

---

* This book is part of the series by Praeger Publishers, the "Praeger Library of U.S. Government Departments and Agencies," which currently

Yet there is a unity in these diverse agencies. These government organizations are no more independent of each other than parts of the body. Aesop tells a fable of former days, "when all a man's limbs did not work together as amicably as they do now, but each had a will and a way of its own." So they conspired together to deprive the belly of its food. "Ere long, they all began, one by one, to fail and flag, and the whole body to pine away. Then the members were convinced that . . . they must work together, each in his proper sphere, for the common good of all."

So too, the federal government is made up of many parts bound to each other in a unified whole with the shared purpose of serving the nation, and the Department of Labor takes its place—one of the parts striving for the "common good."

---

includes nearly forty books. While books in the series touch on most of the highlights and many details about U.S. Government departments and agencies, even such an extensive series cannot fully cover the entire web of federal organizations and activities.

XII

Relations with the Public

The Constituency of the Department of Labor

One of the most intriguing questions concerning the Department of Labor is: Whom does the Department represent? There are many approaches to this puzzle, depending on which historical period is involved and who is answering the question. One recent Secretary of Labor observed that the Department has four chief clients: organized labor, unorganized labor and the working poor, minority workers, and the business community. Undoubtedly, the most important, difficult, and ambivalent relationship of all is that of the Department with organized labor and the labor movement in the United States.

RELATIONS WITH ORGANIZED LABOR

The Department of Labor was created by the American labor movement. The National Labor Union in the 1860's and the Knights of Labor in the 1880's were its champions. Finally, in 1913, the American Federation of Labor (AFL) lobbied through Congress the bill creating the Department of Labor for the purpose of serving the interests of working men and women. And, when it seemed that President William Howard Taft might veto the bill, AFL President Samuel Gompers pleaded successfully with the President for the new Department, which would serve as a voice of labor. Gompers was the midwife at its difficult birth.

In 1913, the inherent dangers of the theory that the Department of Labor should be the "voice of labor" were evident. No one could have possibly been a worse prophet than Congressman William Sulzer, the sponsor of the bill creating the Department, when he said, "My bill . . . excites no opposition from any source. . . . Give labor this boon and the 'labor question' will be reduced to the minimum."

In fact, from the beginning the Department of Labor aroused a hurricane of opposition. Shortly after it was established, one newspaper called it "only the tail of the Federation of Labor kite." Most employers during strikes deliberately avoided mediation by the Department. Some newspapers denounced William B. Wilson, first Secretary of Labor, as an anarchist and a dangerous agitator when the Department, during a copper strike in Michigan, published figures that showed that the Calumet and Hecla Mining Company had made huge profits but refused to bargain in good faith with its workers or to accept mediation through the Department. In a murderous strike in 1913 and 1914, the Colorado Fuel and Iron Company rejected the Department's effort at peaceful conciliation, because behind "the soft voice of Secretary Wilson" was the "hand of Esau." Coal mine operators told the President of the United States that men selected by the Secretary of Labor to investigate the strike would be "partisans of the men who made necessary the presence of federal troops in the strike district."

The antagonism of employers against the Department of Labor threatened its destruction shortly after President Warren G. Harding was elected. Although the Department survived, it became largely impotent. Herbert Hoover, as Secretary of Commerce, had far more influence than Harding's

Secretary of Labor James J. Davis in formulating federal labor policy.

A good example of the crucifixion of a Department of Labor oriented toward the labor movement came during the conservative Eightieth Congress in 1946, when many congressmen opposed the programs of the Department in any shape, manner, or form. As Ewan Clague, then commissioner of Labor Statistics, explained, employers distrusted both the Secretary of Labor and the Conciliation Service. Frank Keefe, chairman of the House Appropriations Committee, attacked Edgar Warren, head of the Service, writing on the margin of his copy of the budget, next to the listing of the Conciliation Service, "Warren is a pinko." When President Truman's Secretary of Labor Lewis Schwellenbach valiantly tried to defend Warren, a congressman told him that the Appropriations Committee was "going to cut the heart out of the Department."

And, indeed, the Eightieth Congress denuded the Department of Labor, leaving it like a plucked chicken.* Although the Eightieth Congress was particularly harsh, during most of the first four decades of the Department's history, its close relationship to the labor movement made it a shining target whenever a conservative administration came into power.

The Department of Labor and the Public Interest

The period from 1953 to 1972 saw the transition of the Department of Labor from a labor-clientele Department to a public interest Department dealing with labor and manpower

---

* Congress began by removing the Conciliation Service—a function that had been placed in the original Department of Labor in 1913—from the Department. Congressman Keefe also tried to cut out entirely the $300,000 budget of the Women's Bureau. But the Bureau was saved when "irate women" raised a "hullabaloo." The Speaker of the House told Keefe, "Damn it, Frank, are you trying to ruin the Republican Party for $300,000?" The Bureau of Labor Statistics (BLS), which was the largest component of the Department, was not so fortunate. Keefe told Commissioner Clague, "We've got statistics running out of our ears. . . . Let's get rid of them." The BLS budget was cut by 40 per cent, and 700 of its 1,700 employees were fired on short notice.

functions. However, it was not a planned transition. In 1953, after only eight months in office, Secretary of Labor Martin Durkin, former president of the Plumbers and Pipefitters union, resigned when the Eisenhower Administration failed to fight for amendment of what he considered the "slave-labor" Taft-Hartley bill.

Durkin's resignation left the Eisenhower Administration in a quandary. It had to appoint a new Secretary in a hurry, and any union leader who would have taken the job would have been attacked as a traitor to the union cause. The Republicans turned to James P. Mitchell, who had known Dwight Eisenhower during World War II, had a good record as a manpower expert for the armed forces, and had been personnel administrator for a large corporation. Consistent with his background, Mitchell followed a policy that viewed the Department of Labor as nonpartisan.

The succeeding Secretaries between 1961 and 1972 continued to pay tribute to the philosophy of nonpartisanship. Of these, Arthur Goldberg, who became Secretary of Labor before he was promoted to the position of Supreme Court Justice, had been the closest to the labor movement, having been a successful union lawyer. But he told the Senate committee that confirmed his appointment, "I can no longer speak in association with or for the labor movement." Although conceding that he could not "brainwash" himself from previous associations, Goldberg assured Congress of his firm resolve to serve the public interest in as objective a manner as any human being could do. As an example of his severing of all ties with unions, he gave up a handsome lifetime pension from the Steelworkers' Union.

Secretary Willard Wirtz also operated on the principle that the government departments were not administered on a special interest basis and that the Department of Labor was no longer a class department. The things that unite labor and management, he said, had become more important than those that divided them.

Because most unions had attacked Republican Presidential candidate Richard Nixon in the election campaign of 1968, they had misgivings about Nixon's choice of Secretary of Labor, George Shultz, a dean from the Graduate Business School of the University of Chicago. But AFL-CIO president George Meany found Shultz "a cut above the average professor," and the two men developed a close working association. Here and there a ripple of controversy disturbed an otherwise calm relationship, but in a general way Shultz won acceptance from both business and labor and seemed to prove the effectiveness of a nonpartisan Department.

The Department of Labor was beginning to overcome its reputation as a biased prolabor agency. Its new role enabled it to take on responsibilities in manpower training, occupational safety and health, and other areas of activity not so controversial as labor-management relations. The Department prospered as a public interest agency and achieved, during the years after 1953, a growth and influence that a generation earlier had seemed unattainable.

Flaws in the Public Interest Theory

The fairly recent success of the Department of Labor as a nonpartisan department has been explained by the fact that economic class distinctions in America have become blurred. As a consequence, in spite of occasional violence, strikes today are tame and civilized affairs when compared to the savage barbarity of earlier industrial conflicts. To a large extent, labor is no longer a "have not" class, and workers are as much interested in defending the Establishment as in fighting it. Several Secretaries of Labor have told union leaders that the original mandate "to foster, promote, and develop the welfare of the wage earners of the United States" can be better achieved through a nonpartisan than through a partisan department.

However, workers still have some special economic interests to defend. Unions are concerned with the administration of the

Landrum-Griffin Act, which deals with union government. They are opposed to Section 14b of the National Labor Relations Act, which bars the closed shop, as well as Section 8b, which prohibits secondary boycotts, which often hurt innocent third parties. The construction trade unions, in particular, are sensitive to the Davis-Bacon Act, under which the Department of Labor often makes the union rate the prevailing wage that must be paid on government and government-assisted construction. Unions also fight hard for the right of strikers to receive unemployment insurance, and defend when appropriate their eligibility to benefit from government relief and welfare programs. And most labor leaders breathe fire when compulsory arbitration is proposed, even when it is given such a euphemistic name as "final offer selection" or "mediation to finality."

Among the most controversial labor issues to face any Secretary of Labor, or for that matter any President of the United States, is the issue of wage and price controls. Although primarily a weapon against inflation, controls also redistribute income and raise the vital question of who gets how much. Labor grudgingly submitted to controls during the national crisis in World War II, though the development of fringe benefits eased the pain. During the Korean War, labor leaders charged that a wage freeze was "unfair, unworkable, unjust." William Green, aging president of the AFL, virtually got a new lease on life from his exhilarating effort to fight controls. In the 1960's, when reporters asked AFL-CIO president George Meany about one aspect of wage stabilization, he retorted, "There's ladies present." Walter Reuther, president of the United Auto Workers, was not so restrained when, allegedly, he gleefully told President Lyndon Johnson that the Chrysler auto strike had "knocked the ———" out of the wage-price guidelines. And on August 19, 1971, James Hodgson accompanied Presidential emissary George Shultz to a meeting of the Executive Council of the AFL-CIO where Shultz tried to explain the freeze on wages. One union president told Shultz, "When you take your ass out of here, get measured for a pair of tin pants, because you are going to need them."

On many matters vital to labor, the labor movement would rather have a Department of Labor that acts as the voice of labor rather than a so-called public interest department. A sad and dramatic case can be made that the Department of Labor faces a cruel paradox. A prolabor department runs the risk of crippling attacks by conservative employers and legislators. But a nonpartisan department might lose its major client —labor. The Department seems to be in the unenviable position of being damned if it is partisan and damned if it is nonpartisan.

The Lessons of History

Fortunately for the Department of Labor, facts do not always fit such neat theories. The question has often been posed: Which is better—a public interest department or a client-oriented department with a Secretary chosen from the ranks of labor? The answer provided by history is "It depends."

There have been times in American history, ranging back to the period of the first Bureau of Labor Statistics in Massachusetts, when government labor agencies were brutally manhandled because of their labor ties. During other periods, such as World War I, the labor union credentials of the Secretary of Labor proved to be a tower of strength in rallying labor behind national goals. Similarly there were occasions when the Secretaries of Labor from outside the labor movement achieved great success, particularly during the period from 1953 to 1970. Conversely, there were instances when lack of sufficient labor support proved disastrous. Recently, Secretary of Labor James Hodgson worked hard "to play it down the middle," but the alienation of the president of the AFL-CIO proved to be his undoing. (See page 89.)

Such apparently contradictory historical examples do not mean that relations with the labor movement are not important. They indicate that there are also other factors, such as the personal ability and vigor of the Secretary and his staff, as well as the extent of harmonious relations with the President, with Congress, and with opinion-shaping media. In addition, factors beyond control—ranging from sheer chance to the social, political, and economic climate—have an important bearing. Predicting the success or the failure of a Secretary of Labor chiefly on the basis of whether or not he comes from the ranks of labor is nonsense.

Another doctrine with a kernel of truth that has been very much exaggerated is that a Secretary from the ranks of organized labor is a partisan of organized labor. It is true that a background in the labor movement creates a knowledge and understanding of the needs and the aspirations of working people. But many observers feel that all Secretaries of Labor, whether union officials, social workers, college professors, lawyers, or businessmen, have sought impartiality. The first Secretary of Labor, who had spent his whole life fighting for labor causes, made it clear in his first annual report that

> The great guiding purpose . . . that should govern the Department at every turn and . . . be understood and acquiesced [in] by everybody—is the . . . promotion of the welfare of the wage earners of the United States.
>
> In the execution of that purpose, the element of *fairness* to every interest is of equal importance, and the Department has in fact made fairness between wage earner and wage earner, between wage earner and employer, between employer and employer, and between each and the public as a whole the supreme motive and purpose of its activities.

Other Secretaries of Labor have, in different words, echoed and re-echoed their determination to be fair.

Recent History

President Nixon nominated Peter J. Brennan, president of the New York Building Trades Council, to become the thirteenth Secretary of Labor, for the term starting in 1973.

Peter Brennan, like William Wilson, the first Secretary of Labor, has spent his life working with labor causes. And, just as AFL president Samuel Gompers cleared the choice of William Wilson as the first Secretary of Labor, so the selection of Brennan was cleared with AFL-CIO president George Meany and with other prominent labor leaders. Brennan announced that as Secretary of Labor he would fight for labor's rights and would not be "forsaking the worker." However, Brennan's clearest public position taken prior to his appointment, which indicated support of the President's policies on U.S. extrication from the Vietnam war, demonstrates an approach with concern for national public interest.

President Nixon has reversed the recent trend of appointing a Secretary of Labor from outside the labor movement. The President's choice in 1972 of a Secretary of Labor from the ranks of labor is in line with the goal of the labor movement since the Civil War.

Relations with Unorganized Labor and the Working Poor

In the first annual report of the Department of Labor, Secretary William B. Wilson observed that there was no "implication that the wage earners in whose behalf this Department was created consist of such only as are associated together in labor unions." The Department, he said, was established in the interest of all workers. "The act of its creation," he specifically explained, was moreover "not only as a law for promoting the welfare of the wage earners of the United States" but also a "command for doing so in harmony with the welfare of all industrial classes."

In the United States, workers organized in labor unions have always been a relatively small part of the labor force. In 1913, when the Department was established, only 7 to 8 per cent of the labor force was unionized. The Depression in the 1930's wreaked such havoc with unions that, by 1933, the ratio had declined to about 5 or 6 per cent. Even after the great organization drives and the growth during the later 1930's and the period of World War II, only about one-quarter of the working population belonged to unions.

Although a substantial portion of the unorganized labor force belongs to better-paid professional and white-collar groups, the unorganized also include most of the disadvantaged workers—the working poor, the "forgotten" men and women at the bottom of the economic pyramid. A major obstacle in providing for the welfare of these unorganized workers is the very fact that they are unorganized. They have few spokesmen to express their desires. In a general way, organized labor voices some of the aspirations of the unorganized, and, to a surprising degree, unions in the past have fought for, and today continue to fight for, programs from which union members gain only indirectly. But, in large measure, the disadvantaged among unorganized labor depend on the moral sensitivity of society as a whole and the public service orientation of government agencies. One of those agencies, the Department of Labor, since its establishment, has in many ways provided services for disadvantaged workers.

One of the periods of greatest service by the Department to the unorganized and the working poor occurred during the Great Depression of the 1930's. The greatest part of the departmental effort at that time was aimed at providing minimum standards for wages, hours, and working conditions. The goals established for workers included steady work in private enterprise and, when such work was not available, emergency employment on public projects. The Department promoted Social Security to meet the needs of workers incapacitated by accidents, old age, or lack of employment opportunity.

Again in the 1960's, the Department was on the firing line in the War on Poverty. Because most union members are well above the poverty level, the major beneficiaries were the working poor, who were generally unorganized. The manpower development and training programs (see Chapter VI) had as their chief objectives raising the skills of disadvantaged workers and placing them in jobs where they could become economically self-sufficient members of American society.

Following the initial thrust of the antipoverty programs, the Nixon Administration has continued to encourage departmental provision of a broad range of services for the unorganized and disadvantaged workers. These include classroom training in remedial education and occupational skills, on-the-job training, short-term employment and other job opportunities for special age groups and the temporarily unemployed, and a transitional Public Employment Program (PEP). (See Chapter VI.) The services have as their goal helping able-bodied people to become self-supporting. Along with this direct aid to unorganized workers, the federal government is emphasizing state and community involvement in their problems so that solutions can be tailored to local needs.

Relations with Minorities

An appropriate slogan summarizing the history of Department of Labor relations with minority workers might be "Nothing ethical is impossible." Employment discrimination against minorities was so great in the past that equal opportunity seemed an impossible dream. Nevertheless, the Department undertook what it could to make the dream a reality.

In the Interest of Black Workers

The Department of Labor has made bringing blacks into the mainstream of American economic life one of its primary goals. The northward trek of blacks, which began at the time of World War I, has continued, and, by the 1970's, the ratio of blacks in the South had declined from 90 per cent of the country's black population to about 50 per cent. Because the destinations of most migrants have been the central neighborhoods of large metropolitan areas, blacks have increasingly become nonagricultural workers. However, though conditions are incomparably better than they were at the turn of the century,* blacks are still concentrated at the lower level of the occupational scale. Nearly 40 per cent of black men work as laborers or janitors or in other low-level occupations, while 30 per cent of employed black women are in unskilled and menial occupations.

Some of these statistics can be explained by a gap in educational opportunity. Correspondingly, the improved situation of blacks is partly accounted for by the rising level of their educational background. If education were the only explanation of differences in economic status, it would be only a matter of time before equality could be achieved. However, the conclusion of some careful students is that some of the differences are caused by factors that are more difficult to overcome. One of them is discrimination.

Equal employment opportunity is now one of the major objectives of the federal government in the United States. It is easier, however, to enunciate such a principle than to carry out effective programs for its implementation. Once, forward-

---

* The condition of black workers was particularly pathetic before World War I, when about 90 per cent of the black population lived in the South. An example of the peonage of black agricultural laborers is provided by an account from the autobiography of a black farm worker in Georgia printed in a weekly magazine, *The Independent,* in 1904:

> When I was about ten years old my uncle hired me out to Captain
> ———. I had already learned to plow, and was also a good hand at picking cotton. . . . I was put to work on the farm, with some twenty or thirty other negroes [sic]. . . . The men got $3 a week and the women $2. . . . Unknown to my uncle or the Captain I went off to a neighboring plantation and hired myself out to another man. The new landlord agreed to give me forty cents a day and furnish me one meal. . . . The Captain came over to the new place. . . . I heard my new boss say: "I beg your pardon, Captain. I didn't know this nigger was bound to you, ..." So I was carried back to the Captain's. That night he made me strip off my clothing down to my waist, had me tied to a tree in his backyard, ordered his foreman to give me thirty lashes with a buggy whip across my bare back, and stood by until it was done. . . . When I reached twenty-one the Captain told me I was a free man, but he urged me to stay . . . I signed a contract—that is, I made my mark— for one year. The Captain was to give me $3.50 a week, and furnish me . . . a one room log cabin similar to those used by his other laborers.

looking people advocated "color blindness" or merely not paying attention to a person's race when hiring. "Quota" was a dirty word because it meant a gate that shut out deserving potential employees. But discrimination was too deeply rooted to be eradicated without quotas. And quotas, like gates, can let people in as well as keep them out.

However, in a nation dedicated to the principle of democracy of opportunity and an aristocracy of merit, hiring quotas, whether positive or negative, create problems—such as reverse discrimination or hiring on the basis of race or religion instead of ability.

In this intricate sociological and economic web, the Department of Labor is working with creative concepts of "affirmative action plans," manning tables, good-faith efforts, and hiring goals, which are not based on racial quotas, and which, it is hoped, will not substitute one injustice for another. (The specific efforts of the Department in the struggle for equal opportunity, both in its hiring of its own staff and in its monitoring of hiring practices of government contractors through the Office of Federal Contract Compliance, are described in greater detail in Chapter X.)

Maximum Feasible Participation

One of the controversial questions concerning programs for minorities and the poor has been: How much should the disadvantaged participate in managing the programs' activities? In the 1960's, the belief was widespread that, if minorities and the poor participated in the planning and running of programs allegedly in their behalf, they would be more effective in dealing with their counterparts than would bourgeois bureaucrats and social workers. The Economic Opportunity Act of 1964 embraced this belief when it provided for "maximum feasible participation" by recipient groups.

The idea of downtrodden people participating in activities shaping their destinies was certainly not new. The Department of Labor during World War I brought in black leaders to help bring their people into war production. During the 1930's, Secretary of Labor Frances Perkins had on her staff a black adviser who sought to give blacks a chance at high-level as well as low-level jobs. Under the manpower programs of the 1960's, the Department worked with many ethnic, religious, and racial groups through representatives of Mexican-American groups, American Indian agencies, and especially leaders in black communities. By such means, the programs could reach minorities and the poor more effectively than through more conventional government channels.

SER and the OIC are two of many examples of efforts at "participatory democracy" in the Department's manpower-training programs. "SER," an acronym for the words "Service," "Employment," and "Redevelopment," forms the Spanish verb "to be." The program deals with poor Mexican Americans whose wretched condition has in many cases been caused by poor education, difficulty with the English language, discrimination, or lack of job skills. Many Mexican Americans are unemployed or in low-paid jobs. Two large organizations of Spanish-speaking Americans, the American G.I. Forum and the League of United Latin American Citizens, operate SER. Its education, training, and job-placement programs are supported through a Department of Labor contract. SER helps Mexican Americans in their efforts "to be" part of the economic mainstream.

"OIC" stands for the Opportunities Industrialization Centers, which were developed by Leon Sullivan, a Baptist pastor in Philadelphia, who eloquently persuaded many blacks that their economic salvation lay in self-help. The OIC's motto is "We Help Ourselves." Applicants accepted for training are *not* paid allowances as are trainees in many other manpower programs. Much of the administration and training is done by volunteers, and the community itself raises some of the money needed for the program. However, the financial burden is too great to be supported entirely by voluntary contributions, and the federal government aids leaders, most of whom are black.

Trainees not only learn skills such as electronics, auto repair, secretarial work, and so on, but they also take courses in black history, good grooming, and a variety of other subjects designed to develop self-respect and confidence. Such self-help is aimed at trainees who are motivated by their desire to make their own way.

The most visible programs in which minorities and the poor have participated in planning and management were directed by the Office of Economic Opportunity (OEO) rather than the Department of Labor. The Department had advocated an attack on poverty through massive work and training programs, but Presidents John F. Kennedy and Lyndon B. Johnson decided on more broadly based programs including health, education, legal services, and other activities. Moreover, the Presidents thought that a new agency might not be as inhibited in handling pioneering and innovative activities as old-line agencies such as the Department of Labor. However, there were important manpower components within the OEO with which the Department was inextricably involved.

Much of the work of the OEO was performed through nearly five hundred Community Action Programs (CAP's), which were agencies that broadly represented the community and mobilized resources to attack poverty. There was a CAP in every one of the fifty largest cities in the nation. While it is impossible to make a general statement applicable to all CAP's, by and large, these programs illustrate the adage that the road to hell is paved with good intentions.

In some areas, established politicians were able to win control of the program. In other areas, antipoverty warriors tried to organize the poor into instruments with which to attack the social system and create new institutions. In several CAP's, racial conflict ensued as blacks tried to oust whites from key positions. And, when some blacks made it to the top, they, in turn, were denounced by other blacks for selling out to the white power structure.

Two of the most serious defects of the CAP's were overselling and underperforming. Even well-trained and experienced managers have difficulty in handling big organizations and large sums of money. Generally, slum dwellers, unskilled workers, and people who live in poverty do not have ready-made management skills. Here and there a project was successful, but failures and financial scandals were numerous and monumental. In Syracuse, New York, for example, black leaders ran a Crusade for Opportunity, which spent $7 million out of their $8 million budget for salaries. Federal aid to the poor too often meant more money for new middle-class black bureaucrats who became insiders in the new system.

Daniel Patrick Moynihan, who during part of this period was an assistant secretary of Labor and was concerned with the problem of poverty, was dismayed at the failure of the CAP's. He observed, in a book appropriately called *Maximum Feasible Misunderstanding,* "At the risk of oversimplification, it might be said that the CAP's most closely controlled by City Hall were disappointing, and that the ones most antagonistic were destroyed."

The idea that the poor and minorities must be motivated through participation in planning, policy, and operating programs for their benefit has lost some of its attractiveness. There is certainly validity in allowing people to have some voice in activities designed for them, but, in Moynihan's words, "We may discover to our sorrow that 'participatory democracy' can mean the end of both participation and democracy."

The Nixon Administration has cut back many social programs in which minorities and the poor participated in management and operations. The President believes that in the past too much money was wasted. The Department of Labor is therefore funneling funds to communities, which will have more to say as to where, when, and how federal manpower funds will be used.

In theory at least, communities should spend manpower money more efficiently, because they are more familiar with local conditions. Funds that normally went to the Urban League, the OIC, and SER and for manpower aspects of

CAP's are being given in block grants to mayors, who allocate money for specific local manpower needs. This does not necessarily mean that minorities and the poor will have no influence on how the money is spent, but it does mean that they will have to work through locally elected officials in making their claims.

RELATIONS WITH BUSINESS

Time and again throughout its history, the Department of Labor has tried to overcome the antipathy of the business community by insisting that the welfare of wage earners can be fostered in such a way that the prosperity of employers is safeguarded. It is the "duty of the department," the first annual report noted, to develop friendly relations "with employers and their organizations to the extent to which they themselves permit." One of the strongest efforts to preach the harmony of interests came during the 1920's. "Employer and employee are like a lock and a key," sermonized Secretary of Labor James J. Davis. One is useless without the other. "If one gains, both must gain; if one loses, both must lose; if one dies, both must die."

Roger W. Babson, famed as a financial adviser, was also a brilliant publicist for the Department during its early days. He glorified what the Department can do for the business community. It can provide information on the cost of accidents and how to prevent them, and it can deter strikes by showing how expensive they are. And, "if some agitator in your city is making trouble in your plant," Babson wrote, in nine cases out of ten, the Department of Labor can "pull off" the troublemaker. Babson's most important argument, however, was that, of all public agencies, the Department of Labor can be most useful in flattening out business cycles.

This probusiness position, created partly as an antidote to charges of a prolabor bias, was toned down in later periods. The Department emphasized impartiality in controversial matters and pointed to the professional services it might provide for business. Apprenticeship could make available a better supply of skilled workers, the Employment Service could help put the right person in the right job, and the Bureau of Labor Statistics (BLS) could provide useful and objective statistical information.

An incident in 1948 illustrates the reliance of business on some of these BLS statistics. An economy-minded Congress had sharply cut the BLS budget in 1947 and was readying another crippling cut for 1948. On May 24, 1948, General Motors signed a contract with the United Auto Workers, which included a historic "escalator" clause, a pioneering way of adjusting wages to increases in the BLS Consumer Price Index. Commissioner of Labor Statistics Ewan Clague confided in an oral historical interview that one of his "senator friends—and I never knew quite who—. . . got hold of General Motors and sent word, 'Look, you'll have to protect the budget of this bureau because you are basing your industrial relations for the next two years on this thing.' " When the appropriation went to a House-Senate conference committee, the cut was rescinded. Clague observed, "I'm sure it was business pressure that brought that about, because that's the only thing that would have influenced these men, the pressure from business. So, the General Motors contract saved us that last cut, which would, of course, have wrecked the statistical work of the Bureau."

During the 1960's and early 1970's, the Department developed working relations with the business community in many manpower-training programs. It enlisted the support of major corporations like International Telephone and Telegraph Company and Litton Industries, which were given contracts to run large residential Job Corps camps. In a somewhat different effort that involved on-the-job training, the Department of Labor worked with the National Alliance of Businessmen on the JOBS (Job Opportunities in the Business Sector) program. Nation's Business, in September, 1970, applauded the development of labor-business cooperation and quoted Secretary of Labor Hodgson as saying, "We have got to realize that seven out of every ten jobs in the country are in private industry." Without business cooperation, the Secretary said, we would be "swimming upstream with every single activity."

Both business and government at that time were captivated by a fascinating dream of combining social idealism and business profit by placing the hard-core unemployed in jobs and thus reducing unemployment. Unfortunately, many manpower programs were oversold by their proponents. The result has been disillusionment and a counterattack that threatens to dismantle the entire JOBS program. It is true that there have been discouraging failures, but there have also been successes. The destruction of both the good with the bad in the program might be tantamount to "throwing out the baby with the bathwater." There is still a chance that the government-business partnership in manpower programs may contribute to improving the quality of American economic life.

Repeated efforts of cooperation notwithstanding, many employers remain hostile to the Department of Labor. For example, Secretary of Labor James P. Mitchell, who had a corporate as well as a government background, was assailed by some business organizations as a captive of labor. Similarly, though Secretary Hodgson in the early 1970's was attacked by labor for leading a *Putsch* with Department of Labor policymakers whose names read like a *Who's Who in Business,* the Department still failed to gain the confidence of most businessmen.

Some businessmen have attacked the Department's administration of the Occupational Safety and Health Act. (See Chapter VIII.) Although everyone favors safety, small businessmen have been critical of complicated regulations and have protested that the cost of required safety equipment is too high. Minimum-wage programs have come under fire from business representatives who claim that the problem of exploited workers has largely disappeared and that a high minimum-wage level prices many young and unskilled workers out of the market. These workers, instead of receiving low wages, are unemployed and receive no wages at all. Budget-minded businessmen have criticized what they call excessive government spending on manpower programs for contributing to inflation. They select "horror stories," which are examples of mistakes and are not typical. The East Harlem, New York, Concentrated Employment Program, for example, had a goal of training 1,400 enrollees but after mismanagement and dropouts only 6 people were actually placed in jobs.

Despite the difficulties, many observers feel that the Department of Labor has generally struggled to follow an even-handed policy. Unfortunately, its image as a partisan of labor has gotten in the way of good relations with the business community. Although informed businessmen know better, the "gut reaction" of many employers is that the Department of Labor is inherently against business.

THE DEPARTMENT'S CONSTITUENCY

The concept of a "public" or a "constituency" of a department of labor lends itself better to societies with more rigid class lines than to the United States, where the goal is an open and upwardly mobile society in which yesterday's unskilled laborer may be today's technician and tomorrow's professional or employer. Relations with constituencies such as organized workers, the working poor, minority workers, or business interests can make departmental administration direct and meaningful, particularly when buttressed by tradition. However, a government agency should not have as its purpose administrative convenience, nor should it be an immutable institution.

The Department of Labor has a tradition of service to its publics that is worth preserving. Yet the challenge of its national role lies in harmonizing the interests of the special groups with which the Department has relations with the interests of American society as a whole. Promotion of the welfare of workers, the first Secretary of Labor noted in 1913, must be "in harmony with the welfare of all . . . legitimate interests."

XIII

The Department and International Labor

A natural question is: Why should the Department of Labor be involved in foreign affairs? Is not this the realm of the Department of State, the Agency for International Development (AID), and other foreign policy and operations agencies of the government? However, the growing importance of manpower in the economic life of foreign countries is reflected in international programs of concern to the Department of Labor.

The Department exerts an influence on labor and manpower aspects of American diplomacy in a variety of ways. It is intimately involved in U.S. participation in international organizations such as the Organization for Economic Cooperation and Development (OECD) and a number of organizations associated with the United Nations. Perhaps the Department's most important international role arises from U.S. affiliation with the International Labor Organization, which fosters world progress by promoting social and economic justice. In addition, the Department sponsors programs of technical assistance to developing countries by providing training in the United States in labor administration for citizens of those countries and by sending American labor experts overseas to guide their labor ministries. The Department also helps to select labor attachés for American embassies abroad and works with the Department of State to familiarize personnel in American embassies and consular offices with manpower problems. In recent years, the Department of Labor has become involved with the labor aspects of U.S. foreign trade policy. In this connection, it helps American workers who lose their jobs because of foreign competition.

The Department of Labor's international work is focused in the International Labor Affairs Bureau (ILAB), which evolved from a high-level Office of International Labor Affairs created in 1947, when U.S. involvement in world affairs was near its high-water mark. The Bureau is now headed by a deputy under secretary—an important position, but not as prestigious as that of former directors of the Bureau, who were assistant secretaries appointed by the President. Much of ILAB's work involves coordination and liaison with AID, whose funds have been cut in recent years so that it now concentrates on fewer programs in fewer countries. The corresponding reduction in ILAB's work in that area has been offset by an expanded role in the labor aspects of international trade.

Government labor officials in the United States were internationally minded even before there was a Department of Labor. The first state labor agency in the United States was the Massachusetts Bureau of Labor Statistics established in 1869. (See Chapter I.) Its first report compared foreign and American labor conditions. The first federal labor agency was the Bureau of Labor in the Department of Interior, established in 1884. Its first annual report studied industrial depressions in the United States, Great Britain, France, Belgium, and Germany. When the Department of Labor was created (without Cabinet status) in 1888, its commissioner was authorized to obtain information "from different foreign nations." In 1893, he reviewed social insurance and workmen's compensation in Europe. In 1900, the commissioner of Labor published a monumental study of wages in various occupations in the United States and in about a hundred foreign countries, colonies, and provinces. The law establishing the Department of Labor in 1913 provided for continuing these international functions.

THE INTERNATIONAL LABOR ORGANIZATION

With the rise of the United States to the status of a world power after World War I, it seemed that American labor would become a force in international labor affairs. Samuel Gompers, the nation's leading trade-unionist, was a member of the U.S. peace delegation at Paris and chairman of a special treaty group that drafted the constitution of the new International Labor Organization (ILO), with the purpose of improving the lives of working people all over the world. The first meeting of the ILO was held in Washington, D.C., on October 29, 1919. The U.S. Secretary of Labor, William B. Wilson, presided.

Then, in a wave of reaction, the United States turned its back on international cooperation. The Senate rejected membership in the League of Nations, and the American people, in the election of 1920, endorsed the repudiation. Because the ILO, in the minds of most Americans, was tied to the League, the Department of Labor stopped participating in the ILO formally, though its officials in the 1920's looked in on meetings in an entirely personal capacity.

When Frances Perkins became Secretary of Labor in 1933, she convinced President Franklin Roosevelt that the United States could join the ILO without getting involved in the League of Nations. As a result of her lobbying, Congress in 1934 approved American participation in the ILO.

The United States cooperated closely with the organization. Two Americans have been director-general. One of these, former U.S. Under Secretary of Labor David A. Morse, directed the ILO for twenty-one years, from 1948 to 1969.

Several ILO conferences were held in the United States. Secretaries of Labor have been strong supporters of the organization, and, in recent years, the United States has paid for about one-fourth of its budget, which in the early 1970's ran to about $30 million a year.

Membership in the ILO has grown from 45 to more than 120 nations. These nations cooperate to achieve goals chiefly in three ways: agreement on international standards, conduct of a program of research and publications, and provision of technical assistance.

Labor standards are developed at international conferences and are adopted as conventions or recommendations. Conventions bind those governments that ratify them; recommendations guide governments in preparing their own laws or programs. These standards cover subjects such as the minimum age for underground work, employment of women with families, accommodations for fishing crews, improvement of conditions for tenant farmers and sharecroppers, and pensions for the old or infirm. It may seem curious that the United States has ratified only a few of the approximately 130 conventions adopted by the ILO, though its own standards are generally higher than ILO minimums. The reason is that, in the American federal-state system of government, conventions often deal with subjects reserved to the jurisdiction of the states. The fear lingers that ratification of conventions of the ILO may challenge the sovereignty of the individual states.

The ILO is among the most important sources of world labor data. It gathers information from all parts of the planet. Its factual reports are the foundation that supports its other activities.

The fastest-growing activity of the ILO is its far-flung technical assistance. When the United States adopted Social Security, its social legislation was lagging behind many nations of the world, so foreign experts from the ILO helped set up the American system. But the bulk of assistance now flows from technically advanced to poorer nations, many of which have joined the ILO since World War II. ILO projects in this field range from industrial and vocational training in India and Morocco to starting rural cooperatives in Bolivia and Afghanistan. Programs of this type give meaning to passionate devotion to human rights and better living standards throughout the world.

One reason why the ILO has survived longer than any other body set up by the World War I peace treaty may be its tripartite organization. The ILO from the first was structured into three divisions: one representing employers, one representing workers, and one representing governments. The fact that the three interest groups involved are equally represented has been a source of strength, but it has also been a source of weakness. As far back as 1927, an effort was made in the ILO to throw out Italian delegates on the ground that Fascist trade unions could not represent workers and had no place in a body with bona fide trade union representatives. Similar challenges rang through ILO conferences in many subsequent years, including 1972, when some opposition to seating Greek delegates developed. When the Soviet Union joined the ILO in 1954, some ILO delegates were offended by the idea of "free" worker and "free" employer representatives from communistic countries.

A new crisis emerged in the early 1970's. The last straw was appointment by a new director-general of the ILO of a Russian as one of his assistant directors. The AFL-CIO had complained for many years that the ILO appeased the Communists by the way it handled charges of forced labor in the Soviet Union and by accepting the credentials of state-dominated unions and employer associations as genuinely representative of labor and private management. George Meany, head of the AFL-CIO, charged that a Soviet assistant director could turn hundreds of ILO employees into Communist agents. He proved astonishingly effective in getting through Congress a motion to kill the American financial contribution to the ILO for the last half of 1970.

For a while, the role of the United States in the ILO hung in the balance. The Secretaries of State, Labor, and Commerce studied proposed courses of action. President Richard Nixon then recommended that the United States pay its dues but adopt specific objectives for the ILO that, if not reasonably achieved, would be cause for later withdrawal from the organization.

The reasons for remaining in the ILO are strong. Withdrawal would leave a clear field for the Soviet Union to promote its ends in the organization without the countervailing effect of American participation; it would cost the United States friends in many countries; it could start a process of undermining the entire United Nations system; and it would mean the loss of an opportunity for the United States to work for the benefit of workers in the Free World.

Perhaps the counsels of conciliation are prevailing. The United States is again paying its dues, but money is not the real issue. The United States is also yielding a little on the idea of an ILO composed solely of truly tripartite national delegations, which is a desirable goal but almost impossible for countries with authoritarian forms of government. On the other hand, the United States is gaining concessions. And, if the ILO is sometimes used as a sounding board for Soviet propaganda, in a larger sense it is also a window where the Free World can display to other nations the advantages of a private-enterprise society.

THE DEPARTMENT'S OVERSEAS TECHNICAL ASSISTANCE

The Labor Department's international technical assistance program is bidirectional. It involves not only sending experts abroad to work in developing countries but also receiving labor administrators from those countries for training in the United States. The emerging countries need a variety of skills, including specialties in labor and labor-related fields.

Formerly, the Department of Labor sent experts overseas

on an *ad hoc* basis to assist in these fields. The professionals who went abroad were motivated by reasons ranging from an itch to travel to missionary zeal. Most were imbued with idealism and a desire to help less-developed nations. Yet there were problems. Some men left important jobs in the United States that were hard to fill. Others encountered language barriers or lacked the necessary technical skills. Even people with the best intentions, unless they were fully prepared for their assignments, faced obstacles.

One of the difficulties that arose in helping foreign countries solve their manpower problems stemmed from efforts to introduce American methods into countries that were not ready for them. For example, an expert on apprenticeship knew the American system, in which young men of about twenty years of age started a program of on-the-job learning with a job virtually assured when they completed their apprenticeship. When this expert was assigned to a Latin American country, he found that apprentices there were twelve to fourteen years old and went to an institute for apprentices chiefly for the stipend, the uniform, the prestige, and the free lunches. Most youngsters did not finish their courses, and, even when they did, they frequently could not find work in the field for which they had theoretically been trained. The background possessed by the U.S. expert impelled him to believe that his best contribution would consist of encouraging the local communities to adopt the U.S. system.

In order to avoid such situations, an effort was made to base project selection on feasibility studies. But problems with overseas technical assistance activities continued to occur when overseas visitors talked to American experts who, though they knew their subjects well, were naïve about conditions in the countries for which the projects were planned. The visitors and the experts carried on amiable dialogues, using the same words but meaning different things. These discussions resulted in such mix-ups as establishment of an employment service in a nonindustrialized country that had more important needs, and application of sophisticated statistical techniques in a primitive nation where most people could not even count.

To provide more realistic projects abroad and at the same time avoid disrupting programs at home, the Secretary of Labor in 1964 created the Department of Labor International Technical Assistance Corps (DOLITAC), made up of technicians who are committed to serve abroad where needed. They are professionally competent and have usually demonstrated through previous experience their ability to work in underdeveloped countries.

DOLITAC technicians have filled hundreds of assignments in many countries of the world. Sometimes things still go wrong. But DOLITAC has improved the quality of overseas assistance and has provided valuable help to many countries and peoples throughout the world.

Foreigners also learn American know-how by coming to the United States for special training. Most of the time, the U.S. Government or an international agency pays their expenses. The Bureau of Labor Statistics has long been famous throughout the world for its professionalism, and its courses have attracted many statisticians from abroad. The International Manpower Institute of ILAB serves foreign nationals by bringing to the United States professionals and administrators from developing countries involved with manpower problems. Other foreigners benefit from tailor-made training in labor standards, industrial relations, employment service operations, and so on. Classes for young workers and workers' education tours for labor leaders are also arranged.

This extensive program extends upward to the VIP's. Ministers of labor or their equivalents, other high officials, and even prime ministers of many countries visit the Department of Labor. A special office plans individual programs for such important guests. Dinners, receptions, and other courtesies are provided when appropriate. Usually, the Secretary of Labor or one of his chief assistants meets with these dignitaries.

Visitors from abroad bring back to their own countries information that may help them with their manpower and labor programs. At the same time, Department of Labor personnel deepen their understanding of international political, social, and economic conditions by contact with these visitors. American experts and foreign visitors from all social classes tend to develop a mutual understanding that benefits workers both in America and overseas.

As part of its program of encouraging economic development abroad, the Department of Labor makes a special point of assisting the development of labor ministries in Latin America. At the Inter-American Conferences of Labor Ministers held every three years, Secretaries of Labor emphasize the role of labor departments in the nation-building process. Representatives of Latin American labor ministries meet regularly with "donor" agencies for technical assistance—primarily with AID, the Department of Labor, the Inter-American Development Bank, the World Bank, and the ILO.

Labor Attachés in American Embassies

The system of maintaining labor attachés at State Department posts overseas originated during World War II and expanded during the cold war with the Soviet Union. Most American unions have vigorously supported U.S. foreign policy, and union leaders sometimes play a role in the selection of labor attachés. ILAB also participates in the State Department's system of selecting, training, and promoting labor attachés.

Because many observers believed that Communists wanted to make unions throughout the world instruments of Soviet policy, U.S. labor attachés usually cooperated closely with the anti-Communist International Confederation of Free Trade Unions in efforts to prevent achievement of that Communist objective. One critic of American international labor policy thought that labor attachés went too far in these efforts. Aside from their "legitimate labor information activities," he complained, attachés spent U.S. Government money to win supporters for anti-Communist policies in foreign lands. Classic examples of such activities, he expounded, could be found in Japan, where "elements within the right-wing labor movement are given free trips to America . . . or in the Philippines, where the U.S. Embassy from the beginning supported [labor leaders of questionable integrity simply because they favored] British-American policies."

George Meany, president of the AFL defended such arrangements on the ground that the Communists were so dangerous that anti-Communists had to be supported wherever possible. He pointed to the winning of control of trade unions by a Communist minority in Czechoslovakia:

> They tied up the city of Prague for twenty-four hours. No telephone, no bus, no radio, no hospital service, no milk, no mail service or anything else. . . . They wanted in and they got in. They only wanted one position, minister of internal security. . . . Within seven days they had the entire country.

In the bitter world of political realities, Meany looked upon labor attachés as warriors against Communist influence everywhere.

Such activities may make labor attachés, along with other State Department officials at overseas posts, targets of militant radicals. In an unusual incident in 1970, several Guatemalan rebels kidnapped the American labor attaché, took him deep into the country blindfolded and on horseback, and warned that he would be executed unless leftist prisoners were freed. Two prisoners were freed and flown to Mexico, whereupon the rebels released the attaché as promised. "It was an interesting experience," he commented, "but one I could have done without."

The life of the labor attaché is not always so adventurous.

Much of his time is taken with a round of social and other routine duties—entertaining important American visitors, talking to officials of the host government, associating with local labor leaders, gathering data, making out reports, and the like. Since anti-Communist activities of the post–World War II period have abated, labor attachés have been concentrating on positive aspects of international labor activities. The attaché is a specialist, a reporter, an adviser. He keeps the American Ambassador posted on labor and manpower developments in the area where he is stationed and forwards information to the Department of Labor and many other interested U.S. Government agencies. The Department in return helps him with a variety of problems.

The attaché also "works the other side of the street." He informs foreign governments, management, and labor officials about American developments. The attaché may advise a foreign government on how to set up a statistical system or an employment exchange, or he may talk to management on American standards of safety and health on the job, or he may explain to both unions and employers how their American counterparts deal with labor-saving devices. He "shows the flag" and endeavors to have people abroad think well of the United States.

In recent years, every assistant secretary of Labor for International Affairs has argued strongly for a better labor-attaché system, with more numerous appointments and more thorough training for the attachés in economics, labor problems, and manpower. The labor factor in foreign relations, they have asserted, used to be neglected. Foreign-assistance programs were written as if workers and future training needs were not part of the picture. The needs for good housing, good labor standards, and good labor relations were seldom considered. Only when there was trouble did the "labor factor" attract the attention it deserved. The solution to the problem, the Department of Labor insists, is more and better labor attachés at overseas posts.

LABOR AND INTERNATIONAL TRADE

A dream of many people throughout the world is that the removal of trade barriers will bring world prosperity. They believe that those nations that can provide the best products and the best services at the lowest cost will exchange them for other goods and services that other nations produce more efficiently. In this way, no partner to a trade loses and all partners in the transaction are better off.

Although a technologically advanced country such as the United States may lose some labor-intensive industries to nations with lower wage scales under such a concept, consumers gain by being able to buy cheaper goods from abroad and thus enjoy a higher standard of living. Labor as a whole also gains as it moves into capital-intensive industries, which usually pay higher wages and provide better working conditions. At the same time, emerging countries take the first steps toward industrialization and find relative wealth and happiness by exporting less sophisticated types of manufactures along with agricultural products and raw materials.

The Department of Labor traditionally has supported the policy of trade expansion along these lines. Secretary of Labor Arthur Goldberg actively lobbied for the Trade Expansion Act of 1962, which laid the groundwork for a new and expanded trade program. Goldberg argued for relaxation of restrictions against Japanese imports because, in the event of such relaxation, Japan would buy more from the United States than it sold to it. Although history has proved Goldberg to be a bad prophet, the program adopted at Goldberg's recommendation did include a safeguard mechanism designed specifically to assist American workers who were economically harmed by rising imports.

Trade Negotiations

The Department of Labor was one of several U.S. Government agencies that participated in the multifaceted international trade negotiations growing out of the Trade Expansion Act. Probably no other country had government labor officials so closely identified with the discussions. The Department was acutely aware of the impact of expanded trade on jobs and sought to protect the interest of workers in those industries most vulnerable to increased imports. The textile and shoe industries both suffer from intensive competition from low-wage countries. They employ large numbers of workers who have only moderate skills and use relatively simple equipment.

Assistance to the textile and apparel industry was one of the major programs adopted during and after the trade negotiations of the 1960's. The key was an international agreement known as the Long-Term Cotton Textile Arrangement. This arrangement, which has been renewed several times, provides for the development of trade in a way that will avoid disrupting the markets of importing countries, while at the same time allowing a gradual expansion of trade by exporting countries. United States Department of Labor officials were among the chief American negotiators of this arrangement.

Under its terms separate bilateral agreements between nations are permitted for the regulation of trade in textiles and apparel products. The United States has entered into more than thirty such agreements. Arrangements of this kind can pose delicate problems. Although on the surface they seem to involve dry statistics and technical matters, the results of negotiations may affect the economic well-being of millions of people.

For example, about 1 million Japanese workers and their families depend on the textile industry. This fact can exert considerable political pressure on the Japanese Government. On the other side, textile imports could threaten industries that provide about 10 per cent of all manufacturing jobs in the United States. Jacob Potofsky, progressive head of a clothing workers' union, protested that textile imports from low-wage countries could undermine the jobs of American workers who were paid from six to forty times as much as the pittances doled out to textile workers in the Far East. His union did not conquer sweatshops and child labor, he said, so that it could "sit idly by and see itself liquidated by imports."

Significant increases in shoe imports also cost American jobs. A tale of two towns—Iuka, Mississippi, and Malmantile, Italy—illustrates the problem. In 1955, a large American corporation built a plant in the decaying Mississippi town. The plant's 850 jobs brought a kind of prosperity. The same corporation imports shoes from Malmantile, a poor town with a population of 1,800, where nearly everyone from childhood to old age cuts, stitches, finishes, and packs shoes. Although few Iukans get more than $2 an hour, that amount is a fortune compared to wages paid at Malmantile. American shoes cost $4 a pair to make; similar Italian shoes, $2. As a result, many Iukans were laid off. When a Malmantile producer learned that the United States might cut shoe imports to protect its own workers, he said, "That can be the end of the world. Our people would starve."

With the economic well-being of people the world over at stake, trade negotiations are a way of averting a "war of the jungle." Leaders of many nations seem to agree that voluntary arrangements governing levels of trade in certain industries are a wiser alternative than an international economic conflict in which more jobs may be lost in industries hurt by foreign restrictions on U.S. exports than are saved by restricting imports. The Department of Labor influences trade negotiations by estimating their effects on the jobs of American workers. And, in instances where some jobs are sacrificed for the common good, the Department has an even more important role in providing assistance and trying to develop new jobs for the workers who bear the bulk of the burden.

Help for Victims

The Trade Expansion Act of 1962 provides that trade-adjustment assistance shall be provided to businesses injured by imports and that the Department of Labor shall assist workers who have lost their jobs because of competition from imports. Even if the expansion of trade is good for the nation as a whole in the long run, individual workers may suffer in the short run. An employee who loses his job because of foreign competition does not find comfort in the fact that fellow Americans can buy more for their dollars or that exports may create a higher-paying job for another worker in another industry in another place.

The 1962 Trade Act authorizes the Department of Labor to pay weekly cash allowances to employees who become unemployed because of imports that benefit the United States as a whole. In practice, no workers have received assistance for many years. The obstacle was that only those workers who lost their jobs because of specific tariff concessions could become eligible. It was not easy to show such measured cause-and-effect relationships.

In the agreement between the United States and Canada that virtually eliminated tariffs between the two countries on automobiles and auto parts, these rigid requirements of proof for firms and workers in the automobile industry were modified. The President, rather than as previously the Tariff Commission, was to determine eligibility for compensatory assistance. The President delegated this authority to a board of three Cabinet secretaries of which the Secretary of Labor was designated chairman. No auto companies received assistance, but about two thousand auto workers got benefits running to a total of about $4 million.

Secretaries of Labor George Shultz and James Hodgson continued to work for more assistance. They argued that individual workers should not be sacrificed on the altar of expanded international trade. Their concern was not with technicalities of eligibility, but with helping men and women thrown out of work by imports.

In November, 1969, the Tariff Commission found that trade concessions were a partial reason for increased imports of steel transmission towers made in Italy and welded pipe manufactured in Japan. In the first certification of its kind under the Trade Expansion Act, the Department of Labor announced that six hundred workers who had lost their jobs in three steel plants in Pennsylvania and California were eligible for adjustment assistance. Other certifications followed. In 1972, about twenty-eight thousand workers were covered. Most of the workers certified were engaged in the manufacture of shoes, pianos, window glass, textiles, and some steel and electronic products. But, considering the size of the problem, this program is a drop in the bucket. Legislation still needs to be liberalized if most workers hurt by imports are to be protected.

Today, many workers who become unemployed because of imports are eligible for a variety of benefits. The federal government provides funds that are turned over to the state employment services, which, in turn, pay workers 65 per cent of their weekly wages for a period of up to fifty-two weeks, with payments for additional weeks to workers who are learning new jobs or who are over sixty years of age and retiring. The maximum benefit in the early 1970's was about $90 a week. The Department of Labor goes farther than merely maintaining income. It tries to get workers back on payrolls. The U.S. Employment Service tests people for job aptitudes, provides counseling, retrains workers, finds new jobs for many of them, and even pays moving expenses to new places of employment.

When Congress, in 1884, debated the proposal to establish a Bureau of Labor, one of the major debates was over the effect of foreign trade on the welfare of labor. The debate is still going on.

XIV

The Challenge of Change–
Forecasting the Future

When we think about change in material aspects of life, we tend to think of great advances in science and technology rather than such seemingly prosaic matters as changes in the labor force. But manpower changes probably have a more dramatic impact on our lives than exploration of space. If you had lived at the time of the American Revolution, the odds are that you would have worked on a farm. By the time the Department of Labor was established in 1913, farm workers had already been reduced to less than a third of the labor force. Yet farm work was still so important that the first Secretary of Labor, William B. Wilson, when he personally designed the original official seal of the Department, featured a farmer's plow and a blacksmith's anvil. Today, only about 4 per cent of the labor force works in agriculture, and most American college students have never seen an anvil.

One responsibility of the Department of Labor is to forecast changes in the labor force. Based on past trends, here are some manpower predictions for the 1970's:

The 1970's will be a period of economic growth accompanied by an increase of about 15 million in the labor force, to reach a total of about 100 million workers by the end of the decade. These workers most likely will have higher real wages and will live better than workers today. They will continue to move, in the words of one union leader, "from beer and hamburgers to martinis and steaks." But trends in the late 1960's, such as the declining rate of gain in productivity, the changing work ethic, and the deteriorating quality of work, suggest a slow-down in progress toward a higher standard of living. On the other hand, productivity may improve because of the dramatic increase in the number of workers in the prime group of those twenty-five to thirty-four years of age, who will be better trained and better educated than their counterparts in earlier decades.

Along with this size increase in the prime group, there will be a steep decline in the growth of the teenage work group. Youth unemployment has grown from about one and a half times the national average in 1930 to more than five times the national average in 1970. The United States is the only major country that has failed to bridge the gap between school and work. The low teenage population growth rate of the early 1970's will help to reduce youth unemployment, which in the past contributed so much to social unrest.

The manpower crystal ball also shows that blacks and other minorities will continue to enter the mainstream of American economic life. By 1970, many more blacks had moved into skilled and white-collar occupations, and the proportion of blacks in better jobs had increased significantly since 1960. Although the gap between blacks and whites in earnings and unemployment rates had narrowed, the blacks were still at a sharp disadvantage in 1970. The gap should continue to narrow during the decade, even though better education among blacks may be partially offset by, first, the general decline in the value of a college degree as a way of qualifying for better jobs and, second, the backlash among white workers who fear that their jobs are threatened by blacks. Looking back, blacks have come a long way. Looking ahead, they will continue to make economic gains. But in 1980 the economic position of blacks and other minorities will still lag behind that of whites.

Women also have special work problems that will continue to be prevalent. Married women and women with children will pour into the work force in increasing numbers as improved means of birth control and changing attitudes toward sex roles allow more careful family planning. A declining birth rate should provide more resources for each child. Preschool care may become one of the great growing businesses of the future. Along with the increasing numbers and proportion of women at work, there will be a modest trend toward women's moving into professions, managerial positions, and skilled jobs. The American economy will gradually deal more fairly with women.

One of the marks of an improved society is a shift in the population's employment from farm and factory jobs to professional, white-collar, and service occupations. This trend is not uniform in all fields; for example, there may be reduced opportunities to enter teaching careers. But, in general, white-collar workers, who first equaled blue-collar workers in number in 1966, by 1980 probably will outnumber blue-collar workers by 50 per cent. At the same time, farm labor will have continued its sharp decline and America's food supply will be produced by only 3 per cent of the work force.

TWENTIETH-CENTURY PLANNING

Forecasts in America are serious business because of the nation's deep faith in the ability of mankind to improve itself. By anticipating problems, forward-looking Americans feel, it may be possible to shape the future.

But forecasting is also a hazardous business. For example, though manpower specialists foresaw the growing role of women workers, almost all underestimated the degree of their importance in the labor force. Very few experts predicted accurately the population explosion after World War II, followed by the sharp drop in birth rates in the 1960's.

And trying to shape the future is even riskier than forecasting. Although far afield from manpower planning, a striking example of how planning may go astray comes from Communist China's drive to increase its food supply by waging a war on sparrows. In a great campaign one year, the peasants of China killed off most of the sparrows who had nibbled at their crops, only to find that the next year their food supply was even smaller because the sparrows no longer ate the worms who destroyed an even greater proportion of the crops than the sparrows did.

Similar dangers lurk in planning manpower programs and general economic programs that have an impact on labor. Attempts in the early 1970's to curb inflation may have caused increased unemployment. Such planned programs as a war on poverty can have various effects on the incentive to get jobs. Concerned efforts to increase productivity may under some circumstances mean that for each 1 per cent improvement in productivity there may be 1 per cent fewer jobs in the economy.

Yet, with all their errors, economic forecasters are more often right than wrong, and planners who are realistic may overcome many obstacles. It is possible that, with fine tuning, inflation may be curbed at the same time that unemployment is declining, that welfare payments may be successfully designed to stimulate incentives to work, and that productivity may be linked to increasing domestic and foreign markets, creating more rather than less employment. Policy-makers who understand the intricacies and pitfalls of economic planning can perhaps devise programs that, while aimed at solving today's problems, are flexible enough to meet the challenge of change. The War on Poverty of the Johnson Administration may be a case in point.

One of the great challenges to America in the twentieth

century is the abolition of poverty. Of even greater importance in a larger perspective is the flowering of the idea that a man or woman, by personal effort, can play a decisive role in determining his or her own station in life. Not so long ago, most human beings were born as slaves, serfs, or low-paid workers who lived in poverty, often lacking the basic needs of food, clothing, and shelter. Moreover, they had no chance of rising out of their situations. They could not, of their own free will, move from the place where they were born or better their economic and social status.

In an economy of scarcity, most human beings had to live at the edge of a miserable subsistence. By contrast, modern technology has created a society of surpluses. Yet even today there are economically deprived countries, such as Bolivia, Bangladesh, and many other nations, where people, though legally free, are enslaved by poverty. They live in another world, far from the dizzying pinnacle of plenty, where, as the richest country in the world in the richest era in history, America is at the height of affluence.

Grinding poverty, like that known through the ages and still known in some parts of the world today, is not prevalent in the United States. Nevertheless, there are still millions of men, women, and children in various parts of the country who do not share the affluence and social mobility of their fellow Americans. Most of these "other Americans" are from rural areas, or are from minority groups, or have inadequate educations or other disadvantages. More than 5 million families, or 10 per cent of all Americans, live below a poverty line established by the U.S. Government.

Poverty is relative. In some places where few people have television sets, telephones, a chance for a high school education, or medical care, the lack of such advantages causes no problem. It is a mark of progress that the concept of a socially acceptable minimum income includes a basic standard of ever increasing goods and services. In the United States in the early 1970's, a nonfarm family of four that did not have an income of about $4,400 a year was considered living at poverty level. This was high in terms of the historical mean income or the standards of poorer nations, where the poverty line is drawn where starvation begins. But $4,400 in the 1970's is too little to allow a family to participate in the "American way of life."

Planning Jobs and Incomes

Since the 1930's, one of the chief weapons in the conquest of poverty has been government support or income maintenance. At the start of these programs, when unemployment increased, welfare relief payments increased. When unemployment dropped, relief rolls also dropped. In the 1960's, however, for the first time, the number of welfare clients increased both in times of prosperity and in times of business recession, with a resultant explosion in welfare rolls. What was happening was that standards for public assistance were being revised and extended to include many poor people who had been formerly ineligible. As the distinction between income from work and income from welfare was blurred, more families applied for welfare.

A series of government programs in the early 1970's was aimed at bolstering the work ethic by making it more profitable to work than to go on welfare. Manpower programs offered training, public jobs, and other supplements to the incomes of the working poor. Yet such incentives do not reach the millions of poor who are too old, too young, or too sick to work. Besides being ineffective, some social programs also antagonize some working Americans who object to helping drug addicts, alcoholics, unmarried mothers, and others they consider to be "undeserving" poor.

Although there has been a tendency to expect too much from manpower programs, it is also important not to underestimate them. In times of prosperity, manpower programs can help to reduce inflation, increase productivity, and open jobs for many disadvantaged workers. In times of recession, manpower programs can provide income with dignity. Prospective workers, instead of rotting away in despair, can build skills for future employment. Although there are aspects of poverty that manpower programs cannot reach, government manpower activities do meet many of the needs of the poor who are able and willing to work.

The Challenge of the Future

Since the Department of Labor was created in 1913, there have been many changes in the world of work, most of them for the better. The Department of Labor has also changed. Although some original functions, such as defending the public interest in conflicts between management and labor, remain important, other activities, such as curbing child labor and sweatshops, are no longer burning issues.

Most significantly, the Department of Labor today, as never before, is at the forefront of efforts to deal with one of the most important issues of our times—the protection and development of human resources. Waste of human ability is more serious than waste of physical resources. The Department of Labor is increasingly concerned with the safety and healthfulness of the places where people work. It is concerned with provision of training to improve skills that increase productivity and help the poor to help themselves out of poverty. The Department struggles with the task of winning opportunities for blacks and other minorities to get jobs and promotions. Such issues had not come to the forefront in 1913. Although problems and programs have changed and expanded, the mission of the Department remains the same one set forth in the Act creating it: "To foster, promote, and develop the welfare of the wage earners of the United States."

Appendix A
Careers in the Department of Labor

The diverse functions of the Department of Labor create opportunities for qualified men and women with a variety of backgrounds. Almost all college majors are represented in the Department. Economists, mathematicians, public or business administration specialists, sociologists, safety engineers, and English majors can find rewarding careers in the Department.

Jobs available in the Department include the following:

- *Economist.* Applicants can qualify with a bachelor's degree that signifies at least twenty-one semester hours of courses in economics and three semester hours in statistics, accounting, or calculus. Experience may be substituted for a degree if the course requirements are met.
- *Manpower Development Specialist.* A manpower development specialist is involved with programs in the areas of manpower resources, requirements, development, and utilization. An applicant must have appropriate experience or have a bachelor's degree that signifies at least twenty-four semester hours in one or a combination of the following subjects: economics, personnel administration, public or business administration, industrial management, industrial relations, industrial engineering, psychology, sociology, political science, education.

- *Budget Examiner and Claims Examiner.* A bachelor's degree or appropriate experience plus Federal Service Entrance Examination eligibility is needed to qualify for the entrance level.
- *Investigator.* Investigators in the Department are primarily concerned with obtaining compliance with wage-hour, safety and health, and labor-management legislation. Investigator positions are primarily located outside the Washington, D.C., area. Requirements for investigator positions include a bachelor's degree with at least twenty-four semester hours of credit in any one or combination of the following subjects: accounting, economics, industrial relations, labor legislation, statistics, law, business administration, political science, sociology, journalism. Equivalent experience and education may be substituted for that requirement.
- *Employment Service Adviser.* An employment service adviser assists in developing policies, standards, programs, and procedures in aiding employment security agencies. Requirements are related experience or a bachelor's degree based on course requirements of at least twenty-four semester hours of study in one or a combination of the following: personnel, public or business administration, government, industrial relations, industrial engineering, psychology, counseling, economics, sociology, political science.

Other positions available in the Department of Labor include those of personnel management specialist, digital computer programer, attorney, management analyst, and statistician. Capable high school graduates may qualify for a variety of clerical and subprofessional jobs.

All jobs in the Department are filled with the people best qualified for the positions, regardless of race, color, creed, sex, politics, or national origin. Most jobs in the Department are filled through the Civil Service system. Selections are based upon potential ability as demonstrated by education, experience, and performance in competitive examinations.

In addition to on-the-job training, the Department offers a variety of other training opportunities to its employees, including the newly instituted Executive Development Program and assignments to individual learning centers. The Department of Labor intern program offers an accelerated one-year training program for highly qualified Department employees in grades 5 through 12. Each intern will serve on rotation in the various component organizations of the Department, providing a broad knowledge of the functions of the Department.

Most entry-level professional positions in the Department are filled at the GS–5 or GS–7 level. Satisfactory performance can earn promotion to the grade-12 level within three or four years. Up to grade 11 or 12, promotions are based entirely upon performance without competition from other employees. Employees compete for positions above the grade-12 level under the Department's merit promotion system, wherein promotions are based on experience, education, and job performance.

Appendix B

Commissioners and Secretaries of Labor

Agency	Title	Incumbent	State from which appointed	Party affiliation	Period of service	Served under President
Bureau of Labor (in the Department of the Interior)	Commissioner of Labor	Carroll D. Wright	Mass.	Ind.	1884–88	Chester A. Arthur Grover Cleveland
Department of Labor (without Cabinet rank)	Commissioner of Labor	Carroll D. Wright	Mass.	Ind.	1888–1903	Grover Cleveland Benjamin Harrison Grover Cleveland William McKinley Theodore Roosevelt
Department of Commerce and Labor	Secretary of Commerce and Labor	George B. Cortelyou Victor H. Metcalf Oscar S. Straus Charles Nagel	N.Y. Cal. N.Y. Mo.	Rep. Rep. Rep. Rep.	1903–4 1904–6 1906–9 1909–13	Theodore Roosevelt Theodore Roosevelt Theodore Roosevelt William H. Taft

Department of Labor	Name	State	Party	Dates	President
Secretary of Labor	William B. Wilson	Pa.	Dem.	Mar. 6, 1913–Mar. 4, 1921	Woodrow Wilson
	James J. Davis	Pa.	Rep.	Mar. 5, 1921–Nov. 30, 1930	Warren G. Harding Calvin Coolidge Herbert Hoover
	William N. Doak	Va.	Rep.	Dec. 9, 1930–Mar. 4, 1933	Herbert Hoover
	Frances Perkins	N.Y.	Dem.	Mar. 4, 1933–June 30, 1945	Franklin D. Roosevelt Harry S. Truman
	Lewis B. Schwellenbach	Wash.	Dem.	July 1, 1945–June 10, 1948 (died in office)	Harry S. Truman
Acting Secretary of Labor	David A. Morse	N.J.	Dem.	June 11, 1948–Aug. 12, 1948	Harry S. Truman
Secretary of Labor	Maurice J. Tobin	Mass.	Dem.	Aug. 13, 1948–Jan. 20, 1953	Harry S. Truman
	Martin P. Durkin	Ill.	Dem.	Jan. 21, 1953–Sept. 10, 1953	Dwight D. Eisenhower
	James P. Mitchell	N.J.	Rep.	Oct. 9, 1953–Jan. 20, 1961	Dwight D. Eisenhower
	Arthur J. Goldberg	Ill.	Dem.	Jan. 21, 1961–Sept. 20, 1962	John F. Kennedy
	W. Willard Wirtz	Ill.	Dem.	Sept. 25, 1962–Jan. 20, 1969	John F. Kennedy Lyndon B. Johnson
	George P. Shultz	Ill.	Rep.	Jan. 22, 1969–July 1, 1970	Richard M. Nixon
	James D. Hodgson	Cal.	Rep.	July 2, 1970–Feb. 1, 1973	Richard M. Nixon
	Peter J. Brennan	N.Y.	Dem.	Feb. 2, 1973–	Richard M. Nixon

A Bibliography on the Department of Labor, Including Some General References on Labor History and Problems

ADAMS, LEONARD P. *The Public Employment Service in Transition, 1933–1968; Evolution of a Placement Service into a Manpower Agency.* Ithaca: New York State School of Industrial and Labor Relations, Cornell University, 1969. (Cornell Studies in Industrial and Labor Relations, v. 16.)

American Labor: From Conspiracy to Collective Bargaining. Advisory editors: Leon Stern and Philip Taft. New York: Arno Press, 1969–71. Series 1:60 v.; series 2:45 v. Reprints of noteworthy but generally unavailable or out-of-print works.

ANDERSON, MARY. *Woman at Work: The Autobiography of Mary Anderson as told to Mary N. Winslow.* Minneapolis: University of Minnesota Press, 1951.

ATKINSON, RAYMOND C., et al. *Public Employment Service in the United States.* Chicago, Published for the Committee on Public Administration of the Social Science Research Council by Public Administration Service, 1968. (Committee on Public Administration, Social Science Research Council. Studies in Administration, v. 5.)

BABSON, ROGER W. *Recent Labor Progress, with Special Reference to the Work of the Federal Government under James J. Davis, Secretary of Labor, as Outlined in the Annual Reports of the Department of Labor.* New York: Fleming H. Revell Company, 1924.

BABSON, ROGER W. *W. B. Wilson and the Department of Labor.* New York: Brentano's, 1919.

BABSON, ROGER W. *Washington and the Depression, Including the Career of W. N. Doak.* New York: Harper, 1932.

BAILEY, STEPHEN K. *Congress Makes a Law: The Story Behind the Employment Act of 1946.* New York: Columbia University Press, 1950.

BALL, JOSEPH H. *The Implementation of Federal Manpower Policy, 1961–1971: A Study in Bureaucratic Competition and Intergovernmental Relations.* New York, 1972. (Thesis, Columbia University. Prepared under a grant from the Manpower Administration, U.S. Department of Labor.)

BERNHARDT, JOSHUA. *The Division of Conciliation: Its History, Activities and Organization.* Baltimore: John Hopkins Press, 1923. (Institute for Governmental Research. Service monographs of the U.S. Government, no. 20.)

BOK, DEREK C., and JOHN T. DUNLOP. *Labor and the American Community.* New York: Simon and Schuster, 1970.

BREEN, VINCENT I. *The United States Conciliation Service.* Washington: Catholic University of America Press, 1943. (Catholic University of America. Studies in Economics, v. 11. Thesis, Catholic University.)

CASSELL, FRANK H. *The Public Employment Service: Organization in Change.* Ann Arbor, Michigan: Academic Publications, 1968.

CHAPPLE, JOSEPH M. *"Our Jim"; A Biography.* Boston: Chapple Publishing Company, 1928. (Biography of James J. Davis.)

CLAGUE, EWAN. *The Bureau of Labor Statistics.* New York: Praeger Publishers, 1968. (Praeger Library of U.S. Government Departments and Agencies, No. 13.) (Contains a bibliography with many references not included in this bibliography.)

Conference on Unemployment and the American Economy, 2d, Boulder, Colorado, 1964. *Employment Policy and the Labor Market,* edited by Arthur M. Ross. Berkeley: University of California Press, 1965.

Conference on Unemployment and the American Economy, 4th, New York, 1966. *Toward a Manpower Policy,* edited by Robert A. Gordon. New York: J. Wiley, 1967.

CORMIER, FRANK, and WILLIAM J. EATON. *Reuther.* Englewood Cliffs, N.J.: Prentice-Hall, 1970.

DAVIS, JAMES J. *The Iron Puddler: My Life in the Rolling Mills and What Came of It.* Indianapolis: Bobbs-Merrill, 1922.

Employment Security-Review. v. 1–30; September 1934–November/ December, 1963. Washington: U.S. Government Printing Office, 1934–63. (Title varied: *Employment Service News; Manpower Review; Employment Service Review.* Issued by the U.S. Employment Service and, from 1943–45, the U.S. War Manpower Commission.

Superseded by the *Employment Service Review* and the *Unemploy-ment Insurance Review*.)

Employment Service Review: A Monthly Journal of Federal–State Employment Service Programs and Operations. (v. 1–5; January/ February, 1964–December, 1968. Washington, U.S. Government Printing Office, 1964–68. 4 v. Issued by the U.S. Bureau of Employment Security in cooperation with the State Employment Security Agencies. Superseded by *Manpower*.)

ESTEY, MARTEN S., *et al.* (eds.). *Regulating Union Government.* New York: Harper & Row, 1964. (Industrial Relations Research Association. Publication no. 31. Covers the background and administration of the Labor-Management Reporting and Disclosure Act.)

FINE, SIDNEY. *Sit-down: The General Motors Strike of 1936–37.* Ann Arbor: University of Michigan Press, 1969.

GALARZA, ERNESTO. *Merchants of Labor: The Mexican Bracero Story. An Account of the Managed Migration of Mexican Farm Workers in California, 1942–60.* San Jose: The Rosicrusian Press, 1964.

GINZBERG, ELI. *Manpower Agenda for America.* New York: McGraw-Hill, 1968.

GINZBERG, ELI, and HYMAN BERMAN. *The American Worker in the Twentieth Century: A History Through Autobiographies.* New York: Free Press of Glencoe, 1963.

GOMPERS, SAMUEL. *Seventy Years of Life and Labor: An Autobiography.* v. 2. New York: E. P. Dutton, 1925.

GOULDEN, JOSEPH C. *Meany.* New York: Atheneum, 1972.

HABER, WILLIAM, and DAVID H. KRUGER. *The Role of the United States Employment Service in a Changing Economy.* Kalamazoo, Mich.: W. E. Upjohn Institute for Employment Research, 1964. (Studies in Employment and Unemployment.)

HABER, WILLIAM, and MERRILL G. MURRAY. *Unemployment Insurance in the American Economy: An Historical Review and Analysis.* Homewood, Ill.: R. D. Irwin, 1966.

Institute of Labor and Industrial Relations. (University of Michigan-Wayne State University.) *Policy Papers in Human Resources and Industrial Relations,* no. 1–18. Ann Arbor: 1967–70. 18 v. (Several of these deal with Department of Labor programs.)

KENNEDY, JOHN F. *A Nation of Immigrants.* Rev. ed. New York: Harper & Row, 1964.

LAPOMARDA, VINCENT A. *Maurice Joseph Tobin, 1901–1953: A Political Profile and an Edition of Selected Public Papers.* Boston: 1969. (Thesis, Boston University, 1968.)

LEBERGOTT, STANLEY. *Manpower in Economic Growth: The American Record Since 1800.* New York: McGraw-Hill, 1964.

LEIBY, JAMES. *Carroll Wright and Labor Reform: The Origin of Labor Statistics.* Cambridge: Harvard University Press, 1960. (Harvard Historical Monographs, 46.)

LEVITAN, SAR A. *The Great Society's Poor Law, A New Approach to Poverty.* Baltimore: Johns Hopkins Press, 1969.

LEVITAN, SAR A., and GARTH L. MANGUM. *Federal Training and Work Programs in the Sixties.* Ann Arbor: Institute of Labor and Industrial Relations, University of Michigan-Wayne State University, 1969.

LEVITAN, SAR A., et al. *Human Resources and Labor Markets: Labor and Manpower in the American Economy.* New York: Harper and Row, 1972.

LIVERNASH, EDWARD R., et al. *Collective Bargaining in the Basic Steel Industry: A Study of the Public Interest and the Role of Government.* Washington: U.S. Department of Labor, 1961.

LOMBARDI, JOHN. *Labor's Voice in the Cabinet: A History of the Department of Labor, from Its Origin to 1921.* New York: Columbia University Press, 1942. (Studies in History, Economics and Public Law, ed. by the Faculty of Political Science of Columbia University, no. 496. Issued also as thesis, Columbia University.)

MCADAMS, ALAN K. *Power and Politics in Labor Legislation.* New York: Columbia University Press, 1964. (An account and analysis of the legislative process by which the Landrum-Griffin bill became a law.)

MANGUM, GARTH L. *The Emergence of Manpower Policy.* New York: Holt, Rinehart and Winston, 1969.

MANGUM, GARTH L. *MDTA: Foundation of Federal Manpower Policy.* Baltimore: The Johns Hopkins Press, 1968.

Manpower. Washington: U.S. Government Printing Office. Issued monthly since January, 1969, by the Manpower Administration, U.S. Department of Labor.

Massachusetts Bureau of Statistics of Labor. *The Working Girls of Boston.* (From the Fifteenth Annual Report of the Massachusetts Bureau of Statistics of Labor, for 1884, by Carroll D. Wright.) Boston: Wright and Potter Printing Company, 1889.

Monthly Labor Review. Washington: U.S. Government Printing Office. Issued monthly since July, 1915, by the U.S. Bureau of Labor Statistics.

MORSE, DAVID A. *The Origin and Evolution of the I.L.O. and Its Role in the World Community.* Ithaca: New York State School of Industrial and Labor Relations, Cornell University, 1969.

MORTON, HERBERT C. *Public Contracts and Private Wages: Experience Under the Walsh-Healey Act.* Washington: Brookings Institution, 1965.

MORTON, J. E. *On the Evolution of Manpower Statistics.* Kalamazoo, Mich.: W. E. Upjohn Institute for Employment Research, 1969. (Upjohn Institute for Employment Research. Studies in Employment and Unemployment.)

MOYNIHAN, DANIEL P. (ed.). *On Understanding Poverty: Perspectives from the Social Sciences.* New York: Basic Books, 1969.

NATHAN, RICHARD P. *Jobs & Civil Rights: The Role of the Federal Government in Promcting Equal Opportunity in Employment and Training.* Prepared for United States Commission on Civil Rights by the Brookings Institution, Washington, D.C. Washington: U.S. Government Printing Office, 1969. (U.S. Commission on Civil Rights. Clearinghouse Publication no. 16.)

PERKINS, FRANCES. *The Roosevelt I Knew.* New York: Viking Press, 1946.

Princeton Manpower Symposium, Princeton University, 1965. *Unemployment in a Prosperous Economy: A Report.* Edited by WILLIAM G. BOWEN and FREDERICK H. HARBISON. Princeton: 1965. (Princeton University, Industrial Relations Section. Research Report Series no. 108. A critique of parts of the 1965 manpower report to the President, which dealt with unemployment and proposals to alleviate it.)

RIIS, JACOB A. *How the Other Half Lives: Studies Among the Tenements of New York.* New York: Charles Scribner's Sons, 1890.

ROURKE, FRANCIS E. *Reorganization of the Labor Department.* Ann Arbor: University Microfilms, 1952. (Thesis, University of Minnesota. Discusses the varying role of the Department from 1913 through the Reorganization Plans of 1950.)

RUTTENBERG, STANLEY H. *Manpower Challenge of the 1970's: Institutions and Social Change.* Baltimore: Johns Hopkins Press, 1970. (Policy Studies in Employment and Welfare, no. 2.)

RUTTENBERG, STANLEY H., and JOCELYN GUTCHESS. *The Federal-State Employment Service: A Critique.* Baltimore: Johns Hopkins Press, 1970.

SCHNAPPER, M. B. *American Labor: A Pictorial History.* Washington: Public Affairs Press, 1972.

SHOR, EDGAR L. *The Role of the Secretary of Labor.* Chicago: Library, Department of Photographic Reproduction, University of Chicago, 1954. (Thesis, University of Chicago.)

SHULTZ, GEORGE P., and ROBERT Z. ALIBER (eds.). *Guidelines, Informal Controls, and the Market Place: Choices in a Full Employment Economy.* Chicago: University of Chicago Press, 1966.

SHULTZ, GEORGE P., and JOHN R. COLEMAN. *Labor Problems: Cases and Readings.* 2d ed. New York: McGraw-Hill, 1959.

SHULTZ, GEORGE P., and ARNOLD R. WEBER. *Strategies for the Displaced Worker: Confronting Economic Change.* New York: Harper and Row, 1966.

SPARGO, JOHN. *The Bitter Cry of the Children.* New York: Macmillan, 1906.

SUNDQUIST, JAMES L. (ed.). *On Fighting Poverty: Perspectives from Experience.* New York: Basic Books, 1969.

TAFT, PHILIP. *Organized Labor in American History.* New York: Harper & Row, 1964.

TERRELL, JOHN U. *The United States Department of Labor: A Story of Workers, Unions, and the Economy.* New York: Meredith Press, 1968.

U.S. Bureau of Labor Standards. *Growth of Labor Law in the United States.* Washington: U.S. Department of Labor, 1967.

U.S. Bureau of Labor Statistics. *Black Americans: A Decade of Occupational Change,* by SYLVIA SMALL. Washington, 1972. (Bulletin no. 1731.)

U.S. Bureau of Labor Statistics. *A Brief History of the American Labor Movement.* 1970 ed. Washington: U.S. Government Printing Office, 1970. (Bulletin no. 1000, rev. 1970.)

U.S. Bureau of Labor Statistics. *Publications of the Bureau of Labor Statistics, 1886–1967: Numerical Listings, Annotations, Subject Index.* Washington: U.S. Government Printing Office, 1968. (Bulletin no. 1567.)

U.S. Congress. House Committee on Appropriations. Hearings on Appropriations for Department of Labor and Health, Education, and Welfare. Washington: U.S. Government Printing Office. (Issued yearly.)

U.S. Congress. House Committee on Education and Labor. *The Role and Mission of the Federal-State Employment Service in the American Economy.* Report, Eighty-eighth Congress, Second Session. Washington: U.S. Government Printing Office, 1965. (Committee Print.)

U.S. Congress. Senate Committee on Appropriations. Hearings on Appropriations for Departments of Labor and Health, Education and Welfare. Washington: U.S. Government Printing Office. (Issued yearly.)

U.S. Congress. Senate Committee on Labor and Public Welfare. Subcommittee on Employment and Manpower. *The Manpower Revolution: Its Policy Consequences; Excerpts from Senate Hearings before the Clark Subcommittee.* Edited by GARTH L. MANGUM. Garden City: Doubleday, 1965.

U.S. Department of Labor. *The American Workers' Fact Book.* Washington, 1960. Includes appendix: The United States Department of Labor.

U.S. Department of Labor. *Annual Report.* Washington, U.S. Government Printing Office. (Issued yearly since 1913.)

U.S. Department of Labor. *The Anvil and the Plow: A History of the United States Department of Labor, 1913–63,* by W. B. WILSON and others. Washington, 1963. (Told in the words of ten Secretaries of Labor as taken from their annual reports.)

U.S. Department of Labor. *Publications of the U.S. Department of Labor: Subject Listing.* Washington: U.S. Government Printing Office. Issued annually since 1964; prior to then, at irregular intervals.

U.S. Department of Labor. *United States Department of Labor:*

Twenty-five Years of Service, 1913–38. Washington: U.S. Government Printing Office, 1938.

U.S. Library of Congress. Legislative Reference Service. *Readings on Public Employment Services.* Compiled for the Select Subcommittee on Labor, Committee on Education and Labor, House of Representatives, Eighty-eighth Congress, Second Session, December, 1964. Washington: U.S. Government Printing Office, 1965.

U.S. President. *Manpower Report of the President, Including a Report on Manpower Requirements, Resources, Utilization, and Training by the United States Department of Labor.* Washington: U.S. Government Printing Office. (Issued annually since 1963.)

WEBER, ARNOLD R., *et al.* (eds.). *Public-private Manpower Policies.* Madison, Wis.: Industrial Relations Research Association, 1969.

WILHELM, CLARKE L. *William B. Wilson: The First Secretary of Labor.* Ann Arbor, Mich.: University Microfilms, 1967. (Thesis, Johns Hopkins University.)

WIRTZ, WILLIAM WILLARD. *Labor and the Public Interest.* New York: Harper & Row, 1964. (A collection of speeches given by the former Secretary of Labor.)

WOLFBEIN, SEYMOUR L. *Education and Training for Full Employment.* New York: Columbia University Press, 1967.

WOLFBEIN, SEYMOUR L. *Employment, Unemployment and Public Policy.* New York: Random House, 1965.

WOLFBEIN, SEYMOUR L. *Work in American Society.* Glenview: Scott, Foresman, 1971.

WYKSTRA, RONALD A., and ELEANOUR V. STEVENS. *Labor Law and Public Policy.* New York: Odyssey Press, 1970.

Index